SPEAKER'S TREASURY OF SPORTS ANECDOTES, STORIES, AND HUMOR

SPEAKER'S TREASURY OF SPORTS ANECDOTES, STORIES, AND HUMOR

Gerald Tomlinson

PRENTICE HALL
Englewood Cliffs, New Jersey 07632

Prentice-Hall International (UK) Limited, *London*
Prentice-Hall of Australia Pty. Limited, *Sydney*
Prentice-Hall Canada, Inc., *Toronto*
Prentice-Hall Hispanoamericana, S.A., *Mexico*
Prentice-Hall of India Private Limited, *New Delhi*
Prentice-Hall of Japan, Inc., *Tokyo*
Simon & Schuster Asia Pte. Ltd., *Singapore*
Editora Prentice-Hall do Brasil, Ltda., *Rio de Janeiro*

© 1990 *by*

Gerald Tomlinson

10 9 8 7 6 5 4 3 2 1

Library of Congress Cataloging-in-Publication Data

Tomlinson, Gerald.
  Speaker's treasury of sports anecdotes, stories, and humor /
Gerald Tomlinson.

    p.   cm.
  Includes bibliographical references.
  ISBN 0-13-824764-1. — ISBN 0-13-826942-4 (pbk).
   1. Sports—Anecdotes. 2. Sports stories. 3. Public speaking-
-Handbooks, manuals, etc.   I. Title.
GV707.T64 1990
796'.02'02—dc20   89-38752
                                                      CIP

ISBN 0-13-824764-1

ISBN 0-13-826942-4 PBK

PRENTICE HALL
BUSINESS & PROFESSIONAL DIVISION
A division of Simon & Schuster
Englewood Cliffs, New Jersey 07632

PRINTED IN THE UNITED STATES OF AMERICA

ACKNOWLEDGMENTS

The great majority of stories, anecdotes, and quotations in this book are based on materials that have appeared in sports periodicals, newspapers, or books. A much smaller number are from individuals, particularly from sports information directors throughout the country. I would like to express my appreciation to the following persons, each of whom has provided the substance or text for at least one entry in the book: George Beres, former Sports Information Director, University of Oregon; Tom Bonerbo, Sports Information Director, Fairleigh Dickinson University/Madison; Helen T. Burns, Assistant Director of Communications/Press Relations, Hamilton College; Vic D'Ascenzo, Sports Information Director, Fairfield University; Charles DeCicco, Director, Public Relations, The City College of The City University of New York; Tom Hall, Assistant Sports Information Director, University of California/Davis; John E. Heisler, Sports Information Director, University of Notre Dame; Butch Henry, Assistant Athletic Director for Media Relations, University of Arizona; Bob Noss, Sports Information Director, Saint Louis University; Russell Rice, Assistant to the Athletic Director, University of Kentucky; Matt Rogers, Sports Information Director, Sam Houston State University; Benjamin M. Sherman, Sports Information Director, University of Delaware; Sports Information Office, Texas Christian University; Sports News Office, Baylor University; Bill Whitmore, former Sports Information Director, Rice University; Bob Winn, Assistant Athletic Director/Communications, Memphis State University; Michael J. Wolf, Sports Information Director, Washington University; Charles Young, Sports Information Office, Dartmouth College.

HOW TO USE THIS BOOK

Whenever you are called upon to give a speech, one of your goals is to make it as interesting as possible. Whatever your topic, you want people to pay attention to what you say and to get your message. Whoever the people in your audience are, you want to appeal to them and to touch their minds and hearts.

Is there any single content area of universal appeal—any surefire way to create a speech or illustrate a point—that will ensure the success of your presentation? Probably not, but there is one content area that comes close: sports.

Almost any audience you encounter will appreciate a story about baseball, football, basketball, golf, hockey, or horse racing. Close personal experience with the sport is seldom necessary. Athletics are so much a part of our culture, so much the focus of our media, that someone like Orel Hershiser, let's say, or even Bronko Nagurski is probably more widely known than virtually anyone in business, the professions, religion, or art.

By and large, Americans know sports. The subject has built-in acceptance. And stories that involve sports lend themselves ideally to inclusion in speeches, whether the speeches are general or specific, inspirational, or technical.

What better way to introduce the topic of motivation than with a football anecdote about Cornell University's startling, if unsuccessful, two-tower defense against field-goal attempts? (page 103)? What better way to illustrate the importance (or perhaps the limits) of self-confidence than with the baseball story of Heinie Mueller's willingness to compare his batting prowess with that of Judas Priest? (page 227)? What better way to conclude a speech dealing with priorities than with a comment on the topic from football coach Vince Lombardi? (page 198)?

There are two basic ways to organize a collection of resource materials for speakers. This book makes use of both of them. The first way is by means of subject categories: achievement, challenge, discipline, honesty, and so on. This is the basic organizational plan here, and the book contains 72 such categories. This framework provides a clear, easy-to-use format for locating and identifying the exact story, anecdote, or comment you need for a specific purpose in a specific speech. It is the most familiar organizational scheme for a speaker's collection of sources. Time and experience have proved it to be the most useful.

You will notice as you begin to use the book, however, that categories do overlap. And individual stories often seem to fit quite well into two, three, or even more categories. For example, the tale of 44-year-old hockey manager Les Patrick coming off the bench, donning the pads, and playing brilliantly at goal in the Stanley Cup playoffs appears under the category Courage (pages 45–46). It surely illustrates courage. But the story might also be used to make a valid point—to name other categories—about assistance, experience, intensity, or maturity. The truth is that you may find a story that aptly illustrates a point you want to make but that does not thereby match the category it is listed under. If so, use it! The categories are storage bins, not straitjackets.

The stories and anecdotes in the book do not attempt to make specific content connections for you. They do not try, for example, to tie a story about Arnold Palmer to a speech dealing with the manufacture of brass doorknobs. To do so would be unnecessarily limiting, first of all, and more important, it would imply a knowledge of speaker, audience, and topic that no compiler can pretend to have. The entries have many applications. They fit many circumstances. They are open-ended, and only you, the user, can say, "Ah, ha! This Jimmy the Greek story under publicity (pages 204–205) is just what I need to emphasize my point about the success of our company's ad campaign for Glint toothpaste."

Only you, the speaker, can make the right connections. You will make them by analogy in most cases, and since you have probably done this many times before without a sourcebook, you will find it easy enough. Of course, if you are making a general, perhaps semi-humorous speech about motivation, you will have to speculate less about good analogies than you will if your topic is specialized, serious, and unrelated to sports. (At the other extreme, if you are talking about sports directly, the entire book is immediately and clearly applicable. Your only concern then becomes choosing the story itself, not puzzling over its utility in illustrating a point about, say, introducing air conditioners to the Inuit market.)

As noted earlier, there is a second method of categorizing entries in this book. It is the chronological (calendar or almanac) method. When you give a speech, you give it on a particular day. Speakers have long found it helpful to tie the date and its events to their speech topic. In doing so, remember: a nearby date is often just as useful as the exact date. If a story, event, personality, anecdote, or comment is well suited to your topic, use it, even if the date is a week in the past or a week in the future. You can fit the story into your talk without making it seem in any way out of place.

The two calendars—one dealing with sports events, the other covering sports figures' birthdays—should prove helpful to you in finding answers to these familiar speakers' questions: How do I start? How do I illustrate major points? How do I hold my audience's interest? How do I end? These are critical questions for any speechwriter, any speechmaker, any speech—and this book's combination of the subject-category approach *and* the almanac approach will give you unparalleled access to high-interest materials for creating, strengthening, and enlivening your speeches.

An important feature of the book, one you will use frequently, is the index. Let's say you have decided to use Ted William's birthday, August 31, as a takeoff point in your speech. The Speaker's Calendar of Sports Stars' Birthdays mentions a dramatic incident in Williams's baseball career. That may be enough for your purpose—but it isn't everything the book contains about the Boston Red Sox slugger. If you check the index, it will lead you to a more detailed story about Williams that you might want to use in conjunction with your birthday opener.

The index serves another purpose, too, besides locating and cross-referencing resources. It also provides help on the pronunciation of difficult names by using a simple respelling system familiar to users of *The Sporting News* publications. Under the index entry for Carl Yastrzemski, for instance, you will find "(Yuh-STREM-skee)." Only difficult-to-pronounce names are respelled in this way. The pronunciation of "Carl" is not shown because it is assumed that users already know how to say it. Even if a name is unfamiliar, the pronunciation guide does not appear if it closely and unmistakably follows the spelling of the name.

Something probably should be said about the veracity of the anecdotes and quotations in the book. In sports, this is a tricky matter. A number of entries are straight humor and obvious fiction. No one is likely to accept as fact the horse-racing story on page 242 ("Your horse is on the phone"). It is humor, pure and simple. Other stories may also be fiction, but less obviously so. The Yogi Berra oeuvre is filled with questionable tales. As Bob Uecker noted in *Catcher in the Wry* under "one of the things [that] will happen every spring," Berra "will be credited with a funny remark that was originally uttered by a nightclub comedian." True enough, and worth keeping in mind.

Sports stories, anecdotes, and one-liners are so commonly repeated and picked up on the rubber-chicken circuit that it is literally impossible to track most of them down or to give credit to the actual originator. Moreover, sportswriters sometimes get things wrong in the first place. "Because of his celebrity status," one biographer wrote recently, "Peter Revson [the late auto racer] has been interviewed and misquoted and misunderstood many times."

Multiply Revson by a thousand or more; it's a hazard of the limelight. And Mickey Herskowitz, the sportswriter, observed in a candid moment, "I did not know then how often Tex [Maule] made up quotes." So you see. . .

A few famous coaches/players/managers/speakers have been entirely open in commenting on the sources of their funny stories and memorable lines. Bear Bryant was one who willingly, almost insistently, credited other people for gems that the press was eager to attribute to him. But, remember, the stories he disclaimed may *already* have been third-, fourth-, or umpteenth-hand by the time they got to him. The best Bryant could do was point to his own immediate source, not necessarily to the originator of the tale or quip.

Despite all these caveats about fiction masquerading as fact, a good many true, accurate, and appropriately credited stories, anecdotes, one-liners, and quotations can be found following this preface. But certifiable gospel? No such claim is made, even though here and there an attempt has been made to set the factual record straight. One such case involves that famous old Babe-Ruth-calling-his-homer story (page 179). But, on the whole, the stories in the subject-category section of the book should be viewed and used for what they are—stories, maybe true, maybe not, but undeniably part of our rich sports literary and anecdotal heritage.

The calendars, on the other hand, are intended to be factually accurate. Any errors that appear in them are unintentional.

The book contains 1,303 carefully chosen sports entries for speakers. These are drawn from the vast reservoir of sports history, tradition, literature, myth, and humor. As its title suggests, the book is a treasure trove of sports materials to use—verbatim or adapted—in speeches that one hopes will sparkle, captivate, and inform. The range of sports is broad, 54 types of activities in all, though with a definite emphasis on major sports. In the book you will find sports-related content for virtually every kind of speech you are likely to make. You will also find a lot of good stories to use in everyday conversation for many years to come.

Gerald Tomlinson

CONTENTS

ABILITY

Auto Racing

Jim Clark, who came from the border country of Scotland, may have been the best grand prix racing driver of all time. There will always be arguments about the best at anything—and there will always be new challengers for the crown.

Certainly, Jim Clark was one of the best. He had every physical, mental, and emotional trait it took to become a great driver. He won the first auto race he entered. His tremendous potential was quickly evident to those who followed auto racing.

He kept being pushed ahead in the sport. Shy and unself-promoting, he sometimes doubted that he was ready for the next step. When asked to drive a D-type Jaguar, he said it was far too quick for him, that it scared him to death.

Maybe, but he agreed to drive it. And when he did, he set an almost unbelievable record. Driving the Jaguar for the first time on an old airfield circuit he had never driven before, he became the first sports-car driver to lap any British circuit at an average speed of 100 miles per hour.

It can truly be said of Jim Clark that, early in his career, he didn't know how good he was. His ability was awesome.

ABILITY

Auto Racing

Al Unser, four-time winner of the Indianapolis 500, could offer no clue about the source of his outstanding driving skills. He said, "All I know is that I drive as fast as I can down that straightaway and turn left when I hit the corner."

ABILITY

Baseball

Ron Gardenhire was one of those ballplayers that a team has to have but who never make much of a splash. He played shortstop for the New York Mets in the early '80s. During spring training, he talked about his lack of recognition. "Nobody's ever said I've got a lot of talent," he said. "They just say, 'He'll run through a brick wall for you.' " Ron looked resigned. "Strawberry has talent," he said. "Hernandez has talent. But I'm just a threat to a brick wall."

ABILITY

Baseball

Double Joe Dwyer spent most of his baseball career in the minors. He saw some of the great players on their way up. But like most career minor leaguers back in the '30s and '40s, he saw a lot of players who were going nowhere.

There was a third baseman, for instance, whose batting average hovered around .200 and whose fielding was not much better.

"Well," said Double Joe, "he's not much of a third baseman, but he's a pretty fair shotputter."

"Is that right?" asked the young sportswriter.

"Yeah," Joe said. "He can put away those shots pretty good."

ABILITY

Baseball

Many baseball fans know about Pete Gray. He was the one-armed outfielder who played for the St. Louis Browns in 1945, the last year of World War Two. He hit only .218 for the Browns, and there was some muttering that his presence on the team had cost St. Louis the pennant. The Browns had gone to the World Series the year before without him.

It's a shame that Gray is remembered mainly as a failure, because for a man who had lost his right arm in a childhood accident, he was a remarkable ballplayer.

No doubt the cynics are right in a way—Gray wouldn't have played professional ball except for the war. But they're wrong in another way. He could play at the professional level. Just a few steps down from the majors, Pete Gray held his own very well.

As a rookie in his mid-20s, he hit .381 for Three Rivers, Quebec, of the Canadian-American League. It earned him a promotion to Memphis of the Southern Association. In 1943 he came to bat 453 times for the Memphis Chicks. He collected 131 hits for a batting average of .289.

The next year was his best. In 1944, again with the Memphis Chicks, he led the league in stolen bases with 68. He hit .333 in 501 times at bat. He had 21 doubles, 9 triples, 5 home runs, and 60 runs-batted-in.

So his signing by the Browns was a bit more than the publicity stunt it's sometimes pictured as being. There was reason to think he could play baseball at the wartime major-league level.

It's true that when Gray was in the outfield, runners had a slight edge. The brief moment it took him to transfer the ball from his glove to his hand probably cost his teams a run or two.

But don't sell the guy short. Pete Gray was no bum. There were plenty of less competent two-armed outfielders in the wartime leagues. At Double-A, which the Southern Association was in those days (it was called "A-1"), he was a bona fide star.

ABILITY

Baseball

Joltin' Joe DiMaggio, a lifetime .325 hitter for the New York Yankees, found it easier to perform than to explain his performance. He said, "There's no skill involved. Just go up there and swing at the ball."

ABILITY

Basketball

When Hall of Fame basketball player Bob Pettit tried out for his high school's junior varsity, he didn't make the team. Discouraged but not defeated, he rigged up a basket in his backyard and practiced for hour after hour. He felt he had the ability to play high school basketball—and, if not, he would develop it.

He eventually made the varsity and became its sought-after star. By the time he graduated from high school, he was six-feet-nine and had the skills to match his height. At LSU, Pettit gained national headlines. For the St. Louis Hawks, he was the standout player on a team that was almost, but not quite, as good as the fabulous Boston Celtics of that era.

Like many another all-time great athlete, he didn't let early discouragement persuade him that he lacked innate ability. He knew better.

ABILITY

Football

You'd think the tremendous talent of a great football player would be obvious. Usually it is, but now and then it isn't.

Take Johnny Unitas. Although he starred in high school, Notre Dame turned him down because he weighed only 145 pounds—too slight for college football. After playing at the University of Louisville, he was picked in the ninth round of the NFL draft—but was cut before he played so much as an exhibition game.

He then worked as a pile driver and played sandlot football for six dollars a game. The Baltimore Colts signed him on as a back-up quarterback—mainly because he cost nothing. Only when the starter George Shaw broke his leg did Unitas get a chance to play.

His first game was terrible. His second game wasn't. By the time he retired in 1973, Johnny Unitas had played 18 seasons in the NFL. He had compiled a long list of passing records. He had once quarterbacked the Colts to 47 straight wins through four seasons.

By then nobody doubted that Johnny Unitas had what it takes to play pro football.

ABILITY

Football

Thousands of words have been written on what it takes to be a great football player. One thing is clear: outstanding performance demands a combination of skills.

Bob Lilly, former star tackle for the Dallas Cowboys, tried to explain it. "On the field," he said, "you're quite reserved. You have to have fantastic concentration. You must be aggressive, but you can't go completely nuts because you'll just make a lot of mistakes. It's a difficult balance."

ABILITY

Horse Racing

Bill Shoemaker, America's greatest jockey, said, "There is no such thing as a natural rider. Some guys have a knack. Horses run better for them. . . . I felt I had the knack. . . ."

ACCURACY

Baseball

Baseball men will tell you that Steve Dalkowski, not Nolan Ryan or Walter Johnson, was the fastest pitcher who ever lived.

There's no proof one way or the other. But there's plenty of evidence that Steve Dalkowski was a pitcher with blinding speed. One year, playing for Stockton in the California League, he struck out 262 batters in 170 innings. That's almost 14 batters a game. The trouble was that he also issued 262 walks.

And that was his problem. Control. One sportswriter said Dalkowski could easily throw the ball through a barn door—except he couldn't hit the door. It was the simple truth. Dalkowski once pitched a one-hitter and lost the game 9 to 8.

The Baltimore Orioles tried hard to make Dalkowski into a major-league pitcher. For one golden stretch of 52 innings with the Elmira Pioneers, under manager Earl Weaver, he found the range. In those 52 innings, he struck out 104 and walked only 11. But Dalkowski soon reverted to form. He couldn't slow down, and he couldn't get his smoker over the plate.

Baltimore tried everything. Nothing worked.

They built a target for him, using 2-by-4s, with six feet of solid wood on each side and an opening in the middle that was slightly larger than the strike zone. It seemed like a good idea, but Dalkowski demolished the frame while trying to find the opening.

Fast as he was—and potentially as great as he was—Steve Dalkowski never pitched an inning in the major league. You won't find him listed in *The Baseball Encyclopedia*.

But for nine seasons as a struggling pro, the little five-foot-nine fireballer from New Britain, Connecticut, terrorized batters all the way from Kennewick, Washington, to Pensacola, Florida.

ACCURACY

Football

Ron Bell was a college running back that the Pittsburgh Steeler scouts liked for his ability, but downgraded for his attitude. "Fine physical skills, but doesn't use them," one scout wrote. "Ran the fastest 4.7 I have seen."

A reporter asked Bell about that assessment.

Ron said, "I guess it means I ran a 4.6."

ACCURACY

Football

When William (The Refrigerator) Perry was a freshman at Clemson, he weighed 290 pounds. That was okay with his football coach, but when he showed up as a sophomore weighing 330 pounds, the coach decided to put him on a diet.

So far, so good. The diet consisted of bananas and milk. But there was one serious hitch—no limits were specified. Perry knew exactly what he was supposed to eat, but not how much. Students in the college cafeteria caught sight of The Refrigerator sitting at a table heaped with bananas and crowded with cartons of milk.

He just kept eating those bananas and drinking that milk—and gaining weight.

ACCURACY

Golf

Harry Vardon is a half-legendary figure in the annals of golf. If modern golfers know anything factual about him at all, it probably concerns the Vardon grip—the grip that nearly every golfer uses today.

But in his heyday, which means at the turn of the last century, Harry

Vardon was known for something else. He was known for accuracy. Vardon was so accurate, they said, that he couldn't play two rounds of golf over the same course on the same day. Why? Because—get this—his afternoon tee shots would fall in the divot holes he'd made in the morning.

Now, if he was that good, why didn't he just adjust his shots a few inches one way or the other on the second round? But never mind. The truth is that Vardon *was* accurate. Here's a tale about his accuracy that has come down through the years.

On an exhibition tour of the United States in 1900, Vardon was talked into hitting shots into a net at the Jordan Marsh department store in Boston. The idea was to display his skill in a general way.

Vardon had a better idea. There was a valve handle on a fire extinguisher that projected through the netting. He decided to aim for it. Since the handle was only about an inch across, the probability of hitting it with any consistency would seem to be nil.

But this was Harry Vardon. He hit that valve handle so often that the store manager finally had to beg him to stop targeting it. The manager was afraid his store would be flooded.

If this sounds like a Paul Bunyan tale, remember that Harry Vardon told the story himself, and he was not one to exaggerate. To him, golf was strictly mechanical, and accuracy was no more than the proof of proper mechanics.

ACHIEVEMENT

Baseball

When Ted Williams joined the Boston Red Sox as a young outfielder, he was told, "Wait till you see Jimmy Foxx hit." His immediate reply was, "Wait till Foxx sees me hit."

He wasn't kidding. Ted Williams, with his phenomenal eyesight and perfect timing, put in 19 seasons in the major leagues and led the American League in hitting six times. His lifetime slugging average is second only to Babe Ruth's.

Many ballplayers spent what would have been important parts of their careers in military service in World War Two or the Korean War. Williams was one of them. As an Air Force fighter pilot, he served three years in World War Two and most of two more years in the Korean War.

Those would probably have been very good baseball years for Williams. In 1941—the season before World War Two—he was batting .39955—which is .400—going into the final day of the season. Manager Joe Cronin asked him if he wanted to sit out the doubleheader that day to protect his .400 average—the first since 1930 and the last one to the present day.

Williams said no. He played. And he lined six hits in eight trips to the plate to finish the season with a .406 average.

The Korean War caused him to miss most of the 1952 and 1953 seasons. In the mere 43 games he played in those two years, his batting average topped .400, and his slugging average was a lofty .900.

No one can say what Ted Williams would have done had he played full seasons in 1943, 1944, 1945, 1952, and 1953. It's a safe bet, though, that his career statistics would have been even more impressive than they are. The seasons surrounding these years were his very best.

ACHIEVEMENT

Basketball

In Wilt Chamberlain's best year as a pro, he averaged more than 50 points a game. No one else has ever approached that figure. Most NBA scoring leaders average in the low or mid 30s.

Frank McGuire, the coach of the Philadelphia Warriors, predicted that his star would someday score 100 points a game. That day came. The game was played at Hershey, Pennsylvania, on March 2, 1962, with Philadelphia as the home team and the New York Knicks as the visitors.

Chamberlain had been very hot that year. In one game he had poured in 78 points to set a new record. In the game at Hershey, he had two great advantages. The first was that the center playing against him, Darrall Imhoff, was not up to the job. The second was that Chamberlain was sinking nearly all his free throws, which was unheard of.

By the end of the half, Wilt had 41 points. By the end of the third quarter, he had 69. Four minutes into the fourth quarter, he had 79—and a new record.

His teammates began feeding him. He went over 80, over 90. The Knicks tried fouling other players to keep Chamberlain from scoring. McGuire had his subs foul Knicks' players to get the ball back. Even so, near the very end of the game Chamberlain went two full minutes without a point. It looked as if he might be stopped at 92.

Then he started in again. Three quick field goals, and he was hovering at 98. With 46 second left, he took a high pass near the net and jammed it through.

That was his scoring for the night—100 points. In addition to his 36 field goals, out of 63 attempted, he had scored 28 of 32 free throws. It was a once-in-a-lifetime achievement.

ACHIEVEMENT

Golf

Ponce de Leon went from St. Augustine to Key West in 1513—which isn't all that many strokes, considering the distance.

ACHIEVEMENT

Tennis

Billie Jean King was ranked number one in women's tennis for many years. She had mixed feelings about the achievement.

She said: "The trouble with being number one in the world—at anything—is that it takes a certain mentality to attain that position in the first place, and that is something of a driving, perfectionist attitude, so that once you do achieve number one, you don't relax and enjoy it."

ACHIEVEMENT

Track

Many of the track stars of yesterday are only dimly remembered names today. Their records have long since been broken and rebroken. As the great British middle-distance runner Sebastian Coe said, "World records are only borrowed."

ACHIEVEMENT

Track

Ron Clarke, the Australian long-distance runner, took part in 313 races over an eight-year period. He won 202 of them and set 17 world records. Still, there was a feeling in Australia that he couldn't win the big races—the Olympics, the Commonwealth Games. And it's true enough that he didn't.

There were the usual excuses: high altitude, tropical heat, injuries. The public bought none of it. In fact, there was a more basic problem than bad luck, a philosophical one. Clarke was a front-runner. He believed that the best runner in a race had an obligation to set the pace.

The conventional wisdom, as you know, is that front-runners get beaten. It's smart to stay back. And the conventional wisdom held true for Ron Clarke in his most important races.

Now, it may take a front-runner to appreciate a front-runner. Both John Landy of Great Britain and Emil Zatopek of Czechoslovakia were front-runners like Clarke. Landy was the second man to run the four-minute mile. Zatopek won three gold medals at the 1966 Olympics in Helsinki. Both regarded Clarke as one of the great competitors of his time.

Landy once stopped in the Australian Championship Mile race to help the fallen Clarke. He thought he had spiked Clarke while trying to avoid him. Incredibly, finding he hadn't, Landy resumed the race 60 yards behind the field, overtook everyone, and finished first.

Zatopek's concern for Ron Clarke's frustrations was equally touching. Clarke spent some time in Prague in 1966, visiting Zatopek. When Clarke left, the Czech star pressed a small box into his pocket. On the plane, Clarke opened the box. In it he found Zatopek's Olympic gold medal for the 10,000-meters in Helsinki. It was inscribed "To Ron Clarke, July 19, 1966."

Then Clarke recalled Zatopek's last words as he left Prague. "Not out of friendship," the Czech runner had said, "but because you deserve it."

When Ron Clarke thinks back on his track record, he remembers his 202 victories. He also remembers Landy and Zatopek. And he can easily forgive the typical response when his name is mentioned in Australia. "Ron Clarke? He's the bloke who never won anything, isn't he?"

ADVICE

Baseball

Willie Mays began playing for the Birmingham Black Barons when he was 17 years old. The Barons were one of the best teams in the old Negro leagues.

Mays' manager was Piper Davis, and Willie gave Piper much of the credit for turning him into a pro ballplayer.

One day Mays hit a home run off Chet Brewer, one of the league's best pitchers. The next time up, Brewer blazed a fastball into Willie's arm.

The Barons' 17-year-old centerfielder lay on the ground. He was in pain and crying. Piper knelt over him and said, "Don't let this guy show you up." He told Willie to get up and run to first base . . . then to steal second base . . . then to steal third.

Willie got up and raced to first. On the next pitch he stole second. As he led off the bag, ready to break for third, it struck him just how good Piper's advice was.

Chet Brewer had tried to show him up. It hadn't worked. The goat of the hour wasn't Willie Mays. It was Chet Brewer.

ADVICE

Baseball

Bill Terry, the National League's last .400 hitter, had no trouble hitting against Dizzy Dean.

One day in his first at-bat, he lined a shot off Dean's leg. It went for a single.

The second time up, he drove a screamer to center field. It missed the pitcher's ear by inches.

In his third appearance at the plate, Terry again lined a sizzler toward Dean. It almost tore the glove off Dean's hand.

At this, Pepper Martin trotted over from third base. "Diz," he said, "I don't think you're playing him deep enough."

ADVICE

Baseball

There were days when Frankie Frisch, manager of the Pittsburgh Pirates, was heckled mercilessly. This was one such day. A fan in the grandstand kept second-guessing Frisch's decisions and generally making a nuisance of himself.

Near the end of the game, Frisch walked over to the man and politely asked him for his name and business address.

The man seemed a little surprised, but readily handed the Pirates' manager a business card. "But I'm curious," the fan said. "Why do you want to know?"

"Because," Frisch said, "I'm going to be at your office the first thing tomorrow morning to tell you how to run your business."

ADVICE

Basketball

Red Holzman, the New York Knicks' basketball coach, remembered the time he had to release a ballplayer while on the road. It was early in his coaching career, before the big-money days, and he had a small room in a small hotel.

The player to be let go was a hulking six-foot-ten, 250-pound bundle of raw aggression. But Red prided himself on his ability to let a guy down easy in situations like this. He invited the ballplayer to his room. Holzman's smooth talk didn't quite work. The player turned green, then mean, then obscene. He stood up and advanced menacingly on the coach. Red retreated slowly to the door. The overwrought hulk followed him, toe to toe, glowering down, pressing all the way.

With his back against the doorknob, Holzman had no room left. He reached back, opened the door, and wished his ex-team member good luck and good-bye. Fortunately, the guy left, and Red breathed a sigh of relief.

He offered some advice to other coaches based on this experience: "Never release a guy in a small room," he said. "Always do it in an open area—a dance floor, a gym, a football field."

ADVICE

Golf

On the day the president of the company retired, his employees presented him with a golf club membership and a new set of clubs. The president had never played the game, but he decided the time had come to take it up.

On the first hole, he asked his caddy, "What am I supposed to do?"

"Do you see the flag down there, sir? You hit the ball toward the flag."

The president swung. And—can you believe it?—his drive went straight and true. The ball landed about three inches from the hole.

"What do I do now?" he asked.

"You hit the ball into the cup," said the caddy.

The president looked slightly annoyed. *"Now* he tells me."

ADVICE

Golf

As Buddy Hackett tells it, fellow comedian Jimmy Durante was no golfer, try as he might. On one particular day, Durante's first round was hellacious. When the Schnoz stepped up for the 18th hole, his score had already soared to well over 200. He took a 12 on the final hole and turned to his partner.

"What should I give the caddy?" he asked softly.

"Your clubs," his friend replied.

ADVICE

Horse Racing

Sometimes it may pay to heed even the most unlikely advice.

Red Smith tells the story of Bay View, an ordinary racehorse that sometimes rose to the occasion and ran a good race. One of those races was the Santa Anita Handicap, which at the time carried the world's biggest purse.

Up in the pressbox that day, Ed Burns of the *Chicago Tribune* groaned as Bay View romped home the winner. And well he might. Ed had planned to bet a few dollars on the race. That morning he'd received a telegram from J.G. Taylor Spink of *The Sporting News*. It read: "Don't overlook Bay View, no matter what the price."

Before the race, Ed had intended to follow Spink's advice. But at race time, when he looked at the tote board and saw Bay View at 60 to 1, he changed his mind. Horses running at those odds just don't win the big races.

"Some handicapper," he thought, stuffing the money back in his pocket. "Spink can really pick 'em."

Well, the odds on Bay View held, and the horse paid $118.40 to win. But not to Ed Burns.

ADVICE

Hunting

Experienced coon hunters say not to worry if you lose a dog while hunting. Just leave your jacket there, and the dog will find it. When you come back the next day, or two days later, the dog will be there waiting for you.

To this advice, the noted outdoorsman and writer Charley Dickey says, "The most jackets I've ever lost that way in a single season is nine."

ADVICE

Track

When Dink Templeton, a well-known track coach, was watching a college meet on the West Coast, a young man wearing track clothes came over to him.

"I need some advice," he said. "I run the hundred, but I'm not satisfied with my time. What can I do to improve it?

"That's easy," said Templeton. "Just run faster."

ASSISTANCE

Football

After a 33–0 loss to their archrivals on homecoming day, a white-faced grad approached the coach of his alma mater's football team.

"How many students do we have enrolled at the university, coach?" The coach thought for a moment. "About 24,000, I think."

The distraught alumnus grabbed the coach by the lapels and yelled, "Would it be asking too much to have two of them running interference?"

ASSISTANCE

Football

It's always gratifying to get help when you need it. Former NFL referee Norm Schachter tells the story about the time he had to referee a preseason football game at the Roundup Fairgrounds in Pendleton, Oregon.

As far as Schachter could see, the Fairgrounds had no dressing room for the game's officials. He asked Dallas coach Tom Landry about it. Landry shook his head. He asked Los Angeles coach Bob Waterfield about it. Waterfield had no idea.

Finally, he cornered a policeman who was working at the field. "I don't know about a dressing room for football officials," the officer said. "This is a rodeo field." But the policeman volunteered to find out. He went to look for help.

He was gone for quite a while. When he came back, he looked pleased with himself. "I don't know where you dress," he told Schachter. "But you come out of chute number three."

ASSISTANCE

Golf

When golfers talk about temper tantrums, they talk about Tommy Bolt. The U.S. Open Champion in 1958, Bolt was known almost as well for his club-throwing he was for his rhythmic swing.

During the 1960 Open at the Cherry Hills course in Denver, he had one of his best-known fits. He was playing well until the 12th hole, but then trouble began. He plopped a shot into a pond and got into an argument with a USGA official about where to place the ball.

Apparently upset, Bolt three-putted the next hole and bogeyed the next. By the 18th hole, steam was coming out of his ears. It didn't help at all when he hooked two drives into the lake. Bolt-watchers could tell that something was coming.

Tommy walked down to the edge of the lake, hesitated a moment, and then threw his driver far out into the water.

To Bolt's surprise—and to the surprise of the crowd around the 18th green—a small boy took off immediately toward the lake. He jumped in and waded to the spot where he thought the driver had dropped. He belly-flopped down, disappeared for a moment, and surfaced with the club.

The crowd cheered. Even Tommy Bolt looked pleased as the boy made his way back to shore.

As the youngster climbed up, he saw Bolt coming toward him. The golfer had a restrained smile on his face. The kid looked surprised. Then he made his intentions clear. He turned and raced away from Tommy Bolt and the specta-tors, out across the fairway, clutching the club he had just recovered.

The crowd, which had just cheered him for being a Good Samaritan, now cheered him for being a rogue. Bolt himself continued to smile grimly.

ASSISTANCE

Golf

Legendary golfer Bobby Jones designed the Augusta National golf course. Every spring the world's great golfers gather there for the Masters Tournament. Down Magnolia Lane, amid the oaks and dogwoods and aza-leas, is one of the trickiest courses anywhere.

When rookie Fuzzy Zoeller came to Augusta in 1979, he knew that his lack of experience on the course would hurt him. So he asked for help—from his caddy.

Zoeller figured that his caddy, Jerry Beard, knew the course a lot better than he did. So Fuzzy just held out his hand prior to each shot and used whatever club Jerry put in it. He would ask, "How hard do I hit it?" Beard would tell him, and Zoeller would swing.

Did the strategy work? It did indeed. Fuzzy Zoeller won the Masters in a playoff that year. People regarded his strategy as strange, even foolish, but Zoeller said that the dumb ones were "the guys who come down here once a year and try to get smart with Mr. Jones's course."

ASSISTANCE

Marathoning

Some kind-hearted assistance cost Dorando Pietri a gold medal in the marathon at the 1908 London Olympics. Well, maybe not. The tiny, gallant Italian could never have crossed the finish line without assistance, but with it he was disqualified.

When Dorando reached White City Stadium, the finishing point of the marathon, he was far in the lead. He had only 385 yards to go for the gold, but it was obvious he was dazed and in trouble. Under the arch, he turned the wrong way. Officials blocked him, and he wheeled and headed in the right direction.

He had nothing left. Nothing at all. His knees began to buckle. His eyes were half closed, and he staggered from side to side like a sodden drunk. He fell, but managed to get up. He fell again, then again—four times in all. Each time he stumbled to his feet and swayed forward.

To the officials beside him, he looked like the picture of death. As he fought against a final collapse, the officials stepped in, grabbed him, lifted, dragged, and carried him across the finish line. He was immediately taken off on a stretcher.

The Italian flag went up in the stadium.

Then the number two runner came breezing in. He was 19-year-old Johnny Hayes of the United States, and he showed no signs of fatigue. He crossed the finish line, apparently happy in the belief that he had won the silver medal.

Now, it's clear enough that brave little Dorando Pietri hadn't won the race. The rules state that a runner has to cross the finish line unaided. Dorando had tried to do that. How he had tried! But he hadn't succeeded. The officials had stepped in and helped out.

And so Dorando Pietri was disqualified, and Johnny Hayes of the United States won the gold medal.

Back in New York City, a young songwriter, just a year older than Johnny Hayes, had followed the story with interest. He wrote a song about it. In years to come, this talented young American would write a lot of other songs, including "God Bless America."

But on the occasion of the London Olympics, Irving Berlin wrote a less patriotic air—one that is now pretty much forgotten, although it became his first big hit. He called it "Dorando."

ASSISTANCE

Track

Ireland's Ron Delany won the 1500-meter run at the Melbourne Olympics in 1956. He had some help.

It was a close, exciting race. The twelve finalists were closely bunched coming into the final lap. The official who was to signal the start of the last lap failed to ring the bell.

With less than eight yards separating the first and last place runners, Ron Delany was in tenth place and boxed in. His coach, Jumbo Elliott of Villanova, had told him to relax in such a box.

He did, but there were only 300 yards to go.

The runner in front of Delany was Gunner Nielsen, who could not hold the pace. Realizing he couldn't win, he glanced back and motioned Delany to pass him on the inside.

Suddenly out of the box, Delany moved up. He sprinted powerfully for the last 120 yards, racing past the other runners in a brilliant closing drive. He won by almost six yards.

CHALLENGE

Golf

Arnold Palmer on the challenge of golf: "Golf is deceptively simple and endlessly complicated. A child can play it well, and a grown man can never master it. . . . It is gratifying and tantalizing, precise and unpredictable; it requires complete concentration and total relaxation. It is, at the same time, rewarding and maddening. . . ."

CHALLENGE

Skiing

Dick Buek's colorful personality, great talent, and untimely death made him a legend on the ski runs of the world.

Nick Howe, another fine skier, remembers his introduction to the legend.

When Howe first went up the chairlift at Sun Valley's Cold Springs run, he saw a small building part way down the slope. It looked like a pumphouse buried to the eaves in snow. No one had skied in that direction.

The second time Howe rode the lift he saw that someone had crossed over to the pumphouse from the center of the run and drawn a message in the snow on the roof. It said: "O.K. BUEK."

When Howe went up the third time, he saw a single skier's tracks headed down the run toward the pumphouse. They went directly at the building, climbed its sloping roof, sliced through the message, and ended.

Far below, the snow showed the impact of the skier's landing. The tracks continued in a straight line down the run.

Buek had seen the message and responded.

CHANGE

Baseball

Even Lindsey Nelson, the New York Mets broadcaster, thought the early Mets were the most overpublicized team in baseball. Their first ragtag team of 1962 enjoyed a ticker-tape parade down Broadway. They went on to lose an incredible 120 games against 40 wins. The Mets were bad, bad, bad.

There's one trivia item about the fledgling Mets that has a kind of sad irony. The team's first ticket office, opened in November 1961, was at the Martinique Hotel. The name may not mean much to out-of-towners, but to New Yorkers the word Martinique became almost a synonym for hell. A respectable commercial hotel in 1961, it declined into the most notorious of all the city's welfare hotels in the 1980s. By the time the Mets had become respectable, the Martinique was bad, bad, bad.

Still, there's an interesting story about the original ticket office. The Martinique is seven blocks south of the Metropolitan Opera House. When a sign went up in the Martinique that read "Mets Ticket Office," it was inevitable that a few people would stop in to buy tickets to *Don Giovanni*.

About all the Mets' ticket manager could do was to ask them if they wouldn't rather see third baseman Don Zimmer or coach Don Heffner.

CHANGE

Baseball

Loud were the wails when Astroturf first made its appearance in Houston's Astrodome. The outrage continues today. Many players, sportswriters, and fans, then and now, have argued that the only proper surface for baseball is natural grass, not a green carpet.

As Phillies star Dick Allen put it, "If my horse can't eat it, I don't want to play on it."

CHANGE

Basketball

Coaches tend to get upset when a ritual goes awry. No one gets more upset than Indiana basketball coach Bob Knight.

The fans at Assembly Hall in Bloomington, Indiana, had established a ritual for Steve Alford's free throws. Or rather, Alford had established one. He would wipe his socks, wipe his shorts, dribble three times, and then shoot. The procedure never varied.

The Indiana fans developed a chant to accompany this ritual. It went, "Socks . . . shorts . . . one-two-three . . . swish!" Alford was an outstanding free-throw shooter, and the swish usually happened.

In any case, it was a well-established routine. The crowd had given their chant hundreds of times.

But in the first half of a close game against Illinois, Steve Alford missed the first of two free throws. Bob Knight exploded. Why didn't those idiots keep quiet and let Steve concentrate? He went over to the cheerleaders. "I'm holding you people responsible for that!" he shouted. And more.

The cheerleaders got the message. So did the fans.

In the second half the game was still close. With 31 seconds left, the score was 68 to 67, Indiana leading.

Steve Alford drew a foul and stepped to the line for two free throws. Now the crowd had a new message. When he was ready to shoot, the fans let out a soft "Shhhhhhh."

Curiously, that didn't work either. Alford, who sank more than 90 percent of his free throws in college, missed one of two this time.

But the score held at 69 to 67. Indiana won, and for the moment at least Bob Knight was happy.

CHANGE

Basketball

Spectator sports have always been a branch of entertainment, but it wasn't until television came along that sports stars began being paid movie-star salaries. Old-time players still marvel at the dollar differences between then and now.

Take Nat "Sweetwater" Clifton, who starred with the New York Knicks and Detroit Pistons in the 1950s, just before the salary explosion. Clifton, who got his nickname because of his preference for 7-Up and Coke over beer or liquor, played with the Harlem Globetrotters for a few years and then moved on to the Knicks. His starting salary with the Knicks was $7,500. Like all players in those days, he did his own negotiating—and never made more than $10,000 a year.

After his pro basketball days, Sweetwater Clifton took a job driving a cab in Chicago. He got other offers of employment but refused them because he wanted to stay near his invalid mother.

Looking back on his basketball career, he regrets that he never made much money. He doesn't hold it against the owners, though. He says, "The guys I negotiated with . . . were nice guys. They gave me whatever I asked for. I just didn't ask for enough."

CHANGE

Cycling

In 1840 a Scottish blacksmith named Kirkpatrick Macmillan introduced crank-driving and pedals to the already popular bicycle. And he was quite a rider of the new machine, pushing it all the way up to 14 miles an hour.

At that speed he often went flying past the local stagecoaches. Such unseemly speed dismayed the drivers and passengers. It also attracted the notice of local police, who forthwith arrested him for what they called "furious driving on the road."

CHANGE

Hockey

Hockey has always been a violent sport. Old-timers say it used to be a lot more violent than it is today.

At one time, Sprague Cleghorn was the undisputed champion of body-checks, charging, cross-checks, elbows, butt-ends, and fists. Once when the rampaging Cleghorn was recovering from a broken leg, his wife swore out a warrant for his arrest. She said he had attacked her with his crutch. Face it, the guy was just plain aggressive.

Another tough player in the early days of the National Hockey League was King Clancy, who played for the Ottawa Senators and the Toronto Maple Leafs. Clancy was small but pugnacious, famous for starting fights on the ice and then losing them.

One afternoon, long after his retirement from coaching and refereeing, King Clancy was watching the Maple Leafs lose a playoff game to the Boston Bruins. Both teams were playing well, but it was all too clean and upstanding for the 70-year-old Clancy. He resented the gentlemanly changes that he felt had transformed hockey.

"The game's just not the same," he lamented. "We don't have a soul who'll walk out there tonight when the whistle blows and hammer somebody into the seats."

CHANGE

Horse Racing

Danny's clothes were looking a little sharper. He shaved more often. There was a new air of prosperity about him.

"Has Danny started winning on the horses?" I asked.

"Naw," my friend said. "He finally figured out a way to leave the track with money—he gave up picking horses and started picking pockets."

CHANGE

Hunting

There's an old story about a knight who is given a magic charm to protect him while he fights fire-breathing dragons. The knight has complete faith in the charm, and he sallies forth bravely to kill 50 dragons in a row. Then, the night before he is to challenge his 51st dragon, he learns that the charm has no real power. Its purpose is only to make him feel secure.

You can guess the outcome. The knight never returns from his encounter with the 51st dragon.

It's much the same, says *Field and Stream* writer Havilah Babcock, with a hunter and his gun. The hunter has to look upon that gun in about the same way the knight looked upon his magic charm. He has to believe in it.

Babcock tells about a shotgun that he borrowed from a neighbor. It was a double-barreled Lefever that had seen better days. Nevertheless, Babcock, to his surprise, found the relic to be an absolute gem, the perfect quail gun. In his first outing, he dropped 13 birds with 13 shots. The next day he brought down 11 of 13.

He just had to buy that old Lefever, and he did. He carried the rickety firearm home in his car as if it were a rare treasure. It was the ultimate quail gun. It was—yes—a magic charm.

The next morning he was getting ready for a hunting trip. He cradled the Lefever lovingly in his arms. And then he noticed something. Something scary. The perfect quail gun had Damascus barrels.

Now, Damascus barrels were the very thing back in the days of black powder. But by now they were obsolete. Nitro loads could blow them apart and, along with the barrels, the hunter.

At first Babcock was depressed. His gun was dangerous and unusable. Still, he had used it for two days with brilliant success. He had dropped 24 of 26 quail with the magnificent antique. He couldn't abandon it now. So, like the knight challenging his 51st dragon, Havilah Babcock sallied forth.

He might as well have stayed at home. He used the gun for an entire week. He bagged nothing at all. His own sad words summed up the post-Damascus revelation. "I couldn't hit a streetcar with it," he said.

CHANGE

Hunting

If you're a hunter and use a scope, you know that scopes and scope mounts can creep. You can be shooting test groups the size of a quarter at a hundred yards only to find that the next day that you've got a group bigger than a hot air balloon.

Keeping a barrel coordinated with a telescopic sight is a trial. You never know what to expect.

Charley Dickey once went off on an elk hunt with a hastily sighted-in 7-mm Magnum rifle. He was getting a basketball group at two hundred yards. That was not what he wanted, but time was running out, he had an airplane to catch, and away he went.

At the airport his cased rifle fell off the luggage conveyor belt onto a concrete floor. Next day, on a horse, he saw his rifle bouncing and vibrating in its scabbard. He was pretty sure that if he got a shot at an elk, the scope would be little more than a bad gamble.

Not to worry. In five days of racing about the mountains with his frantic guide, he never saw an elk. He never had time to sight-in the rifle either. Once he did take the rifle out of the scabbard, and what did he do but drop it. It clattered down a gravel slope.

When he returned home, he knew he'd better check the scope. From a bench at two hundred yards on the local range, he fired five shots. Two friends were watching him, and he says they can verify this—the five shots formed a group the size of a dime.

That banging around on the trip had actually brought the barrel and scope into perfect coordination. If only he had seen an elk. . . .

CHANGE

Marathoning

Women were not allowed to compete in the New York Marathon until 1972 and not in the Olympics until 1984. If the idea was that women wouldn't be competitive with men, then the gurus were wrong.

Consider Grete Waitz, the great Norwegian runner.

When Grete Waitz finished the 1979 New York Marathon, *The New York Times* published an editorial under the heading, "2:27:33—and Waiting." Her time—two hours, 27 minutes, and 33 seconds—was a world record for the 26-mile, 385-yard distance.

Now, it's true that it was a women's record. Bill Rodgers, the men's winner, finished about 16 minutes ahead of Mrs. Waitz.

In marathoning, as in most other sports, the general level of performance tends to rise with each new generation of athletes. So it's never quite fair to make comparisons across the years. The four-minute mile was once regarded as an impossibility. Today it's commonplace.

Nevertheless, fair or not, here's a fact to think about: If Grete Waitz had run the New York Marathon in 1970—and if she had run it in 2:27:33—she would have beaten every man in the race.

CHANGE

Polo

Have you seen any left-handed polo players lately? Probably not, because since January 1, 1974, they've been outlawed.

What's this? Left-handers of the world unite! Why would the United

States Polo Association want to discriminate against left-handers? What brought about the change?

There's a very good reason. Polo horses can gallop at speeds up to 40 miles an hour. Suppose a left-handed player and a right-handed player are racing for the ball from opposite directions. According to the rules, they can't cross the line of the ball—which would mean that the poor horses would be charging at each other on an 80-mile-an-hour collision course.

A number of high-speed collisions convinced the governing body of polo that the rights of left-handers would have to be sacrificed in the interests of safety.

So if you're a left-hander and were thinking about taking up polo, forget it. Go out for baseball. Play first base. Or try tennis. Or some other game where you'll be appreciated.

CHARISMA

Baseball

Sportswriter Jimmy Cannon wrote a one-line sketch on the magic of Babe Ruth: "He was a parade all by himself, a burst of dazzle and jingle. . . . "

CHARISMA

Tennis

It's an axiom that performances in all sports have gotten better over the years. In swimming and in track and field, the facts can be easily documented. In other sports, the improvements aren't so clear. There are still people who say that the oldtimers—the Joe Louises, the Babe Ruths—were the best.

Tennis seems more prone to this nostalgia than many other sports. Bill Tilden, they say, could have beaten anybody playing today. And Suzanne Lenglen—ah, Suzanne Lenglen.

Whenever someone ranks the all-time women tennis players, Suzanne Lenglen appears at or near the top of the list. In her prime, way back in the 1920s, she displayed dazzling ability. She was also the first of the showbiz tennis stars.

Television would not have been kind to Suzanne. Her sallow complexion required heavy makeup, and her nose could have been lifted from the face of an eagle. Yet at a distance—say, from the Wimbledon stands—she looked gorgeous, with perfectly controlled strength and ballerina grace.

Tennis fans adored Suzanne. From the very beginning, she played her starring role to the hilt. When changing ends during a match, she sipped champagne from a bottle she kept on the sidelines. Her father tossed her sugar cubes spiked with brandy. She wore glamorous and ever-changing tennis clothes. Her lipstick, even when purple, matched the color of her headband—and her headband was a famous trademark.

How good a tennis player was Suzanne Lenglen? She was very, very good. Whether she could have beaten the women players of today is a moot question. She might have held her own against Chris Evert or Martina Navratilova. Or maybe not.

What does seem clear is that she could have held her own against anyone today in charm and assurance. She loved crowds as much as they loved her. She knew what they wanted, and it was more than brilliant tennis. She wore the first silk see-through dress. She showed a shocking expanse of bare leg above her stockings. She strolled onto the center court at Wimbledon wearing a brown rabbit skin coat over her tennis dress.

Suzanne Langlen was ahead of her time all right. She was a crowd-pleaser and a great tennis star of the '20s. She might even have won some big matches today. We'll never know.

COMPARISON

Baseball

Rod Carew was one of the best contact hitters in baseball. No matter how the pitcher tried to fool him, Carew would adjust.

A long-time National League pitcher, Curt Simmons, gave the best description of what it was like to face Rod Carew from the pitcher's mound.

"Trying to sneak a pitch past him," Simmons said, "is like trying to sneak the sunrise past a rooster."

COMPARISON

Basketball

Sam Houston State had a competitive basketball team except for one thing—they couldn't hit on their free throws. Halfway through the season, their free-throw percentage was a dismal 61 percent. Time after time, the team went down to defeat by far fewer points that their missed free throws would have provided.

When archrival Southwest Texas State won by a single point on Sam Houston's home court—after ten missed free throws—Coach Jeff Bittman was at his wit's end. Talking to the team didn't help. "It's mostly psychological," he said. "It boils down to confidence."

One out of every six points a game, on the average, is a free throw. So the free throw is important. Said Bittman, "It's like the extra point in football, but we can't fire the placekicker."

COMPARISON

Boxing

Heavyweight champion Joe Louis served in the army during World War Two. While he was driving with another soldier, he was involved in an accident with a truck. It wasn't serious, but the truck driver was furious. He screamed and swore at Louis, who just sat in the driver's seat and smiled.

Louis's friend was surprised by the boxer's calm reaction. Why didn't Joe get out and flatten the guy, he wanted to know.

"Why should I?" Joe asked. "When somebody insulted Caruso, did he sing an aria for him?"

COMPARISON

Football

Coach Woody Hayes of Ohio State was a student of history, especially military history. He kept pictures of generals on his office walls. He sometimes compared players to military leaders.

One of his best quarterbacks, Rex Kern, came from Lancaster, Ohio. "Now, do you know what other great leader came from the same town?" Woody once asked an interviewer. General William T. Sherman, that's who—the man who, in Woody's words, "ran an option play right through the South in the Civil War." Sherman was quick and versatile. He never gave the defense a chance to dig in. Just like Rex Kern, as Woody saw it.

Yep, Kern's quarterbacking resembled General Sherman's. And both men were from Lancaster, Ohio. "Y'see, history is full of such ironies," Woody said.

COMPARISON

Football

Then strip, lads, and to it, though sharp be the weather,
And if by mischance, you should happen to fall,
There are worse things in life than a tumble on heather,
And life is itself but a game of football.

—Sir Walter Scott

COMPARISON

Football

Earl (Red) Blaik coached football at the U.S. Military Academy during the dark years of World War Two and the bright years of Glenn Davis and Doc Blanchard.

He made this comparison: "In its steep physical, mental, and moral challenges, in its sacrifices, selflessness, and courage, football, beyond any game invented by man, is closest to war."

COMPARISON

Horse Racing

Secretariat was a racehorse almost in a class with Man o' War. He won the Triple Crown of thoroughbred racing in 1973. His time in the Kentucky Derby has never been equaled, and his time in the Belmont Stakes has hardly been approached.

You might think that Secretariat's yearlings would bring an astronomical price. Well, they do—but not quite so astronomical as those of a horse named Alydar. At a time when Secretariat's yearlings were selling for an average of $200,000, Alydar's were bringing $500,000.

How come? If breeding is what it's cracked up to be, why wouldn't Secretariat be the absolute king of sires? Why would Alydar—a horse that finished second to Affirmed in all three races for the Triple Crown—be a better father?

Trainer Woody Stephens put the answer simply: "Breeding is a risky game." Although bloodlines are the bedrock of thoroughbred racing, there are no guarantees.

Alydar turned out to be a great sire. Secretariat was very good, but not up to Alydar. And Affirmed, who nosed out Alydar in those Triple Crown races, was a flop.

COMPARISON

Horse Racing

He was having a terrible day at the track.

"I can't understand it," he said. "When I play cards, I always win. But at the racetrack I always lose. Why?"

His friend replied, "Because at the track you can't shuffle the horses."

COMPETITION

Auto Racing

Mario Andretti raced to win. "In any of your competitive sports," he said, "unless you can be a winner, forget it!"

And, with a dash of metaphor, he observed: "I want to climb that tree and get to the very top of it. Some of those limbs up there I know can be awfully flimsy. But you're never going to reach the top unless you step on a few, and hope to hell they don't break. You've got to take those chances...."

COMPETITION

Baseball

Heywood Broun, a New York City journalist, took a more cynical view of baseball than some of his contemporaries. "The tradition of professional baseball," he wrote, "has been agreeably free of charity. The rule is, 'Do anything you can get away with.' "

COMPETITION

Baseball

Tommy Lasorda always thought he would be a major league pitcher. Eventually he became one, but his lifetime record was no wins and four losses. He was great at the Triple-A level, but he never made the final, successful step to the top.

When he became a manager, he found himself explaining the facts of competition to his young players. At Ogden, Utah, he had a kid from Brooklyn who was getting shelled one night. He went to the mound to make a pitching change. The kid was downcast. Back in high school, he said, he could strike out 16 or 17 batters a game.

Lasorda asked him about the batters he didn't strike out.

The kid looked puzzled.

Tommy explained. "Those are the guys who are here now. The guys you struck out are still back in Brooklyn."

COMPETITION

Baseball

Pete Rose on competition: "Somebody's gotta win and somebody's gotta lose—and I believe in letting the other guy lose."

COMPETITION

Football

The Army-Navy football game is one of the classic college rivalries. Army won the 1949 game by a score of 38 to 0, its greatest edge ever. Army also won the battle of the banners that day.

An Army officer on duty at Annapolis had learned of a series of banners that Navy intended to hoist during the game. The banners would poke fun at Army's easy schedule. They would imply that the West Pointers had dropped much of their tough competition, while Navy still faced it.

The Midshipmen were also ready with a parody of the Army fight song. What they didn't know was that the Army men would be ready with some prepared responses to these insults.

After the Middies had kidded Army in song for playing tiny Davidson

College—and for not playing such schools as Notre Dame and Tulane—they raised a huge banner. It read: "When Do You Drop Navy?"

To their amazement, the Cadets' cheering section immediately unfurled a banner of their own. It read: "Today."

Caution might have suggested that Navy would do well to forget about the rest of their banners. But no. They unfurled a second banner. This one read: "Why Not Schedule Vassar?"

The Cadets came back with a response to that one, too. Their banner read: "We Already Got Navy."

COMPETITION

Football

Sometimes competition comes from unexpected sources. In a football game you expect the struggle to be between the two teams. But at a 1954 football game in Northwestern's Dyche Stadium, there was a battle of the bands.

Now, playing of the national anthem used to be standard at major sporting events. But on this particular occasion even the most fervent patriot would have preferred silence.

Just before the two teams took up their struggle, the visiting band from the University of Illinois was on one side of the field, facing Northwestern's band on the other. Instead of unity in music, it evolved into a clash between the bands, which were unwittingly playing the national anthem in two different keys.

The only people unaware of the cacophony were the bandsmen themselves, whose ears were filled with the sounds of their own instruments. They blasted away to the bitter end in a musical version of scraping chalk on a rough blackboard.

COMPETITION

Skiing

Races in Alpine skiing are measured to the thousandth of a second. Sometimes the first ten racers are within one second of each other. According to skier Weems Westfeldt, "If someone like Ingemar Stenmark wins by a margin of one-half second or more, he says, 'What took you guys so long?' "

CONCENTRATION

Boxing

A boxer has to concentrate. He can't let his mind wander. He can't spend time talking with the referee.

Jack Sharkey found that out the hard way. Sharkey's weakness was in taking punches to the body. He didn't like to get hit there.

For his fight with Sharkey, Jack Dempsey naturally decided to fight in close, pummeling Sharkey's body. The strategy worked, and Sharkey began to get hot about it. He turned to the referee and snarled, "He's hitting me low."

At the instant he turned, Dempsey hit him high. Sharkey reeled from the left hook to his chin, toppled to the canvas, and the fight was over.

Later Sharkey complained bitterly. He said Dempsey hit him when he wasn't looking. He was right.

Dempsey had the perfect answer. "Well, why ain't you looking?" he said. "The fight's still on." He figured Sharkey should have been watching him, not the referee. It's hard to argue with that.

CONCENTRATION

Fishing

Does a smart fisherman catch more trout than a dumb fisherman? Ed Zern, the fishing humorist, thought about that question carefully. He concluded that the smart money would be on the dummy. Here's why.

Trout fishing requires absolute concentration. You have to be ready to tighten at once when the fish rises to a floating lure. You have only a split second. You have to be alert.

Zern couldn't imagine an exceptionally bright person— a nuclear physicist, say, or a mathematics professor—paying all that close attention to his lure. The brainy fellow would be thinking about other things. Higher matters. His mind would be wandering.

The slow-witted guy, on the other hand, would be staring dully at that lure. He'd be ready. As soon as a fish rose, the dolt would be ready to set the hook. And he would.

Zern's observation may not say much for brains, but it definitely says something for concentration.

CONCENTRATION

Golf

Ben Hogan's concentration on the golf course was legendary. Once when George Fazio was paired with Hogan in a tournament, Fazio sank a five-iron shot for an eagle-two. The audience greeted this feat with deafening applause.

Hogan walked single-mindedly to the next tee.

When he got there, he pulled out a scorecard and turned to Fazio. "What did you have on that last hole, George?" he asked.

CONCENTRATION

Soccer

Roberto Rivelino was one of Brazil's greatest soccer players. He had outstanding talent and tremendous drive. But he also had a short fuse.

An opposing coach used Rivelino's well-known temper as a part of his game plan. The coach had a player on his team who was an acquaintance of Rivelino's. This player's assignment was to aggravate Rivelino—to kick him a little, to blow on the back of his neck, and so on.

At first Rivelino would take these irritants in stride, maybe even smile at them. But as they continued, Roberto's anger would rise. In time he would be paying more attention to the needling than to the game. He just couldn't concentrate.

As the opposing coach said, "That was how we nullified him."

CONCENTRATION

Tennis

Chris Evert, one of the world's finest tennis players, had tremendous powers of concentration. Like most top tennis players, she started early and played the game single-mindedly.

Once during a junior tournament someone had left a chair near the backline. Whenever Chris went back for a shot, she bumped into the chair. But she never moved it.

After the match someone asked her why she hadn't moved the chair. Chris looked puzzled. "What chair?" she asked.

CONSISTENCY

Baseball

Pinch-hitting is one of the toughest roles in baseball. A pinch-hitter, by definition, is not good enough to be in the starting lineup. Yet he must come off the bench, usually in a critical situation, and deliver a hit—something the best regular players can do only once in three or so at-bats. For a pinch-hitter to come through time after time under this kind of pressure is next to impossible.

But consider the case of Dusty Rhodes, a wayfaring ballplayer for the New York Giants in the 1950s. In 1954 the Giants made it to the World Series, but they went in as 22 to 1 underdogs against the Cleveland Indians. And no wonder. The Indians had won 111 games that year, more than any other team in American League history. Al Lopez's Indians figured to breeze to victory in the Series.

Dusty Rhodes, coming off the Giants' bench as a pinch-hitter, changed their thinking.

In the first game of the Series, Rhodes blasted a pinch-hit three-run homer in the tenth inning to give the Giants the win.

In the second game of the Series, he slapped a pinch-hit single to tie the game in the fifth inning, then homered for an insurance run in the seventh.

In the third game of the Series, he hit a pinch-hit single with the bases loaded in the third inning to drive in two runs en route to the Giants' third straight win.

Rhodes rested in the fourth game. He wasn't needed. The Giants jumped out to a 7 to 0 lead and held on to win the game, thus taking the Series in four straight. No World Series upset before or since has been as shattering as this four-game devastation of the Indians.

And no World Series pinch-hitter has ever come close to the cool consistency of Dusty Rhodes. A journeyman ballplayer before and afterwards, Rhodes dominated the 1954 World Series as a pinch-hitter, batting .667 and leading the Giants to a storybook triumph.

CONSISTENCY

Football

John Madden, former head coach of the Oakland Raiders, said he wasn't interested in the kind of fancy player who occasionally makes a big play.

"I didn't want a big play once in a while," he said. "I wanted a solid play every time."

CONSISTENCY

Golf

Goldman, who was very big in textiles, had never played golf, but he decided the time had come. He bought a fine set of clubs and ventured out on the course.

To his caddy he said, "Listen, I know nothing about this game. What do I do?"

His caddy patiently explained the procedure of holding the club and hitting the ball. He pointed out the distant green and the flag and described the small hole that Goldman would be aiming for.

"Okay, got it," said the textile king. He stepped up and aimed a prodigious blow at the dimpled little ball. The spheroid took off straight and true. It headed on a perfect arc for the green.

The caddy, thunderstruck, followed its course, chased it down, and found it lying in the cup. He stared at the ball for a long moment. An incredible hole in one.

Goldman made his way to the green, casually picked up the ball, and said, "What next?"

The caddy pointed with dumb wonder toward the second hole.

This time the new golfer's powerful swing produced a bad slice. His ball ricocheted off a large tree, but then angled back directly toward the green.

Amazed, the caddy reached toward the cup and, sure enough, found the ball resting in it. Another hole in one for Goldman, this time on a bank shot off a sycamore.

With perfect calm, Goldman picked up the ball and looked toward the third hole. He let go with another strong but awkward flail, and the ball took off on a line. His drive was short, but the ball, as if guided by radar, hopped briskly toward the green. It neared the cup. It stopped an eyelash short.

The caddy went up, stood over it, and sighed in disbelief. Goldman strolled nonchalantly to the green and took a long look.

He smiled at the caddy, shrugged in a matter-of-fact way, and said, "It had to happen. A beginner's a beginner."

CONSISTENCY

Sailing

T.O.M. Sopwith of the Royal Yacht Squadron in England was already known to many Americans when he issued his challenge for the America's Cup.

More than 20 years earlier, he had barnstormed as a stunt flier in the United States. On one memorable day off Coney Island, he had a mishap that dunked him in the ocean. Along with stunt flying, Sopwith had also raced motorboats in this country.

When World War One broke out, he quickly became a leader in the infant aviation industry. His Sopwith Camel is still a favorite of Snoopy's in his dogfights with the Red Baron.

Sopwith's challenge called for a four-out-of-seven series, starting on September 15, 1934, off Newport, Rhode Island. The British entry, the *Endeavour*, had been a consistent winner in England. Its record and appearance made Harold Vanderbilt of the New York Yacht Club a bit uneasy. "*Endeavour* is a fast boat—a very fast boat," he was heard to say.

Still, neither the British nor anyone else from overseas had been able to take home the America's Cup in more than 80 years. Boats from the United States had won consistently. One after another the challengers went down to defeat. But Sopwith's challenge looked like a serious one.

And it was. The U.S. entry, the *Rainbow*, had been chosen only after some seesaw contests with two other boats. Few American yachtsmen were convinced that she was unbeatable.

The *Endeavour* won the first race by two minutes and nine seconds, going away. In the second race, both yachts bettered the old 30-mile course record, but once again the British *Endeavour* won, this time by 51 seconds.

In the third race, the *Endeavour* led at one point by more than six and a half minutes. The situation looked grim. But then some costly mistakes by the crew of the *Endeavour* and some brilliant sailing by the Rainbow's crew turned it around. The Americans won a tough come-from-behind victory. No one was elated, though. Without the British errors, the cup would have been all but lost that day.

The crew of the *Endeavour* never recovered. The American *Rainbow* went on to win the next three races, turning back the British challenge yet again. To some people here and abroad, it began to look as if the America's Cup would remain at the New York Yacht Club forever.

Sopwith's *Endeavour* was almost certainly the faster boat. Only superb sailing by the *Rainbow*'s crew—and a few foul-ups aboard the *Endeavour*—saved the America's Cup for the United States.

CONSISTENCY

Tennis

Frank Sedgman, the Australian tennis player, ranked Jack Kramer as the best competitor he'd ever seen. Other players might have greater natural ability, but Kramer had a priceless gift—consistency. He didn't suffer wild streaks. He didn't make strings of errors. He didn't have lapses of concentration. And he always knew the odds. Game after game, match after match, Kramer kept up the pressure, forcing others into mistakes, seldom making any himself.

COOPERATION

Auto Racing

Racing drivers, according to one psychologist, are extraordinarily tough-minded. They are aggressive, decisive, self-disciplined, and strongly independent. They are not the kind of people you would expect to step modestly aside for another when the World Championship of racing is on the line.

Yet the talented English driver Peter Collins did just that in 1956. He willingly forfeited the world championship and handed it to Argentina's legendary Juan Manuel Fangio.

Here's how it happened.

Collins and Fangio were both driving for Team Ferrari in 1956. It was Peter Collins's first big year of international racing, and the fun-loving Collins may well have been astonished to find himself number one on the Grand Prix circuit and Juan Manuel Fangio, number two. For Fangio was by then considered one of the greatest—if not *the* greatest—race driver who ever lived. He had won world championships in 1951, 1954, and 1955.

In the final race at Monza, Fangio was in trouble. He was stranded in the pits with a car that was being repaired and seemed certain to finish far back.

Fangio's manager flagged Peter Collins in and asked him if Juan could replace him in the cockpit. We don't know what went through Collins's mind at that moment. He was being asked the unthinkable, to relinquish the World Championship to another driver. He may have had mixed emotions—he probably did—but he said yes.

Juan Fangio climbed into the Ferrari and took off. Although he finished second in the race to Stirling Moss, driving a Maserati, he finished first in title points. Fangio had won his fourth World Championship.

COOPERATION

Horse Racing

Steve Cauthen, one of America's great jockeys rode Affirmed to the Triple Crown of thoroughbred racing in 1978.

He explained his success. "The horse weighs 1000 pounds," he said, "and I weigh 95. I guess I'd better get him to cooperate."

COOPERATION

Mountaineering

If you've ever been in a spot where you desperately needed help, think of poor George Hopkins. In October 1941 Hopkins, a stunt parachutist, dropped down on the top of Devil's Tower, Wyoming—a place that has been aptly called "an island in the sky."

A 1,000-foot coil of rope was dropped down to aid him in his descent from the tower. Unfortunately, the rope fell onto some ledges well below the summit. Hopkins had no way to reach it.

This parachute drop was made before the days of helicopter rescues. And at the time, only three teams of climbers had ever made this ascent to the top of Devil's Tower.

It's important to be able to picture Devil's Tower. It looks like an immense upside-down thimble rising 1,300 feet above the tree line. A couple of ranchers had once built a crude ladder to the top, but the ladder was long since gone. The upper 500 feet of the volcanic rock tower requires rock-climbing skills, nothing less. George Hopkins was stuck.

Park officials—for Devil's Tower is a National Monument—had supplies dropped to him by airplane and wondered what to do next.

Jack Durrance, who lived in Hanover, New Hampshire, had climbed Devil's Tower in 1938, establishing what is known today as the Durrance Route. He offered to lead a rescue team to the summit. There weren't a whole lot of options, and park officials eagerly accepted his offer.

Durrance traveled by train from New Hampshire to Wyoming. He found his climbing route wet and partially coated with ice. It wasn't an easy ascent, but Durrance and his team made it.

At the summit they found George Hopkins in remarkably good spirits, none the worse for his six-day ordeal. He was a professional daredevil, of course, and he had always expected a fairly tough descent.

Jack Durrance and his friends gave the parachutist a short course in rappelling. Then down they went. George Hopkins, however dauntless he was, must have been happy that one of the six conquerors of Devil's Tower had volunteered to tackle the peak a second time.

COOPERATION

Track

Chris Chataway and Chris Brasher are not household names, yet they contributed to one of the great sports achievements of all time—the first four-minute mile.

There were those who said the four-minute mark could never be reached. "The fastest possible mile," said Brutus Hamilton, track coach at the University of California, "is a shade under four minutes, two seconds." Jake Weber, track coach at Fordham, was less optimistic. Four minutes and three seconds, he said—not a fraction of a second less.

But when Gunder Haegg of Sweden lowered the mark to four minutes, one and four-tenths seconds in 1945, people began to believe that maybe the four-minute mile *was* possible. One track star who believed it was Roger Bannister of England. He also believed something else—that cooperation among runners could help.

He asked Chris Chataway to set a grueling pace for him. He enlisted Chris Brasher to run a furious last quarter after Chris had loafed through two laps to Bannister's three. Soon the stage was set for Roger's date with destiny. He was eager to get on with it, because John Landy of Australia and Wes Santee of the United States could see the four-minute mile within their reach, too.

On May 6, 1954, in a race at Oxford, England, Bannister was ready. With Brasher and Chataway alternately moving to the lead, Roger held to the fast, demanding pace he needed for the first quarter mile . . . the second . . . the third. With one quarter to go, his time stood at three minutes, five-tenths seconds. Good enough, but still no cinch. His pacers faded, and he was on his own.

We all know the outcome. Bannister put on a blazing final drive, crossed the finish line, collapsed, and waited for the announcement. When it came, only the first four words were audible above the thunderous roar of the crowd:

"The time, three minutes. . . . "

The precise time was three minutes, fifty-nine and four tenths seconds—a triumph of both individual achievement and dedicated cooperation.

COURAGE

Adventure

In the nineteenth century, quite a few people had ridden in barrels beneath Niagara Falls. But no one had ever gone over the Falls in a barrel.

Mrs. Anna Taylor, a 43 year-old-widow, decided to take the plunge. The year was 1901. Mrs. Taylor had a special barrel constructed, with a cushioned interior and a leather harness and arm straps. Most people thought she was crazy.

On October 24, she and her barrel were taken to Grass Island, just above Horseshoe Falls. She was strapped inside. The cover was fastened, and the barrel was pumped full of air. The barrel was towed out into the current, and at 4:05 p.m. the line was cut.

The barrel rolled and tumbled above the Falls. It cleared the treacherous rocks, hung for an instant at the brink, then crashed down 173 feet into the river below. Spectators—there were thousands of them—saw the barrel bob almost immediately to the surface. It looked intact.

As the barrel was swept downstream, it was caught in an eddy. It swirled there for a few agonizing minutes. Then at 4:40 p.m., it was caught and grounded on a rock. Several men struggled to get the hatch off. It wouldn't budge. The top of the barrel had to be sawed away.

Mrs. Taylor, badly shaken, with a three-inch gash in her scalp, climbed out of the barrel. She said later that she had lost consciousness for a time during the plunge. She warned others not to try "the foolish thing" she had done.

Others did try it, of course. Some died in the attempt. But what was the point anymore? Mrs. Taylor, a courageous schoolteacher, had already conquered the Falls in a barrel. She was the first.

COURAGE

Baseball

They don't come any more courageous than Don Zimmer. His story starts way back in 1949, when he was a rookie shortstop for Cambridge, Maryland, of the Class D Eastern Shore League. Zimmer batted a weak .227 and fielded a none-too-impressive .925. Playing at the lowest level of professional baseball, he seemed to have a bleak future. There were 83 players in the league who hit for a higher average than Zimmer . . . and there were 25 leagues at the Class D level . . . and there were five levels of minor-league baseball above that.

Zimmer didn't get a promotion in 1950—just a transfer to another Class D league. But it was there, in tiny Hornell, New York, where he began to show the tremendous potential that would cause Brooklyn Dodger executives to start talking of him as the eventual successor to the great Pee Wee Resse. He raised his batting average to .315. He hit 23 home runs. He often fielded brilliantly, and although he was still error-prone, he was named the league's all-star shortstop.

With Reese a fixture in the Brooklyn infield, the Dodgers could afford to bring Zimmer along slowly—which they did. He went up to Class A in 1951 (skipping two classifications), then to a Double-A in '52, and to Triple-A in '53. By then his name was in *The Sporting News*, and his prospects were golden. For half a season, he tore apart American Association pitching and fielding like a major-league shortstop.

Then, on July 7, 1953—this was before the days of batting helmets—his major-league dreams nearly ended. A curve ball that didn't break smashed into his head. He was unconscious for 11 days. The doctors had to drill two holes in his skull to relieve the pressure of the concussion. When Zimmer came out of his coma, he couldn't recognize his wife. He couldn't talk. He was in the hospital for 31 days, and many people assumed his career was over.

But Zimmer fought back. He returned to St. Paul in 1954 and did well.

Once again Pee Wee Reese's job was mentioned. While Zimmer was playing winter ball in Puerto Rico, a second injury struck. A pitched ball came flying at his head. Involuntarily, he threw up his arm to ward it off. The ball ricocheted off his wrist, cracking it in two places.

He made it to the majors anyway, playing the 1955 season with the pennant-winning Brooklyn Dodgers, though not as a starter. Some Zimmer-watchers felt that the injuries had lingering effects—he hit only .239—and that the stocky little infielder wasn't quite as good as he had been before the beaning.

And then, incredibly, it happened again. Hal Jeffcoat of the Cincinnati Reds hit him in the head with a pitch on June 23, 1956. This time he had a fractured cheekbone and what the doctors feared was a detached retina. He was out of baseball for the rest of the season.

Zimmer, who just wouldn't quit, came back to Brooklyn in 1957. But now there was little question about it: he would never become the bright superstar he had once seemed destined to be. He would simply be a good, aggressive utility infielder—and eventually a highly respected manager (highly respected everywhere except Boston, that is, where his Red Sox played well but never quite well enough).

Many players have suffered injuries and bounced back. But few have suffered a sequence of injuries as serious as Don Zimmer's and fought back so bravely. When Mickey Mantle wrote a book about courage, he made sure to include a chapter about the valiant infielder who never filled Pee Wee Reese's shoes, but who nevertheless made an indelible mark on the national pastime.

COURAGE

Football

The football career of Baylor defensive back Kyle Woods came to end before the 1979 season when Woods, going through a routine tackling drill, suffered a broken neck that left him paralyzed.

Woods showed the same determination in his rehabilitation program that he had as a football player. But it took over a year for his teammates to find out just how determined he was.

The 1980 Baylor Bears started the season with seven straight wins and were ranked sixth in the nation. Then came a shocking upset at home to a San Jose State team that entered the game a 21-point underdog.

Nobody knew how the Bears would react the next week in the traditional homecoming game against nationally ranked Arkansas. One man who hoped he knew was Kyle Woods, who planned to visit his old teammates before the game.

After the Bears finished their pregame warmups, coach Grant Teaff gathered the team in the locker room and gave Woods the chance to speak.

Woods, speaking from his wheelchair, told the players how hard he had been working at rehabilitation. He told them of the pain and problems he had suffered. But through it all, he said, he had learned this: "No matter what happens to you, no matter how bad things might seem, you have to do one thing. You have to take a setback and turn it into a comeback."

With that, Woods showed them what kind of comeback he was making. Grasping the arms of his wheelchair, he locked his arms to raise his body a few inches. Then, with the help of his brother, he stood, wobbly but erect. What followed brought shocked silence, then tears, and then shouts from his teammates.

Woods took a short, shuffling step.

Inspired by his courageous example, Baylor beat the highly regarded Razorbacks 42 to 15 and went on to finish with a 10 and 1 record, winning the Southwest Conference championship and a Cotton Bowl berth.

All because they turned a setback into a comeback.

COURAGE

Golf

One of the most inspirational stories in American sports is Ben Hogan's comeback from a near-fatal automobile accident in 1949. No one supposed that Hogan would ever play tournament golf again after the accident. Ever. His injuries were that serious.

But the very next year Ben Hogan, hobbling on a surgically repaired leg, won the United States Open at Merion, Pennsylvania. A year later he won it again, this time over an Oakland Hills course so tough that only two rounds below par 70 were shot in the entire tournament. One of them was Hogan's 67, which Hogan himself felt was the finest round of his career.

This man who had come back from the brink of death was not through yet. In his third year after surgery, he won every event he played in—the Masters Tournament, the United States Open, the British Open. And not only did he win, he set records along the way. It may have been the greatest year any golfer ever had.

Ben Hogan's return to golf is an example of courage and perseverance that has seldom been equaled in any walk of life. He not only came back, but he came back to win it all.

COURAGE

Hockey

The National Hockey League remained strictly a Canadian league for many years. It was not until 1928 that a U.S. team won the Stanley Cup. That year the New York Rangers, after having won the playoffs against the Boston Bruins, defeated the Montreal Maroons for the championship.

But it took a courageous act by Rangers' coach Lester Patrick to do it. Patrick, a handsome, silver-haired, 44-year-old manager inserted himself into the Rangers' lineup when the regular goalie, Lorne Chabot, was injured.

When they carried the unconscious Chabot from the ice and rushed him to a hospital, Patrick was at a loss. Teams in those days carried only one goalie. Patrick's only hope—permitted by the Stanley Cup rules then in effect—was to find a substitute goalie somewhere and get the opposing manager's permission.

As it happened, Alex Connell, a goalie from Ottawa's NHL team was in the stands. But Eddie Gerard, the Maroons' coach, who had little love for Lester Patrick, said no. He wouldn't accept the substitution.

There was also a minor-league goalie in the crowd. Again Gerard said no.

At that point, a New York sportswriter worked his way into the Ranger huddle and said, "Hey, Les, why don't you put on the pads yourself?"

And so Les Patrick put on the pads.

There's a good photograph of him as a goalie for that game. This was in the days before face masks, you'll recall, so Patrick wasn't disguised like Jason in *Friday the 13th*. In fact, he looks like an aging and distinguished business-man posing as a goalie. He looks vulnerable.

But he wasn't. Even though he had played goal only once or twice in his life, he rose to inspired heights that day. Montreal tried to overwhelm him with a barrage of shots. Patrick deflected them all.

The Rangers scored to take a 1 to 0 lead. Then, with 5:40 left to play, the Maroons finally slammed the puck past Patrick to tie the score. At the end of regulation time, it was 1 to 1.

In sudden-death overtime, the Maroons repeatedly tried and failed to crack the Ranger defense. Then, after seven minutes and five seconds, Frank

Boucher of the Rangers put the puck past the Montreal goalie, and Les Patrick's New Yorkers had their victory. Later, with Chabot back in goal, the Rangers went on to win the Stanley Cup.

COURAGE

Horse Racing

All winning racehorses have courage. Some horses are so good—Citation, Secretariat, and Seattle Slew come to mind—that their courage may never be tested to the limit. But the great thoroughbred War Admiral had it tested all the way.

It was in the Belmont Stakes. War Admiral had already won the Kentucky Derby and the Preakness. Only the Belmont remained in racing's Triple Crown.

War Admiral, always eager to be off and running, stumbled but managed to recover while leaving the starting gate. That might have slowed a lesser horse, but War Admiral poured it on from start to finish, winning the mile and a half race in record time.

The previous record, by the way, had been held by the almost legendary Man O' War, and Man O' War was War Admiral's sire.

In the winner's circle, someone noticed that War Admiral's lower body was covered with blood. The blood had been thrown up, it appeared, from one of the horse's forefeet. Examination showed that part of a hoof had been sheared off as War Admiral left the starting gate.

The courageous thoroughbred had run the entire race with this serious injury. He had to be retired afterwards for several months in order to recuperate. But it would have taken more than a sheared hoof to keep the gallant War Admiral from running when the chips were down.

COURAGE

Hunting

A hundred years ago there were more than a few grizzly bears in the Coast Range Mountains of California. John Grummet, one of the famous hunters of the day, had a chilling encounter in Stanislaus County, southwest of Modesto.

Hungry for bear meat, Grummet climbed to the summit of a steep chaparral hill. Armed with his trusty Spencer rifle, he worked his way along the summit. Finding a fresh bear track, he followed it into and through a dense thicket. He came to an open space of about half an acre, broken by clumps of wild juniper shrubs.

Grummet heard the snapping of small twigs on the other side of a juniper clump. From past experience he knew that a bear was back there eating juniper berries. He cautiously worked his way around to a position within thirty steps of the bear.

She was a huge grizzly, so intent on her feast that she was unaware of the hunter. Her head was turned away from him. Grummet took deliberate aim at the back of her head and fired. The bear toppled over without a sound.

That was easy enough, but the adventure had just begun. No sooner had Grummet taken a couple of steps forward than a series of snarls and growls and the crashing of undergrowth from beyond the clearing told him he had company.

A second grizzly burst from the thicket opposite, about 75 yards away and charging. Grummet, loading hurriedly, got a cartridge jammed in the breech. He had failed to pull the lever far enough back. With no time to lose, he snapped the lever back, dumped a few cartridges from his pocket beside him, and slipped one into the breech.

When he was ready to fire, the bear was 20 feet away, still charging. Grummet's shot was perfect, and the bear fell dead.

Then he saw a third bear advancing directly behind the second one. Calmer now, Grummet took aim, fired once, fired again. The third bear dropped within ten feet of the second.

It still wasn't over. There was a fourth bear.

This bear acted cautious. He reared up on his hind legs and looked the situation over. Not seeing or sensing anyone, he advanced slowly.

When he was 20 steps away, Grummet fired for the last time. The fourth bear fell to the ground, also dead. The California hunter had felled four large grizzlies without any significant change in his firing position.

Another legendary hunter, Dr. Stanley, would accomplish a similar feat in northern California's Trinity County a few years later. Both men showed exceptional coolness under stress and deadly accuracy with firearms. Anything less than perfect shooting would have ended their hunting careers on the spot.

COURAGE

Tennis

The story of tennis star Maureen—"Little Mo"—Connolly is usually told as tragedy. It could also be viewed as a profile in courage.

Little Mo was a childhood sensation. She expected to be the world's best woman tennis player, and said so. At the age of 16, she won the U.S. tennis championship. At the age of 17, she captured Wimbledon.

That year she won the championships of France, Australia, England, and the United States—the first woman to complete the grand slam. Next year she was just as good, winning for the third straight time at Wimbledon.

A few weeks later, while she was horseback riding in San Diego, a cement mixer crashed into her horse and smashed Maureen Connolly's leg. At the age of 20, she was finished as a top tennis player. She never turned pro.

With a tennis career out of the question, she married and had two daughters, Cindy and Brenda.

Then, still in her late 20s, she went to the doctor for a routine physical examination. She was hoping to have a third child. The doctor discovered cancer. Little Mo, calm and purposeful, fought her last contest, one that she lost after five painful years. By then the cancer had spread to every part of her body.

On the day before she died, Little Mo wrote out a list of books she wanted her daughters Cindy and Brenda to read. Tennis star Mary Hare, who was with her that day, said that despite massive medication "she was in complete charge of herself until the end."

Little Mo's story is a tragedy, of course. Barely out of her teens, she was on the threshold of a great career. But it is also a story of courage in the face of a grim and brutal fate.

DISAGREEMENT

Baseball

Hank Greenberg, when he was general manager of the Cleveland Indians, received an unsigned contract from one of his players. He sent off this telegram: "In your haste to accept the terms, you forgot to sign the contract."

A telegram from the player arrived the next day. It read: "In your haste to give me a raise, you put in the wrong figure."

DISAPPOINTMENT

Baseball

Casey at the Bat *by Ernest Lawrence Thayer*

The outlook wasn't brilliant for the Mudville nine that day;
The score stood four to two with but one inning left to play.
So when Cooney died at second, and Burrows did the same,
A sickly silence fell upon the patrons of the game.

A straggling few got up to go, leaving there the rest,
With that hope which springs eternal within the human breast.
They thought: "If only Casey could get a whack at that,"
They'd put up even money now with Casey at the bat.

But Flynn preceded Casey, and likewise so did Blake,
And the former was a pudd'n, and the latter was a fake.

So on that stricken multitude a deathlike silence sat;
For there seemed but little chance of Casey's getting to the bat.

But Flynn let drive a single to the wonderment of all,
And the much-despised Blakey tore the cover off the ball.
And when the dust had lifted, and they saw what had occurred,
There was Blakey safe at second, and Flynn a-huggin' third.

Then from the gladdened multitude went up a joyous yell—
It rumbled in the mountaintops, it rattled in the dell;
It struck upon the hillside, and rebounded on the flat;
For Casey, mighty Casey, was advancing to the bat.

There was ease in Casey's manner as he stepped into his place,
There was pride in Casey's bearing and a smile on Casey's face;
And when responding to the cheers he lightly doffed his hat,
No stranger in the crowd could doubt 'twas Casey at the bat.

Ten thousand eyes were on him as he rubbed his hands with dirt,
Five thousand tongues applauded when he wiped them on his shirt;
Then when the writhing pitcher ground the ball into his hip,
Defiance gleamed in Casey's eye, a sneer curled Casey's lip.

And now the leather-covered sphere came hurtling through the air,
And Casey stood a-watching it in haughty grandeur there.
Close by the sturdy batsman the ball unheeded sped;
"That ain't my style," said Casey. "Strike one," the umpire said.

From the benches black with people, there went up a muffled roar,
Like the beating of the storm waves on a stern and distant shore.
"Kill him! Kill the umpire!" shouted someone in the stand;
And it's likely they'd have killed him had not Casey raised his hand.

With a smile of Christian charity great Casey's visage shone;
He stilled the rising tumult, he bade the game go on;
He signaled to the pitcher, and once more the spheroid flew;
But Casey still ignored it, and the umpire said, "Strike two."

"Fraud!" cried the maddened thousands, and the echo answered, "Fraud!"
But one scornful look from Casey, and the audience was awed;
They saw his face grown stern and cold, they saw his muscles strain,
And they knew that Casey wouldn't let that ball go by again.

The sneer is gone from Casey's lips, his teeth are clenched in hate,
He pounds with cruel violence his bat upon the plate;
And now the pitcher holds the ball, and now he lets it go,
And now the air is shattered by the force of Casey's blow.

Oh, somewhere in this favored land the sun is shining bright,
The band is playing somewhere, and somewhere hearts are light;
And somewhere men are laughing, and somewhere children shout,
But there is no joy in Mudville—mighty Casey has struck out.

DISAPPOINTMENT

Football

One afternoon when John McKay was coaching Tampa Bay, his Buccaneers lost a heartbreaker.

A reporter asked him what he thought of his team's execution.

"I think it's a good idea," McKay replied.

DISAPPOINTMENT

Horse Racing

Burnett bet the horses faithfully, but he never won. His luck was so bad that even his bookie felt sorry for him.

One day Burnett went to the bookie with his last two dollars. "Put it on Rosewater in the fourth," he said.

"No way," the bookie replied. "The odds on the horse are 150 to 1. It ain't got a prayer. Stop throwing your money away."

"Rosewater in the fourth," Burnett insisted.

The bookie said, "Look, the horse has got no chance. I'll personally give you a million-to-one odds on him. What do you say to that?"

"I'll take it," Burnett said.

Now, as you've probably guessed, Rosewater won the race.

Not by 40 lengths or anything, but somehow the horse made it to the finish line in first place.

Burnett arrived on his bookie's doorstep with a suitcase. He began stuffing thousand-dollar bills into it. But the bookie noticed that his biggest winner ever looked a little downcast. The guy looked sad.

"I don't get it," said the bookie. "You're walking out of here with all this money, and you look like you just lost your last friend."

Burnett stopped and looked at him. "I've been betting the horses all my life," he said. "I never had too much luck. So finally I win a race on a million-to-one shot. And what have I got on it? A lousy two dollars."

DISCIPLINE

Baseball

Leo Durocher saw the problem coming. "How can the manager exert discipline?" he asked. "What is he going to do to a guy with a million dollar contract? Fine him?"

DISCIPLINE

Football

Nobody ever mistook Vince Lombardi for a member of the tea-and-crumpets set. He was a man who understood power, and used it. He imposed total control. The toughest of the Green Bay linemen seldom snarled when matched against Lombardi. "When he says 'sit down,'" said one player, "I don't even bother to look for a chair."

DISCIPLINE

Football

It's easy to enforce team rules when there's no cost involved. The trouble begins when rule enforcement may affect a team's chances of winning.

Like most football coaches, Bear Bryant faced this dilemma more than once. And he always enforced the rules. Even with Joe Namath.

Joe Willie, later Broadway Joe, never worried much about training rules. And early on, in Tuscaloosa, he ran into the rock-hard discipline of Bear Bryant.

Namath and some friends had been out drinking. He admitted it. Bryant told him that nine assistant coaches had recommended penalties, but no suspension. Only one coach, Bryant's one-time player, Gene Stallings, had voted to suspend Namath.

"If it had been me," Stallings said, "you'd kick me off the team wouldn't you?"

Bryant had to admit that he would.

But Joe Namath was a superstar and seemed indispensable to the team. There were two games to go—one against Miami and the other against Mississippi in the Cotton Bowl. The Bear doubted they could win either of them without Namath.

But rules are rules. "You're out for the year," Bryant told his star quarterback. "Maybe forever."

Six thousand fans sent letters of protest. Joe's mother phoned Bryant in tears. The alumni grimly awaited two late-season losses. Bryant held firm.

Jack Hurlbut then quarterbacked the Alabama team to a 17 to 12 win over Miami. He didn't look sensational doing it, though, and sportswriters in the South predicted Namath would be back in action for the Cotton Bowl.

He wasn't. A second quarterback, Steve Sloan, took the field against Ole Miss. He was no sensation either, but Alabama squeaked by Johnny Vaught's favored Rebels by a score of 12 to 7.

Joe Namath returned the next year to lead Alabama to the national championship. And years later he agreed that Bear Bryant was absolutely right to suspend him when he did, and to make the suspension stick. One hundred percent right, he said. No, he added, "make that 110 percent."

DISCIPLINE

Football

Notre Dame has always had a reputation for educating its athletes as well as getting championship performances from them. Discipline is part of the process.

Head football coach Lou Holtz said, "I don't think discipline is forcing somebody to do something. It's showing them how this is going to help them in the long run. You don't go about establishing discipline. You set the rules, and you enforce the rules. . . . Everybody says I'm a disciplinarian, and I'm not. A person who won't do what's necessary isn't a bit better than one who can't."

DISCIPLINE

General

Whitey Burnham coached three sports at Dartmouth College in the 1960s. He produced Ivy League championship teams in soccer and lacrosse, and a number of All-America players emerged in both sports.

Like many fine coaches, Burnham was a man of quiet patience. Yet his calmness and lively sense of humor concealed a tough competitive spirit. He was a firm believer in discipline. He intended to win, and he did win.

His advice to his players reflected his own self-discipline. He said: "Be like ducks—calm on the surface and paddling like hell underneath."

DISCOURAGEMENT

Auto Racing

British cartoonist David Langdon was always impressed by the lightning speed of the pit crews in auto racing. One day, while caught in a traffic jam after the races at Silverstone, he dreamed up a famous cartoon.

It shows two pit-crew members talking at the side of the track. Racing cars are roaring past. One mechanic, with a look of deep discouragement, says to the other: "I'm all thumbs today; took me three and a half seconds to change a ruddy wheel. . . ."

DISCOURAGEMENT

Baseball

From *Baseball's Sad Lexicon* by "F.P.A." [Franklin Pierce Adams]

These are the saddest of possible words:
"Tinker to Evers to Chance."
Trio of bear Cubs and fleeter than birds,
Tinker and Evers and Chance.

Ruthlessly pricking our gonfalon bubble,
Making a Giant hit into a double,
Words that are weighty with nothing but trouble:
"Tinker to Evers to Chance."

DISCOURAGEMENT

Baseball

If Mickey Mantle had hit 61 home runs in a season, there would have been cheers. But Roger Maris? A lifetime .260 hitter. Average home run production except for a couple of seasons. It just seemed wrong.

And Maris suffered for it. He set the record, but it brought him little joy. He got an asterisk after his name because Babe Ruth had hit his 60 in a shorter season. No other record-breaker got an asterisk after his name. Only Maris.

He was understandably downcast. He said, "It would have been a helluva lot more fun if I'd never hit those 61 home runs. . . . All it brought me was headaches."

DISCOURAGEMENT

Baseball

Ron Swoboda of the Miracle Mets wondered about all those locker-room pep talks that used to fire him up. He asked, "Why am I wasting so much dedication on a mediocre career?

DISCOURAGEMENT

Fishing

A father took his little girl fishing for the first time. For a while, she sat patiently in the boat, but at last she put down her pole and said, "I quit."

"What's the matter?" her father asked.

"I just can't seem to get waited on," she said.

DISCOURAGEMENT

Hockey

Hockey star Derek Sanderson didn't believe in hero worship. "If you don't have a hero," he said, "you'll never be disillusioned."

DISCOVERY

Baseball

When Ted Williams came to the majors, pitchers could see right away that he was something special. He cracked 31 homers in his rookie season and knocked in 145 runs. Even the Yankee pitchers worried long and hard about this Splendid Splinter in a Boston Red Sox uniform. They discussed the best way to pitch to him.

The Yanks decided to pitch him high and tight, and then low and away. Spud Chandler, a very good Yankee pitcher, got to test this plan. What did he find out?

"I'll tell you," he said. "I found out that high and tight is ball one. Low and away is ball two, and then you have to throw the ball over the plate. That's when the trouble starts."

DISCOVERY

Basketball

Adolph Rupp took his University of Kentucky basketball team to New York in December 1935 to play NYU in the second collegiate doubleheader ever to be held in Madison Square Garden. The Kentucky Wildcats had won all five of their previous games by impressive margins and were touting sophomore center Leroy Edwards for All-America honors.

In what must rank as one of the roughest college basketball games ever played, NYU's "King Kong" Klein and "Slim" Tergesen used every tactic imaginable to keep Kentucky's big, strong, and deadly scorer out from under the basket.

When films of the game were shown at a meeting of the Rules Committee the following summer, the play of the pivotmen under the basket was so rugged that it shocked some of the coaches who saw it. As a result, the three-second rule was adopted that year to force the pivotman away from the basket.

A ruling concerning illegal screens was also looked at closely by the committee. Such screens had played a large part in the Kentucky-NYU game.

Since arriving at Kentucky four years earlier, Rupp had compiled a remarkable 71 and 9 record by using a strong man-to-man defense and a fast-break offense. The offense featured screening plays that were legal in the

South and Midwest but, as it turned out, were apparently verboten in Gotham.

Time and time again as the Wildcats tried to set up their plays, they were called for illegal screens. At halftime Rupp went up to the official, Jack Murray, and asked what his team was doing wrong.

"You know what you're doing wrong," Murray replied. "And it isn't legal."

With eight seconds to go in the game, and the score tied, Murray called Edwards for setting an illegal screen. The Violets made the free throw and won the game.

Upon his return to Lexington, Rupp was asked what had happened in New York.

Well, he said, "I was heading for home the next morning, a Sunday, and I saw on one of their church signs where the sermon that day was,'I was a stranger and they took me in.' That's all I know about it."

DISCOVERY

Boxing

When Kid McCoy gave up the welterweight boxing title, he did what many other ex-champions have done—he opened a saloon. If he hadn't done that, he might be as little known today as Mysterious Billy Smith or Honey Melody, two other welterweight champs of the day.

But Kid McCoy lives on in song and story, for Kid McCoy was (or may have been) the original "real McCoy."

One night, as the tale goes, a drunk staggered into McCoy's Manhattan bar and promptly began to make a nuisance of himself. He introduced himself with rowdy camaraderie to a small, quiet man in the establishment.

"Hello! My name's Morgan," he boomed. "What's yours?"

I'm McCoy," said the pint-sized owner. Welterweights, as you know, are not very big.

"What? You're McCoy? *The* McCoy?" sneered the drunk, perhaps looking for enough well-muscled bulk to match the reputation. "I don't believe it."

Of course there's one good way to prove you're a boxer, and Kid McCoy, still in fighting trim, proved it. The drunk hit the sawdust with a resounding thud. As he struggled to his feet, he knew he'd been hit by something stronger

than a shot of red-eye. A new respect crept into his manner and his words.
He said, "Okay, mister, I *do* believe it. You're the real McCoy."

DISCOVERY

Football

Sportswriter Red Smith tells this story.

In 1925 Laurence Stallings took an assignment to cover the football game between Penn and the University of Illinois. The brilliant halfback Red Grange would be making his first Eastern appearance.

Stallings was not a sportswriter. He was a novelist, dramatist, war correspondent, and film writer. His best-known work was *What Price Glory?*, a play about the First World War.

On this gray afternoon, Red Grange broke loose on a muddy field, ran for three touchdowns, and set up another. His performance dazzled even the old hands in the press box. But they dutifully began to type up their stories.

Not Stallings. He was in a tizzy. He paced up and down the press box, his hands clasped to his head. "I can't!" he wailed. "I can't write it! It's too big."

DISCOVERY

Fishing

A friend of Patrick F. McManus, the fishing humorist, hit on the idea of achieving immortality by compiling a book of quotations on outdoor sports.

As luck would have it, he was fishing on the very day the idea struck him. He cast a fly that fell about ten feet short of the pool he was aiming for. Nonetheless, a sizable rainbow trout rose to it, and the man reeled in the fish."

"Ah, ha," he thought, "my first quotation: A cast that reaches a fish is never too short."

DISCOVERY

General

Most coaches will tell you that sports build character. Heywood Hale Broun, the sportswriter disagreed. "Sports do not build character," he said. "They reveal it."

DOMINANCE

Baseball

It's an old saw that pitching is 75 percent of the game of baseball. The corollary to that is that an outstanding pitching staff is a big plus on the road to a pennant.

But how about just one outstanding pitcher? Can a dominant pitcher produce a pennant, or at least a solid finish? No. There's proof positive that a single ace won't be able to do it. The proof came in 1972 with the Philadelphia Phillies.

The Phils had just acquired lefty Steve Carlton from the St. Louis Cardinals in a trade for Rick Wise. Carlton had some kind of year. He led the National League in wins, ERA, strikeouts, games started, and games completed. During one stretch, he allowed only one earned run over 63 innings. He won the Cy Young award.

How did the Phillies fare that year? Carlton's 27 wins must have helped, right? Well, not really—because the rest of the Phillie pitching staff won only 32 games. In other words, Steve Carlton accounted for 45 percent of all the games won by the hapless Phillies.

Philadelphia finished the season in last place, far behind Montreal and light years away from pennant-winning Pittsburgh.

DOMINANCE

Baseball

Minor league baseball has always tried to capitalize on the theme of "Catch a Rising Star"—the idea being that most minor league teams have at least one future major leaguer on their rosters. It's probably true, although at the lower levels the future major leaguer may be destined for no more than a cup of coffee in the big time.

Still, with a little luck, your town might land a team like the Ogden Dodgers of 1968. They were in the Pioneer League that year, a Rookie classification, which is the lowest rung of the ladder in professional baseball.

The worst problem for this Utah club was that they had too many first basemen—too many future major-league first basemen, that is. The guy who played the position for the Ogden rookies was 18-year-old Bill Buckner. His .344 batting average led the Pioneer league. Buckner had a fine major league career, but he's probably best known for letting Mookie Wilson's ground ball roll through his legs in the last game of the 1987 World Series.

At third base for Ogden was 19-year-old Steve Garvey. His 20 home runs led the Pioneer League. Garvey became a superstar for the L.A. Dodgers, playing in every All-Star game from 1975 through 1981. He became a pretty fair first baseman too. In 1984, for example, he handled 1,232 chances without an error.

In the outfield for the Ogden team were Tom Paciorek and Bobby Valentine. Both of them were to have long major league careers. Paciorek played many of his major league games at first base; Valentine played a few.

Catch a rising star indeed! With a team like this, you'd think the Ogden Dodgers would walk away with the league championship. You'd be right. They did. In a split season, the Ogden Dodgers won both halves easily, each time with a won-lost percentage of better than .700. They were practically unbeatable.

And no wonder. Their manager was Tommy Lasorda.

DOMINANCE

Basketball

How many times has television coverage of a team sport been canceled because a single superstar wouldn't be there?

It happened at least once.

The superstar was Julius Erving, the famous Dr. J, who was then playing for the New York Nets. Or rather, he wasn't playing. Instead he was holding out in a salary dispute.

CBS had scheduled the opening game of the ABA season between the Nets and the Oakland Warriors. The idea, said Barry Frank of CBS, was to show Julius Erving in action to the national audience.

But Erving wasn't going to be there for the Nets that day—so CBS decided not to be there either. Without Erving the game just didn't warrant the attention.

DOMINANCE

Basketball

Ernest Blood is one of the coaches in the Basketball Hall of Fame in Springfield, Massachusetts. His name may not be familiar to everyone because he coached at the high school level. And how he coached! His lifetime record reads 1,296 wins against only 165 losses.

For six seasons in the 1920s, his Passaic High School teams massacred the opposition in northern New Jersey and the rest of the Northeast. They reeled off 159 consecutive wins before dropping a close game to neighboring Hackensack. One of their victories was a 145 to 5 romp over Williams Prep of Stamford, Connecticut.

How did Professor Blood's teams achieve such dominance? Were the kids in Passaic taller and better coordinated than kids elsewhere? No. The professor had a system—a farm system that consisted of the city's 12 grammar schools. By the time Blood's ballplayers reached high school, they were already well trained in fundamentals.

DOMINANCE

Boxing

When Joe Louis wore the heavyweight boxing crown, it was tough to find good opponents for him. Sometimes promoters looked down into the light-heavyweight class for possible contenders. That's where they found Billy Conn. And earlier that's where they found John Henry Lewis.

John Henry Lewis was a black boxer and a personal friend of Joe Louis. He held the light-heavyweight title for nearly five years. Neither man particularly wanted the match, but both were professionals and agreed to it.

At the weigh-in Joe Louis said, "He's my pal," and "I'll put him away early. I'll make it quick for him."

The end for John Henry Lewis came in two minutes and 29 seconds of the first round. In that brief period he went crashing to the canvas three times. Films of the fight showed that Joe Louis landed 39 punches, many of them solid rights. John Henry Lewis landed three, all of them weak jabs.

DOMINANCE

Football

When people think of big-time football today, they don't think about the Ivy League. There was a time when they did, though. There was a time when the top All-America choices came from Yale, Harvard, and Princeton. No one else played football half so well.

That was a long time ago. Yale's greatest team, by any possible standard of measurement, was the stout but tiny squad of 1888, averaging 169 pounds per man. In 13 games these amazing Old Eli's were unbeaten, untied, and unscored upon. They piled up 698 points to their opponents' none. You can't do much better than that.

Nearly all of the 1888 players went on to become head coaches at other colleges. And two of them are still well known today, the marvelously named Pudge Hefflefinger and the legendary Amos Alonzo Stagg.

DOMINANCE

Hockey

At the turn of the century, the Ottawa hockey team, known as the Silver Seven, dominated the Stanley Cup championships. From 1902 to 1905, they beat back all challenges to their supremacy. Their most interesting opponent during this period was a ragtag team from Dawson City in the Yukon. Why these fellows, who called themselves the Klondikers, decided to take on the smooth-functioning Silver Seven may never be known.

A rich prospector, Colonel Joe Boyle, put up the money for the Klondikers 4,400-mile trip to Ottawa. In December of 1904, they traveled there by bicycle, dogsled, stagecoach, boat, and train. The trip took 23 days. Its rigors, though, were nothing compared to the rigors they would face against the Silver Seven.

The series was a best-of-three. In the first game, Ottawa won easily, 9 to 2. The *Ottawa Journal* found the Klondikers form to be, in their words, "of the most mediocre kind."

Still, the Klondikers had held Frank McGee, hockey's first superstar, to only one goal. They were feeling pretty good. The Klondikers rowdy right wing, a man named Norm Watts, was moved to sneer during lunch at Sam Cassidy's saloon: "Who the hell's McGee? He don't look like much."

It was the wrong thing to say. Frank McGee and the Silver Seven had been toying with the Dawson City skaters in the first game. The second time out they turned mean, especially their young superstar. Frank McGee scored 14 goals as the Ottawa team annihilated the Klondikers, 23 to 2.

The Stanley Cup stayed in Ottawa. Norm Watts learned who Frank McGee was. And from that day to this, no one but McGee has ever scored 14 goals in a professional hockey game.

DOMINANCE

Sailing

The first formal yacht race between the United States and Great Britain took place in 1851. The U.S. schooner *America* set sail against a group of 14

British cutters and schooners in a 53-mile race around the Isle of Wight. In attendance at this forerunner of the America's Cup races was Queen Victoria, who presumably thought at least one of the British yachts would defeat the *America*'s challenge.

From the royal party's ship the *Victoria and Albert*, the Queen dispatched a smaller steam yacht to catch a first glimpse of the leader, which was invisible to her beyond a cliff.

When the steam yacht returned, so they say, the Queen asked, "Are the yachts in sight?"

The signalmaster replied, "Only the *America*, may it please Your Majesty."

"Which is second?" she asked.

"Ah, Your Majesty, there is no second."

DOMINANCE

Softball

Have you ever heard the name Eddie Feigner?

Maybe if you're an old-timer you have. He was a famous softball pitcher on an outfit called "The King and His Court." The King's fast ball was once clocked at 104 miles an hour. That's faster than Nolan Ryan's, and over a shorter distance. Feigner was pretty tough to hit. In his career he threw 530 no-hitters and 152 perfect games.

Some people think of softball as a kind of sissy sport. They think that a good major league hitter would pulverize a good softball pitcher—even one as good as Eddie Feigner.

If you think that, think again. In 1967 a group of Hollywood celebrities took on a team of major league all-stars in a softball game sponsored by NBC. The celebrities, who included James Garner and Bobby Darin, had a ringer out there on the mound. Eddie Feigner.

How did Feigner fare against the baseball all-stars? Well, sort of like Carl Hubbell. Feigner struck out the following players in order: Willie Mays, Willie McCovey, Brooks Robinson, Roberto Clemente, Maury Wills, and Harmon Killebrew.

Not bad for an underhand pitcher in his forties.

ECCENTRICITY

Baseball

Luis Aparicio, a Hall of Fame shortstop, was a shrewd, competitive ballplayer, always looking for a way to beat the other team.

As Bill Lee tells it in *The Wrong Stuff*, Aparicio, while with the Baltimore Orioles, learned that St. Louis Cardinals' shortstop, Julio Gotay, had certain religious eccentricities.

Aparicio decided to try to take advantage of the fact. In an exhibition game against the Cardinals, he arranged some pairs of tongue depressors in the shape of crosses on the second-base bag.

With a runner on first in the first inning, Aparicio hit a grounder to Gotay. It was a perfect double-play ball. Gotay fielded the grounder and crossed to his left to step on second base.

Then he saw the crosses. He screamed. He leaped away from the bag. He made no throw to first. Both runners were safe.

Gotay refused to go near second base until the crosses were removed. After they were gone, the next Oriole batter tripled.

Bill Lee asked Aparicio if he ever used the trick again. Luis said no. He'd try it only in a crucial game, say an All-Star game or the World Series. Gotay never made it to either.

ECCENTRICITY

Baseball

Rube Waddell, a pitcher for the old Philadelphia Athletics, was one of the game's great eccentrics. He was a pretty fair hitter for a pitcher, a distinction that got him in trouble one day.

Philadelphia was behind 2 to 1 in the eighth inning. There were two outs and an A's runner on second base. The baserunner was taking a long lead. The opposing catcher saw his chance and threw to second, trying to pick him off. The throw sailed high and bounced into centerfield.

The A's baserunner took off, rounded third, and headed for the plate. He would have made it easily, but Rude Waddell intervened.

Taking deliberate aim on the throw to the plate, Rube cut loose with a mighty swing of his bat and lined the ball over the rightfield fence.

The umpire ruled interference, of course. He called Waddell out—the final out of the inning.

Connie Mack, the A's manager, had seen Rube's crazy stunts before, but he couldn't understand this one, which could cost the A's the game. "Why did you do it?" he moaned.

Rube had an answer of sorts. "They'd been feeding me curves all afternoon," he said, "and this was the first straight ball I'd looked at."

ECCENTRICITY

Baseball

Germany Schaefer was one of the great zanies of major league baseball. If a player could get into Cooperstown on the basis of jokes and antics, Schaefer would have been enshrined there long ago.

They say you can't steal first base, but Germany Schaefer did. Here's how it happened.

He was playing for the Washington Senators at the time. In a game against the Chicago White Sox, the score was tied in the ninth inning. With two out, the Senators had two men on base—Clyde Milan on third, and Germany Schaefer on first.

On the first pitch, Schaefer broke for second. The catcher paid no attention to him. The important runner was on third.

The pitcher delivered again—and Schaefer broke for first. He went in to the bag with a dramatic slide. The catcher, still holding the ball, just stared at him. Schaefer had been trying once again to draw a throw so that Milan, on third, could score.

It hadn't worked. But the White Sox were furious anyway. What kind of nonsense was this? You can't run the bases the wrong way, they shouted.

But as a matter of fact, when the umpires studied the rule book, they found no restriction on stealing in reverse. They ruled him safe at first.

Now, it seems, Schaefer really had shaken up the catcher. Because on the next pitch, Germany broke for second base—and stole it again! But this time the catcher made a throw to second—at which instant Milan headed home and scored.

There's no plaque in Cooperstown for Germany Schaefer, but you'll find a lot of stories in a lot of books about the man who stole bases in both directions.

ECCENTRICITY

Football

The tales told about Bronko Nagurski in football rival those about Yogi Berra in baseball. While Berra comes off in the stories as as friendly dunce, Nagurski emerges as a man who knew no pain.

Take the time when Bronko was horsing around with a teammate in a second-story hotel room. One thing led to another, and Bronko fell out the window. A crowd gathered on the sidewalk below. Soon a policeman came up and asked what was going on.

"I don't know, Nagurski said. "I just got here myself."

ECCENTRICITY

Golf

The city of Kitchener, Ontario, put on a day for one of its local heroes, golfer Moe Norman. There were speeches, fanfares, and a presentation. Unfortunately, there was no Moe Norman. As on other occasions honoring him, the honoree didn't show up.

From the 1950s through the 1970s, Moe Norman won two Canadian Amateur titles and two Canadian PGA championships. He was a first-rate golfer. He was also a first-rate flake.

Moe saw no need for a caddy. "Bag's not heavy," he would say gruffly.

And he saw no need to win by a wide margin. Once he led by four strokes in a tournament. His ball was on the 18th green, three feet from the cup. Moe intentionally putted the ball into a bunker. He then clipped the ball back onto the green. His final putt gave him the win by one stroke.

There are dozens of stories about Moe Norman. Once, at the Los Angeles Open, he carried a Coke bottle onto the first tee. A thought struck him. He put the ball on top of the bottle, took his driver, and teed off.

He was the only player ever to walk out of the Masters. "Too windy for golf," he said. "Back to Canada, back to Canada."

Moe Norman won't make the PGA Hall of Fame, but his name will be remembered for a long time by the great golfers of Canada and the United States. He was a funny guy in a serious game.

ECCENTRICITY

Hockey

The heroes of hockey are more famous for their belligerence than for their clowning. Even the old-time showmen, such as Eddie Shore, were seldom admired for their sense of humor. A writer in *Collier's* magazine paid tribute to Shore as a drawing card, but added, "What makes him that way [in every city but Boston] is that he will some night be severely killed."

Eddie Shore had a pregame act that they loved in Boston. After the other Bruins had gone on the ice, the band would strike up "Hail to the Chief." Shore would skate slowly to center ice, flamboyant in a toreador's cape. Behind Shore came a proper valet who, at the appropriate moment, would lift the cape from his master's shoulders.

This act helped to pack in the fans at Boston, but naturally it didn't endear Shore to other NHL teams. One of them, the New York Americans, came up with a stunt of their own.

After Shore made his entrance at Boston and the applause had died down, the Amerks skated to center ice carrying a large rolled-up rug. They stopped there to gain the crowd's attention. When the arena was silent, they unrolled the rug.

Inside was Rabbit McVeigh, one of the players on the Amerks. Rabbit reclined there like Cleopatra, his head resting on the palm of his hand. Then he sprang to his feet, pirouetted on the tips of his skates, and flung kisses to the crowd.

It was a great put-down, and Shore decided on the spot to abandon his pregame toreador act. The players went back to high-sticking for their laughs.

ECONOMY

Baseball

Before free agency came to baseball, owners could be draconian in their salary cuts. After a particularly bad season, New York Yankee pitcher Lefty Gomez was asked to take a pay cut from $20,000 to $7,500.

He gave the matter some thought and said, "Tell you what—you keep the salary and pay me the cut."

ECONOMY

Baseball

Branch Rickey had a deserved reputation for being tightfisted.

When players of the St. Louis Cardinals' Gashouse Gang got together for a reunion, Rickey waxed nostalgic. He praised the Gashouse squad as men who loved the game so much they would have played for nothing.

Pepper Martin couldn't resist the opening. He said, "Thanks to you, Mr. Rickey, we almost did."

ECONOMY

Baseball

Enos (Country) Slaughter, the great St. Louis Cardinal outfielder, regarded Branch Rickey as the most knowledgeable man in baseball.

"But he didn't like to pay out money," Slaughter said. "He'd go into the vault to get you a nickel change."

ECONOMY

Football

George Halas, founder of the Chicago Bears and one of the founders of the National Football League, had a well-earned reputation for economy.

Mike Ditka put it best: "Halas," he said "throws nickels around like they're manhole covers."

ECONOMY

Football

Phil McConkey, a wide receiver, was unhappy when the Giants cut him in 1986. He was claimed by the Green Bay Packers, but then when the Packers lost four games in a row, he was even more unhappy. The Giants were on their way to the Superbowl.

After the Giants suffered a couple of injuries, coach Bill Parcells decided he wanted McConkey back. But he didn't want to bargain very much for him—and he didn't have to.

Parcells told McConkey, "We had to give up a blocking dummy and a couple of clipboards for you."

EDUCATION

Auto Racing

After Stirling Moss had retired from grand prix racing, he was asked where he had learned the most about racing. He replied, "The best classroom of all time, I'm convinced, was the spot about two car-lengths behind Juan Manuel Fangio. I learned more there than I ever did anywhere else."

EDUCATION

Baseball

When Hank Aaron signed with the barnstorming Indianapolis Clowns at the age of 17, he hit cross-handed. As Bob Uecker says, that's "like playing a piano in handcuffs."

Aaron changed his grip, but he was always a self-taught hitter. Naturally, after he'd broken Babe Ruth's lifetime home run record, people asked him about his hitting. Sometimes he was asked if he'd like to teach hitting to youngsters.

"I'd like it very much," he said. But he added that he'd try to teach them using *their* style, not his.

Aaron explained: He had a hitch in his swing, he said, and he hit off the wrong foot. It was true. He wasn't a picture-perfect hitter. And, like Stan Musial and a few others with unusual batting styles, he knew that imitating a star wasn't necessarily the best idea for a kid who was learning how to hit.

EDUCATION

Basketball

According to the dictionary, a university is an institution of higher learning that provides facilities for teaching and research. But wait a minute. That leaves something out. Most universities also provide facilities for football, basketball, and other sports—and the education gained in such a place can be very different from the lessons of the classroom.

Tates Locke, former head basketball coach at Clemson, learned his own lesson there—the hard way. He learned that recruiting players for big-time college basketball can get you into big trouble. He tells his story in a book called *Caught in the Net*. It's a grim story of free-spending alumni, cash under the table, and buying one's way to a national ranking.

Yet, one of Locke's tales is so outrageous it's funny. The central figure in it is Tree Rollins, a seven-foot-one-inch high school senior from a small town in Georgia. This gangly kid wasn't actually seeking a facility for study and research. He was looking for the right basketball court. And half the major universities in the South were trying to woo him onto theirs.

The finalists among Tree Rollins's academic suitors were Clemson, Georgia, Jacksonville, Florida State, Auburn, and Kentucky. All were into big-time basketball in a serious way, and they all hoped to enroll this hot prospect called Tree.

Tates Locke, by this time, was into full-scale NCAA rules violations. His plan was to fly into the local Georgia airport in a rich alumnus's Aero Commander plane. The plane would land and quickly pick up Tree, his family, and an assistant Clemson coach. The entourage would then depart for Clemson without having to register at the airport, Locke would thus cover his tracks—for this kind of recruiting was illegal.

As Locke's plane came in for a landing, Locke was upset not to see Tree and his family already waiting. Their absence would mean a delay at the airport, which he didn't want.

What Locke did see, though, was another plane, a Learjet, landing almost simultaneously. On its side were the bold letters FSU—Florida State University. When the FSU Learjet stopped, out trooped the Rollins clan, some with champagne bottles, some with fried chicken, and young Tree himself with a can of soda.

The Rollinses walked a few hundred feet, climbed aboard the well-provisioned Clemson alum's plane, and were on their way.

Fortunately for Clemson, their wealthy benefactor made the highest bid for Tree Rollins's services. Unfortunately for Tates Locke, this wondrous recruiting success aroused the suspicions of the NCAA. It set off an investigation that would eventually result in Locke's dismissal and Clemson's three-year probation.

EDUCATION

Basketball

A basketball scholarship to Indiana State University hung in the balance as a star athlete at Chicago's Englewood High School took a special verbal examination.

He was asked to name the twelve months of the year.

ISU's recruiter breathed a sigh of relief at the result. The kid passed. He named ten.

EDUCATION

Basketball

There are plenty of cautionary tales about the fleeting nature of sports fame. One of the best fictional ones has to do with ex-high school basketball star Rabbit Angstrom in John Updike's novel, *Rabbit, Run*.

One of the best actual ones has to do with Bevo Francis. In the mid-1950s, Bevo Francis made sports headlines across the nation for his phenomenal play at tiny Rio Grande College in Ohio. As a rookie he poured in 116 points in a single game.

Rio Grande's schedule was so easy that the NCAA disallowed that record and other potential Bevo Francis records. Nothing daunted, the Rio Grande basketball coach scheduled—and defeated—such major teams as Butler, Providence, Wake Forest, and Creighton.

Bevo proved just as sensational as a sophomore as he had been as a freshman. He made a big impression at Madison Square Garden, Boston Garden, and the Miami Beach Arena. In one game against Hillsdale College, he scored 113 points.

His future seemed assured. The Boston Whirlwinds offered him $15,000 to go pro. For Bevo that was too much money to pass up, so he quit college after his sophomore year—and all but disappeared from public view. He played low-level basketball for a few years, until 1962, and then at the age of 30 he retired.

It isn't quite accurate to say he retired, though. He had no significant savings from his years of basketball, and like many other ex-jocks he had to look around for a belated second career. He had no college degree and no marketable skills beyond basketball.

He took a job in a steel mill in Midland, Pennsylvania. Years later he was saying wistfully that he still intended to get a college degree someday.

EDUCATION

Basketball

Most sports announcers use their own phrases that fans have come to recognize. Mel Allen used to say, "How about that?" Phil Rizzuto says, "Holy cow!" Warner Wolf is known for two expressions—"Gimme a break," which is the title of his book, and "Let's go to the videotape."

You might think that "Let's go to the videotape" is just an ordinary remark that became attached to Wolf. But as he tells it, there's a practical purpose for the statement. It surfaced because of a mixup.

One night, Wolf was giving the score of a Lakers-Warriors basketball game. Wanting the director to run the videotape, he said, "Okay, let's look at Kareem Abdul-Jabbar versus Nate Thurmond last night."

Nothing happened.

He tried again. "Okay. Let's look at Jabbar last night."

Still nothing.

He yelled at the director, "Hey, Ernie, roll the Jabbar tape."

Still nothing.

In a slow voice fraught with anger, he said, "Okay, let's go to the videotape!"

And thus was born the familiar Warner Wolf expression. As he explains it, a director is a very busy person, doing a dozen things at once. A subtle hint from the announcer may not be enough. The director needs to be jolted with a direct command—one like "Let's go to the videotape!"

EDUCATION

Football

There have been many reforms aimed at making sure a college athlete gets a decent education. But there has always been some conflict in the minds of football coaches whose jobs depend on bone-crushing teams and happy alumni. Do the coaches want scholar athletes? Or do they want to win?

An old story has a college dean asking a few questions to establish the eligibility of an All-America tackle.

"What," the dean asks, "is the sum of eight and six?"

"The big tackle hesitates. He thinks it over. "Thirteen," he says at last.

As the dean shakes his head sadly, the head football coach puts it in perspective:

"Ah, Dean, give him another chance," the coach says. "He only missed by two."

EDUCATION

Football

Vince Lombardi's view of higher education may not have been restricted to a gridiron—but it clearly contained a gridiron. "A school without football," he said, "is in danger of deteriorating into a medieval study hall."

EDUCATION

Hunting

Charley Dickey tells this story about a Louisiana hunting dog named Pierre.

It seems that Pierre, of the Brittany breed, had a curious habit. After a woodcock had been flushed and the hunters had fired, Pierre would go after the game. Sometimes he would be gone a very long time. The curious part was that when he came back, he always brought something with him.

It might be a woodcock, but then again it might not be. It might be an armadillo or a turtle.

Pierre's Cajun owner explained. The dog, he said, was a retriever. Its job was to retrieve. Since the owner was a practical man, he wanted Pierre to bring something back. And Pierre did.

But how was he trained to do that?

No problem, said the owner. It was the reward system. Whenever Pierre brought something back, he was rewarded by not being whipped.

EDUCATION

Skiing

Jean-Claude Killy, the Olympic downhill and slalom champion from France, was asked about his education as a skier. He said, "I learned that you cannot be taught anything by anyone but yourself."

EXAGGERATION

Baseball

Much of Bob Uecker's baseball humor revolves around how weak a hitter he was. Actually, he wasn't all that bad, or he wouldn't have stuck in the majors for six years.

Still, his lifetime batting average of .200 won't get him into the Hall of Fame.

Once in St. Louis, he was being interviewed on Harry Caray's postgame show. Caray asked him whether he worried about whether the official scorer had given him a hit or an error after he'd grounded a hard shot off the shortstop's glove.

Uecker admitted that he'd sometimes glance up at the scoreboard to check.

"I guess you'd like to see them call it a hit," prompted Caray.

Uke replied, tongue-in-check, that he called everything a hit—walks, errors, fielder's choices. If he hit the ball well, he called it a hit.

Caray asked, "Well, by your own system, what are you hitting right now?"

Uecker said, "Six-forty-three."

EXAGGERATION

Baseball

Cool Papa Bell had blinding speed on the basepaths. Some think he was the fastest baserunner ever to wear a professional baseball uniform.

Josh Gibson, who observed him at first hand, said, "Cool Papa Bell was so fast he could get out of bed, turn out the lights across the room, and be back in bed under the covers before the lights went out."

EXAGGERATION

Baseball

Ron Cey, a third baseman better known as "The Penguin," commenting on the increasing girth of L.A. Dodger manager Tommy Lasorda: "We're going to have to start running laps around him."

EXAGGERATION

Basketball

A freshman basketball player at the University of Texas was being questioned in a preseason interview.

"I understand you're pretty good," the reporter said.

"Best there is," the kid said modestly. "Of course, there are pluses and minuses."

"What are the pluses?" asked the reporter.

"Well, I averaged 43 points a game for my high school. Led the team to three undefeated seasons. Made all-state every year."

"That's fantastic! What are the minuses?"

"Only one, really," the kid said. "Being from Texas, I tend to exaggerate."

EXAGGERATION

Fishing

Ed Zern tells about the time he stole a fish. He claims he never stole another one before or since, and he thinks there was a good reason for copping this one.

He was staying at the Antrim Lodge on the Beaverkill in the Catskills. He'd struck up a friendship with a young kid on leave from the army. The kid told him he'd never caught a trout over ten inches.

Zern and the boy fished that day, and the young soldier netted a fair-sized brown trout after a good struggle.

"That's a nice 15-, 16-inch fish," Zern said.

"Wow! Sixteen inches!"

"Maybe more," Zern said enthusiastically, knowing he was stretching the truth, but figuring why not?

That night at the bar, Zern told the crowd about the boy's fish.

"How big was it?" one of them asked.

The kid admitted he didn't have a chance to measure it, but he said, "I'd say 16-, 17-inches."

"Hey," another man said, "I watched you net it from the road, and it looked bigger than that."

"Well," the soldier said, pleased, "It might have been."

A few drinks later, Zern heard the kid describe it as an 18-inch trout. One of the men said, "Wow! I'd like to see that baby."

"Sure," The soldier said. "Soon as I finish my drink"

Zern slipped away and went to the freezer room. He found the soldier's trout. It was in a paper bag with the kid's name on it. By the ruler hanging on the wall near the freezer, the fish measured 14½ inches. Zern added the trout to his own three in the freezer and then threw the paper bag away.

When the boy and a few others came to look at the prize trout, they couldn't find it. "Gone!" the kid wailed. Then he turned philosophical. "Well, if somebody needs a 19-inch trout that bad, he's welcome to it."

EXAGGERATION

Fishing

For a fisherman, he was a master of understatement.

"I hooked into a pretty nice one last summer," he said. "Yes, a pretty nice one indeed. But I had to throw him back."

"Why?" someone asked.

He shook his head sadly. "The water level dropped when I took him out," he said. "It would've ruined the fishing."

EXAGGERATION

Fishing

Mark Twain was returning to New York after a pleasant fishing trip to Maine. A dour Down Easterner sat down in the smoking car beside him. Twain was never at a loss for words, and the two of them struck up a conversation.

The stranger asked if Twain had enjoyed himself in the woods. He said he had. "And let me tell you something," Twain went on. "It may be closed season for fishing up here in Maine, but I have a couple hundred pounds of the finest rock bass you ever saw iced down in the baggage car."

At that point Twain thought to ask the man his occupation.

"I'm the state game warden," came the chilling reply. "Who are you?"

Twain hesitated for just an instant. Then he said, "I'm the biggest damn liar in these whole United States!"

EXAGGERATION

Football

Does anyone remember the New York Titans? They were the forerunners of the Jets, and they were not what you'd call a successful franchise.

One of the Titans' owners was ex-sports announcer Harry Wismer. It was hard for Wismer to admit that his football team was drawing as poorly as it did. In fact, he didn't admit it. Wismer padded the attendance figures—sometimes up to eight times the actual number.

This padding became so obvious that a sportswriter was moved to note: "The attendance was announced at 30,000. Approximately 25,000 of the fans came disguised as empty seats."

EXAGGERATION

Football

Coach Duffy Daugherty was not one for understatement. "When you're playing for the national championship," he once said, "it's not a matter of life or death. It's more important than that."

EXAGGERATION

Football

"Our quarterback lost 10 yards on the first play," said the former UCLA linebacker. "Then we got pushed back another 12 yards or so."

His listener said, "That's pretty bad. Did your offense ever pull itself together?"

"Nope. On third down we took a 25 yard loss."

His listener said, "That's terrible. I'm almost afraid to ask the score of the game."

"Forget the score," said the linebacker sadly. "Three guys in our back-field drowned off Santa Monica."

EXAGGERATION

Horse Racing

"Did your horse win?" I asked Roger.

Roger looked glum. "The horse was so slow," he said, "the jockey carried a change of saddle."

EXAGGERATION

Mountaineering

Edward Kasner, an American mathematician, spent his summer vacations in Belgium. His favorite locale was an outdoor cafe in Brussels, where he spent many happy hours. He claimed to have chosen Brussels as a base from which to organize mountain-climbing expeditions to the highest point in Belgium.

"And what might the highest point in Belgium be?" someone asked.

Kasner's reply: "Twelve feet above sea level."

EXPERIENCE

Football

Some football teams, like some people, just won't learn from experience. Take the Stetson University Hatters of 1947. A 15-yard penalty seemed to teach them nothing at all. It took a whole lot of penalties to attract their attention.

One day the Hatters were playing the so-called Flying Fleet of little Erskine College. On Erskine's second-half kickoff return, one of the Stetson players was called for clipping. An official stepped off a 15-yard penalty, from Erskine's 30-yard line to its 45-yard line.

The Hatters were mad as mad could be. They said the penalty should have been against Erskine, not Stetson. Some of their teammates from the sideline came out to argue the case. This so irritated the referee that he assessed a 15-yard penalty for unsportsmanlike conduct.

He stepped off the yardage, moving the football to the Stetson 40.

This second penalty might have brought a lesser team to its knees, but not the mad Hatters. The level of the argument only increased. Soon the officials threw two of the Stetson players out of the game.

When that still failed to stop the furor, the ref slapped yet another 15-yard penalty on the Hatters. He put the ball down on the 25-yard line.

At that, cooler heads on the Stetson squad prevailed—for the moment. Erskine ran its first play after the kickoff. The play lost a yard, as the Stetson defense swarmed all over the Tigers.

There was a flag on the play. Unnecessary roughness by, you guessed it, the Stetson Hatters. A ten-yard penalty took the ball to the Stetson 11-yard line.

On just one play that lost yardage, the Flying Fleet had sailed 69 yards downfield. On the next play they floated over for a touchdown.

Courtesy, you might say, of the slow-learning tendencies of the terrible-tempered Stetson defense.

EXPERIENCE

General

Whitey Burnham, coach of soccer, lacrosse, and wrestling at Dartmouth College, used to say, "Good judgment comes from experience, and experience comes from bad judgment."

FUTILITY

Baseball

Major league baseball never looked less artistic than it did during World War Two. Many of the top players were in the service, especially during the last two years of the war. By 1945 the level of play had reached its lowest point. Warren Brown, the *Chicago Sun's* sports editor, was asked to pick the winner in the '45 World Series between the Detroit Tigers and the Chicago Cubs. After giving it some thought, he said, "I don't think either one of them can win it."

FUTILITY

Baseball

The 1962 Mets will live in infamy for at least as long as Pearl Harbor does. It was no surprise to anyone that the team could lose 120 games. The surprise was that they could win 40.

Casey Stengel's team that year was an assortment of has-been's and never-were's. One of the famous, or infamous, members of the club was first baseman Marvelous Marv Throneberry. Known far and wide for his errors, Throneberry celebrated a birthday near the end of the season.

Richie Ashburn, later a Phillies sportscaster, but then a Mets' teammate, walked over to congratulate Marv. "We were going to give you a cake," he said, "but we thought you'd drop it."

FUTILITY

Baseball

One of Bob Uecker's stories of despair involves his last days with the Philadelphia Phillies:

"I knew my days with the Phillies were numbered," he says. "I went to the plate one night as a pinch hitter, and when I looked to the third-base coach for a sign, he turned his back."

FUTILITY

Baseball

Sportscaster Lindsey Nelson, along with Bob Murphy, was the voice of the Mets in those long, dark days before the Miracle of '69. The very symbol of the Mets in those years was first baseman Marvelous Marv Throneberry.

Nelson summed up Marvelous Marv in these words: "He was a genius at turning victory into defeat, a puller of boners, a wondrously bad judge of which base to throw to, a juggler of grounders, and a dropper of pop flies. He was not simply a Met; he was the Mets."

FUTILITY

Basketball

Mark Edwards left an assistant coaching job at Washington State, a Pac-10 school, to become head basketball coach at Washington University in St. Louis, a Division III school. His new team had neither basketballs nor uniforms at the beginning. It was a wrenching change.

One of the baskets in the old Washington U fieldhouse turned out to be 9-feet-8-inches high and the other 10-feet-2-inches. In Edwards's first game, chlorine gas from the next-door machine room of the pool threatened to end the game early. After all the fans had been moved to the far side of the court— and all the doors had been opened in subfreezing temperature—the Washington Bears fought on, blowing a lead and losing to tiny Illinois College.

For Edwards it was a grim introduction to his new duties. And chlorine gas was only the beginning. There was a back-breaking loss (said one wag) to the Logan College of Chiropractics. This was followed by a loss to little Concordia Seminary.

Now, here was a prestigious, good-sized university—more than 4,000 students—being humiliated by Lilliputian schools that hardly classed as basketball powers.

The Washington Bears next lost to Harris-Stowe State College, even though their opponents finished the game with four players on the floor. The Harris-Stowe squad was so small that when a couple of players fouled out, the team was left short-handed. And, worse from Edwards's standpoint, the game wasn't even close. Harris-Stowe won convincingly with those four survivors.

Mark Edwards could tell there wasn't much hope for his first season when, in a typically lopsided loss, the Washington center went up and blocked a shot by one of his own guards. The coach couldn't believe what he was seeing. "He goaltended it," Edwards marveled, "just swatted it out as it was going into the basket."

After substituting for the center, Edwards asked the kid, "What in the world are you doing?"

The center said glumly, "He was shooting too much."

Edwards eventually turned the Washington U Bears into a winning basketball team, but he never forgot that first season, where a mere 3 wins in 19 games bordered on the miraculous.

FUTILITY

Basketball

It's become fairly common for a sportswriter to spend a season with a team and write a book based on the experience. One exceptionally good book of this kind is John Feinstein's *A Season on the Brink*, an account of Bob Knight's basketball coaching at Indiana University.

Feinstein talks about Knight's "mind games"—what they are and how they're supposed to motivate. One such game involves—presumably—leaving the future of the team in the hands of the players.

After a heartbreaking loss to the University of Michigan, Knight was furious. Back at Assembly Hall in Bloomington, he blamed everyone on the team, including superstar Steve Alford.

Most of the players had seen all of this before. They were expecting Knight's next move. "You guys sit here for a while," he told them, "and if you still want to have a team, then you come and tell us."

Knight stalked out of the room and joined his coaching staff.

The team captains knew what they had to do. After a short time, they went in to Knight and his staff and said, yes, they'd like to keep playing, and they'd try to improve.

As he watched this scene unfold, author Feinstein asked himself, "What would happen someday if the captains walked in and told Knight, 'You're right, coach, it's hopeless, let's cancel the season'?"

FUTILITY

Football

Football owners sometimes act as if they think every team in the NFL—but especially *their* team—can win the Super Bowl. The fans know better. They realize that where there are winners, there are also losers. It takes a certain maturity, well beyond that of many owners, to cheer on one's failed heroes, as the San Diego Charger fans used to do with the proud banner: "We're number 26!"

FUTILITY

Football

Harvard football fans have often had to keep a stiff upper lip. Their teams, in general, have not been awesome. On the day before Ivy-League-leading Princeton was to play Harvard, the *Crimson*, Harvard's undergraduate paper, faced the likely rout with good humor.

It declared, "Two powerful elevens will take the field in Princeton's Palmer Stadium this afternoon." Then it added, "In a few minutes, they will be joined by Harvard's football players."

FUTILITY

Football

You have to feel sorry for poor Clair Scott. Not only were his Indiana Hoosiers losing badly to the Iowa Hawkeyes, but Scott suffered a personal humiliation that had to set some sort of record.

The Hoosiers, with possession of the ball on their own three-yard line, were out of downs. Clair Scott dropped back to kick. He retreated as far as he could in the Indiana end zone.

At the snap, Scott booted. It wasn't a great kick, but it wasn't terrible either. It was high, and it sailed into the teeth of a 50-mile-an-hour wind.

The punt returner for Iowa waited for the ball on the 25-yard line. He began moving in as the ball drifted back toward the Indiana goal line. He reached the 20 and then the 15. The wind kept blowing. The ball kept drifting, and the Hawkeye punt returner kept coming.

A frantic dash took him over the goal line. His hands grasped the football, and the referee signaled touchdown. History doesn't record whether Clair Scott signaled anything, or said anything. But he must have thought plenty.

FUTILITY

Football

The public address system announced: "Will the lady who left her eleven kids at Texas Stadium please pick them up? They're beating the Dallas Cowboys 14 to 0."

FUTILITY

Golf

Former President Jerry Ford was an enthusiastic golfer but not a great one. Bob Hope, a friend of his, often joked about Ford's wildness on the golf course.

One day Ford responded to the needling: "I deny allegations by Bob Hope that during my last game I hit an eagle, a birdie, an elk, and a moose."

FUTILITY

Sailing

For 17 years after the United States won the Hundred Guinea Cup—now the America's Cup—the trophy gathered dust in the lockers of the New York Yacht Club.

But not everyone had forgotten about its existence. James Ashbury, the owner of the English schooner *Cambria*, expressed a desire to race for the cup. The timing seemed right to him. The British had recently made great strides in the building of sailing ships. In the U.S., the era of sail, of the great clipper ships, was over, and the Civil War had caused yachting to languish.

Ashbury thought the *Cambria* could beat whatever yachts the Americans entered against it. The Americans obliged by entering a total of 23 boats. The date of the 38-mile race was set for August 8, 1870.

The race attracted enormous interest. A large fleet of sightseeing vessels crowded New York Bay. The stock exchanges closed for the day, and Wall and Broad Streets were deserted.

James Ashbury was astonished at the interest his challenge had aroused. He was even more astonished at the outcome of the race. The British *Cambria* was not invincible after all. It finished 27 minutes and 3 seconds behind the leader, the American schooner *Magic*.

That wasn't the worst of it. Not only did Ashbury's entry lose to the *Magic*, but it also lost to eight other American boats—the *Idler*, *Silvie*, *America*, *Dauntless*, *Madgie*, *Phantom*, *Alice*, and the *Halcyon*.

HONESTY

Baseball

Bob Uecker, the catcher turned humorist, notes that a fringe player doesn't miss the cheers when he retires. He never heard all that many cheers. He doesn't miss the money either because, until recently, fringe players weren't paid very much.

Uecker's highest salary in baseball was $23,000 a year. Not long after he left baseball, he says, he was earning more than that from telling people what a failure he was.

HONESTY

Baseball

Hall of Fame pitcher Waite Hoyt won 22 games for the New York Yankees in 1927 and lost 7. The Yankee team that year was probably the strongest in baseball history. The lineup with Ruth, Gehrig, and Lazzeri was loaded with power. So Hoyt wasn't just being modest when he said, "The secret of success as a pitcher lies in getting a job with the Yankees."

HONESTY

Basketball

A lot of old-time athletes scoff at the players of today. They think the greats of their era would run circles around today's pampered highly paid stars.

Not George "the Bird" Yardley who in 1957/58 became the first player in NBA history to score 2,000 points in a season. He scored 2,001.

Yardley doesn't think it makes sense to compare athletes from one period to another. Today they're different physical specimens, he says. "I wouldn't even make a good college team."

HONESTY

Cross-country

It was billed as the longest mass marathon in modern history. The runners were to start from Ascot Speedway in Los Angeles and finish at Madison Square Garden in New York. They would share $48,500 in cash prizes—big money back in 1928.

This "Bunion Derby," as sportswriters called it, soon turned into the biggest fiasco up to the Edsel. Everything went wrong. Expenses soared into the stratosphere. About the only positive aspect of the race turned out to be the honor of its long-suffering sponsor, C.C. Pyle.

No one would have picked Pyle for a hero. A fast talker who sported a derby and pearl-buttoned spats, Pyle was both a promoter and a self-promoter. He expected to make millions on his cross-country marathon. He had deals lined up all along the route.

It fell apart completely. Most of the runners were eager unknowns. Nearly half of the 199 starters dropped out within the first few miles. The Mojave Desert claimed more. Pyle had disastrously underestimated the cost of feeding the runners who ploughed on. Cities canceled promotional contracts. Crowds were small everywhere. By the time 55 runners loped into Ohio, Pyle's marathon was being called the flop of the century.

Few people expected old C.C. to pay the struggling runners a dime—not even to pay back the finishers their $100 entry fee. Pyle had already lost a bundle on the venture, and now the runners would lose their pittance. So people thought.

But Pyle kept the race going. The runners crossed the Hudson on a ferryboat and ran ten times around the track at Madison Square Garden. About five hundred people, the smallest in the history of the Garden, watched them.

What they saw was an exhibition of class that few expected from the fast-dealing, debt-ridden C.C. Pyle. He paid back all the finishers their $100 fees. And, with newsreel cameras whirring, he paid out the entire $48,500 in prize money. He even hired a brass band to liven up the occasion.

HONESTY

Football

A once-great football team in the Southwest Conference was having a disastrous year. Week after week, the team went down to defeat by lopsided scores.

The head coach talked to his players before a game near the end of the season. He said, "Men, we've asked you to win one for your parents. We've asked you to win one for your girlfriends . . . for the college . . . for the alumni. It hasn't worked. So this time, men, just go out there and win one for yourselves."

By halftime, the team trailed 17 to 0.

A disheartened coach launched into what he knew would probably be a futile pep talk. "Men," he said, "I can see you're not going to win one for yourselves. Now, let me level with you. I still want you to go out there and win this game. But not for yourselves. This time think about the coaching staff. Consider the eight wives . . . the 26 children."

HONESTY

Football

When the injury-ridden Chicago Bears needed some backup insurance at quarterback, they hired Ben Bennett, a former Arena Football League player. Said Bennett: "I guess you could refer to me as a worst-case scenario."

HONESTY

Golf

Dan Conners was a fine middle linebacker for the Oakland Raiders, but not much of a golfer. Once, in a golf tournament, he got the booby prize for shooting a 144.

"You should have cheated," coach John Madden told him.

"I did cheat," Conners admitted. "I still shot 144."

HONESTY

Hockey

The New York Rovers, a hockey team owned by the New York Rangers, had been playing poorly. One morning, after an all-night card game, the players were confronted by Lester Patrick, general manager of the Rangers. He gave them a tongue-lashing for their uninspired play.

Having gotten wind of the card game, he snarled, "I want everyone who stayed up playing cards last night to raise his hand."

Rudy Pilous raised his left hand. After a slight pause, he also raised his right hand.

The general manager wasn't amused. "What are you, a comedian?" he asked.

"No, Mr. Patrick," Pilous said. "One hand is for my roommate, Walt Cunningham. He was too tired to make the meeting this morning."

HUMILITY

Baseball

Stan Musial was a dangerous hitter anytime, and he was especially dangerous in the clutch. If you added a rookie pitcher to that equation, you got a situation that favored Musial and the St. Louis Cardinals.

The rookie pitcher in this story seemed to think so. The Cardinals were behind by two runs, but they had just put two runners on base. Into the game came the rookie to face Musial. Stan the Man had gone hitless that day, but that hardly raised the kid's confidence.

The catcher called for a slider. The kid shook it off. The catcher signaled a curve. Again the pitcher shook it off. After two more signs had been rejected, the catcher called time and strolled out to the mound.

"Look, kid," he said, "you've only got four pitches, and you've shaken them all off. What's your plan?"

The kid looked embarrassed, glanced toward the plate, and said, "I want to hold on to the ball as long as I can."

HUMILITY

Fishing

Henry's Fork is a trout stream in eastern Idaho. Ernest Schwiebert, whose knowledge of trout is encyclopedic, calls it perhaps the finest trout stream in the United States.

There's one problem. As a bartender in West Yellowstone said to Schwiebert one night, "Those rainbows over there are tough."

They're tough because they won't go after the standard fly-patterns, the ones that work everywhere else.

One morning Schwiebert saw several fishermen waiting for a mating swarm of mayflies to finish their egg laying. When the mayflies had finished and were drifting just above the water, the trout starting to rise.

The rainbows were everywhere!

Schwiebert noticed one fisherman in particular. The rhythm of his casts became more and more frantic. Surrounded by rising trout, he was catching nothing.

Finally, the frustrated fisherman gave up. He took his bamboo rod and launched it like a javelin into the sparkling waters of Henry's Fork. He turned away and waded out of the stream, scattering trout in all directions.

Schwiebert questioned the unhappy fisherman. What had he been using? "Everything that usually works," the fisherman said. "Renegades, Humpies, Grasshoppers, Royal Wullfs."

"They won't work here," Schwiebert advised him.

"They work everywhere," the man said.

"Not here," Schwiebert insisted.

And it was true. For whatever reasons, the rainbow trout in Henry's Fork—and there are plenty of them—are both choosy and fickle. Hundreds of trout fisherman have fished the Henry's Fork and come up empty.

It's a trout stream that tests and sometimes frustrates the very best fisherman. That's why when Schwiebert sat down to write about it, he called his piece, "The River of Humility."

HUMILITY

Football

Pro football is a tough game, and even rookie phenoms can take their lumps. Look at Gale Sayers. When the great running back of the Chicago Bears was in his first pro season, he got a sudden lesson in humility.

Sayers took a pitchout and slanted off toward Willie Davis, the Green Bay Packers' defensive end. Running hard, he saw Davis shake off the Bears' blockers. By the time Sayers turned upfield, Ray Nitschke, the Packers' big linebacker, had raced in beside Davis.

Sayers barrelled into both of them, and the next thing he knew, he was lifted high off the ground. Willie Davis held one leg, and Ray Nitschke held the other. Sayers heard Davis say cheerfully: "Okay, Ray, make a wish, baby!"

HUMILITY

Football

When Irv Pankey, the L.A. Rams left tackle, tore an Achilles tendon, it gave big Bill Bain a chance for a starting assignment.

Bain took his good fortune with a grain of salt. "All this means is that I make the cut next week," he said. "Look, I know they like Irv more than me. I like Irv more than me, too."

HUMILITY

Football

Lou Holtz, head football coach at Notre Dame, admitted that it's not easy to do a half-hour television show when you've just lost a game. He added, "So one time after we got beat at Arkansas, I started out by saying, 'Welcome to *The Lou Holtz Show*. Unfortunately, I'm Lou Holtz.' "

IMPROVEMENT

Basketball

Red Auerbach of the Boston Celtics was asked who was the greatest basketball player he ever saw. After weighing the claims of both Bill Russell and Larry Bird, he finally named Bill Russell. He had many reasons for the choice. One was Russell's ability to learn and respond.

The Celtics played the Knicks soon after Russell joined the Boston team. Harry Gallatin, a shrewd Knick ballplayer, shut Russell down completely.

Before the next game, the coach told Russell that Tommy Heinsohn would take Gallatin. Bill said nothing until just before the game. Then he spoke up.

"I'd like to play Gallatin," he said. "It won't happen again."

Russell played Gallatin, and indeed it didn't happen again. History didn't repeat itself. Bill Russell took total control. In Auerbach's words, "He *killed* him."

IMPROVEMENT

Basketball

Announcer Al McGuire on how to make basketball more exciting: "Eliminate the referees. Raise the basket four feet. Double the size of the basketball. Limit the height of the players to five-nine. Bring back the center jump. Allow taxi drivers in free. And allow the players to carry guns."

IMPROVEMENT

Boxing

After winning a gold medal at the 1976 Olympics, Sugar Ray Leonard wasn't sure he wanted to enter the world of professional boxing.

"But after they started talking about a million dollars," he said, "I decided they had to be cleaning things up."

IMPROVEMENT

Horse Racing

People tend to remember the blunders that athletes make. In the 1957 Kentucky Derby, Bill Shoemaker, riding Gallant Man, misjudged the finish line and stood up in the irons a sixteenth of a mile too soon. Before he could recover, Iron Liege flashed past Gallant Man and won the Derby.

Shoemaker made no excuses for his mistake, then or later. "I goofed," he said. "I'm sorry."

Few people in the vast television audience or at Churchill Downs would ever forget that astonishing finish. Shoemaker never forgot it, but he did redeem himself in short order. So did Gallant Man.

In the Belmont Stakes, five weeks later—after spectators in the walking ring had taunted Shoe, "Don't close your eyes, Willie"—Gallant Man thundered across the finish line eight lengths in front. His time broke Citation's earlier mark at Belmont and set a new American record for the mile and a half.

IMPROVEMENT

Horse Racing

There's the old verse that a jockey supposedly whispers in his horse's ear:

> Roses are red,
> Violets are blue,
> Horses that lose
> Are made into glue.

Amazingly enough, there's a true story that reverses that sequence of events. It starts with a van on the way to a dog-food factory.

This story will sound unbelievable, but it actually happened.

As the nags were being loaded onto the van, one Harry de Leyer, a man who knew horses, was watching them. To his surprise, he saw a big white horse that didn't really look like dog-food material. He signaled the driver, looked the horse over, and bought it for $70.

The horse was a mess—filthy, missing a shoe, and with collar marks showing he had been in harness. Without spirit or poise at the time, he was at least nine years old.

When cleaned up, the horse became known as Snow Man. De Leyer sold him to a local doctor at a nice profit.

The horse wouldn't stay sold. He jumped the paddock fence and came trotting back home. The doctor built a much higher fence. Snow Man jumped that, too.

At this point the doctor was fed up, while de Leyer realized he had parted with a remarkable jumper. He took the horse back, foregoing his profit.

De Leyer then began schooling the horse seriously. Snow Man proved to be an even better jumper than his owner had imagined—awkward but sensational. In his first big show, Snow Man met the open champion Andante and won. Next he beat Diamante, one of the great international jumpers. He went on to Madison Square Garden and knocked off the reigning world champion, a horse named First Chance.

Within six months, Snow Man had captured the Triple Crown in show-ring jumping. How about that? From dog-meat to world champion in the twinkling of an eye.

That has to be one of the great self-improvement stories of all time—even if it's about a horse

INFLUENCE

Baseball

Baseball players are known to be superstitious. Many are also deeply religious. Just as they don't want to change their socks for fear of jinxing a hitting streak, neither do they want to annoy the Man Upstairs.

One Friday the Brooklyn Dodgers were flying back from St. Louis. Harold Parrott, the club secretary, noticed that Rex Barney, a Catholic, was eating a steak dinner.

Barney explained: "My bishop told me it was okay to eat meat on Friday in extraordinary circumstances where nothing else is available."

Later Parrot relayed Barney's comment to Gil Hodges, who hadn't ordered the steak.

"How high up is this plane? Hodges asked.

Parrot said, "Twenty-two thousand feet."

Hodges thought for a moment. "No steak for me, then," he said. "We're too close to headquarters."

INFLUENCE

Football

Jim Sochor, head football coach at the University of California/Davis, took over a struggling Aggie football team and turned it around in spectacular fashion. After a rookie year in which his team finished second, Sochor led the Aggies to 18 consecutive conference titles, an NCAA record. And he did it without the lure of athletic scholarships.

New York Jets quarterback Ken O'Brien played for Sochor at UC/Davis. So did San Diego Chargers' placekicker Rolf Benirschke. Both commented on the influence that Sochor had on their lives and careers.

Benirschke said, "As I got two or three years into my career, I began to understand that the experience I had at Davis—as an academic athlete— prepared me for life in the pros. Jim's philosophy about trying . . . taught me how to compete. 'Put your best foot forward, and if that doesn't work, that's the way it is, and you get up and do it again.' "

INFLUENCE

Football

Not everyone liked Vince Lombardi. He was often rude, abusive, surly, impatient, and profane. Yet he exerted a tremendous influence over the lives of his players—and, on the whole, his influence seems to have been positive.

Author W.C. Heinz, who collaborated with Lombardi on the book *Run to Daylight*, thought he knew the secret of Lombardi's hold over his men. Heinz wrote: "He knew them not just as football players, but as distinct individuals, each of whom he was determined to make into a better player than that man had ever thought he could be."

INFLUENCE

Football

We hear a lot about the power of the media. When pressed for a concrete example, people often fall back on the first Kennedy-Nixon debate, which may or may not have put Kennedy in the White House.

Even before the days of television, though, the media had plenty of influence. Sportswriters in the early 1900s wielded enormous power. So did the rest of the working press.

Do you remember the story of Grantland Rice and the Four Horsemen of the Apocalypse? Probably you do.

The year was 1924, and Notre Dame's football team handed Army a stunning 13–7 defeat. Now, Notre Dame had a very good team, a very good backfield. Good, but not necessarily the stuff of legend.

Grantland Rice made that backfield great. He made it immortal. He wrote: "Outlined against a blue-gray October sky, the Four Horsemen rode again—Famine, Pestilence, Destruction, and Death. These are only aliases. Their real names are Stuhldreher, Miller, Crowley, and Layden."

That made readers sit up and take notice. A South Bend publicist put the honored backfield on horses. The young men were dressed in football uniforms and wreathed in their new-found glory. Photographs of them went out across the country. The Four Horsemen, averaging 163 pounds (maybe one of them *was* Famine), became instant and heroic legends.

Instant, yet permanent. Even today, more than two generations later, if you say "Four Horsemen," more of your listeners are likely to think of the Fighting Irish of Notre Dame than they are of the Bible's Book of Revelation.

INNOVATION

Badminton

The Duke of Beaufort didn't invent badminton, but he did give the sport its name. At a houseparty in Gloucestershire, England, in 1870, the friends of the Duke—sports lovers, all—decided to call the established game of shuttlecock by a new name. They chose the name of their host's estate—Badminton—and it stuck.

A dozen years later, the British publishing house of Longmans, Green asked the Duke of Beaufort to edit a six-volume encyclopedia of sports. The

Duke was an excellent choice, for he was a master of hounds, a member of the Jockey Club, an outstanding shot, and an excellent fisherman.

When he accepted the editorship, the famous *Badminton Library* was born. Its popularity was immediate. The original six volumes became 28 volumes, each one devoted to a single sport. The Duke himself wrote the hunting volume.

Curiously enough, none of the 28 books dealt with badminton.

INNOVATION

Baseball

Too much discipline, not actual necessity, was the mother of invention for Brother Jasper of Manhattan College. Back in 1882, Brother Jasper was Manhattan's moderator of athletics, baseball coach, and prefect of discipline.

When the Manhattan baseball team played at home, students were not allowed to leave their seats until the end of the game. That was a pretty strict rule for antsy college students, and during one long game in the spring of 1882, the student spectators began to get restless.

Sensing that some kind of rule-bending was better than an outright revolt, Brother Jasper walked over to the stands before the Manhattan team came to bat in the seventh inning. All right, he told the crowd, stand up, stretch, and move around for a couple of minutes.

It worked beautifully. The spectators settled down. So Brother Jasper continued the practice at all Manhattan games thereafter. The custom then spread to baseball fans at the Polo Grounds, where Manhattan played some of its home games.

Today it's universal, although fans rooting for the visiting team don't always realize they should stand up at the beginning of, not in the middle of, the seventh inning.

INNOVATION

Baseball

Captain Abner Doubleday, a Union officer, aimed the first gun fired in the defense of Fort Sumter. During the Civil War that followed, Doubleday rose to the rank of general. He commanded the First Corps at Gettysburg after the regular corps commander was killed by a Confederate sharpshooter.

He might be known today as just one of many Union generals. But, long after his death, a commission named by the presidents of baseball's two major leagues discovered a startling fact: Baseball had not simply evolved out of the old English game of rounders, as many people thought. No, it had sprung from the fertile brain of the late Abner Doubleday.

The exact place was Cooperstown, New York, and the exact year was 1839. It's a charming and persistent myth, and the National Baseball Hall of Fame that grew out of the commission's discovery is a delight to every baseball fan.

As for the history, though, you'll do well to listen to Branch Rickey, the sage old Mahatma of baseball. Said Rickey, "The only thing Doubleday ever started was the Civil War."

INNOVATION

Basketball

Sometimes, innovation is gradual. Other times it occurs in a blinding flash. The innovation may be something truly new, or it may be a throwback to earlier practices. The innovator may be well known or unknown.

On November 22, 1956, Bill Russell played his first pro basketball game as a Boston Celtic. He dazzled the fans and the press that night with something as old as the game and as new as his own mastery of it—the art of defense.

That may sound like an overstatement. It isn't. During the early 1950s, the game of basketball had turned into an offensive jamboree. Scores soared into the stratosphere. The big stars were known, to a man, for their offense.

Russell changed that overnight. Literally. In his very first game, Boston sportswriters marveled at his ability to block shots and to rebound. The headlines stressed his outstanding defense. By Russell's fourth game, there was no question that this tall kid from San Francisco University was going to revolutionize the game.

A headline in a Boston paper summed it up: "Russell Puts Defense Back in NBA."

A curious footnote is that while he was starring on defense, he wanted to talk with interviewers about his offense. It was like a star pitcher in baseball who insists on discussing his bloop single.

Not that Russell couldn't shoot. Indeed he could. But it was his defense from the very start that knocked the writers off their barstools and revised the course of basketball history.

INNOVATION

Basketball

Necessity is the mother of invention. Bob Cousy proved that old axiom for the umpteenth time in a basketball game between Holy Cross and Loyola of Chicago.

With the score tied 57–57 and ten seconds to go, Cousy of Holy Cross was fed the ball and drove for the basket. He couldn't gain that half step he needed on Ralph Klaerich, the man guarding him. Any shot he made after the dribble was sure to be blocked.

Cousy realized that he had to cut to Klaerich's right. But how? Without an instant's hesitation, he reached behind his back with his right hand and flicked the ball to the floor. As it came up on the bounce at his left side, he found it with his left hand and dribbled past the astonished Klaerich. Cousy's left-handed lay-up won the game.

Sportswriters figured that Cousy had been practicing that behind-the-back dribble for quite a while, waiting for the right moment to use it. Cousy said no. He'd never thought of the move until the split-second he was forced to use it. Later, of course, he practiced the technique a lot, and it became one of the weapons in his arsenal when he went on to star for the Boston Celtics.

INNOVATION

Basketball

Once upon a time, the usual scoring play in basketball was the two-handed set shot. By today's standards, the game was too slow to generate much excitement. A sharp, aggressive team might score 50 points a game.

Then along came Hank Luisetti. He developed a one-handed jump shot that startled opposing teams and seemed to work very well. There were plenty of doubters, but Luisetti's coach at Stanford, Johnny Bunn, let him keep shooting the one-hander. Hank led his freshman team at Stanford to an undefeated season.

As a sophomore he was nominated as an All-American. The Stanford Indians won the Pacific Coast championship. Luisetti averaged nearly 17 points a game—not much these days, but impressive back in the late '30s. Others began to imitate Hank's one-handed jump shot.

As a matter of fact, Hank Luisetti's jumper revolutionized the game of basketball. It led to the fast break. It changed the defensive strategy of the game. Much higher scores became commonplace. Basketball was suddenly more exciting to fans than it had been in the old two-handed days.

Hank Luisetti developed the one-handed jump shot simply because he found that it worked for him. Today, few young players know his name. Yet every one of them—high school, college, or pro—uses the shot that seemed so strange when Luisetti first perfected it.

INNOVATION

Basketball

Sometimes a new idea comes in a single flash of inspiration. More often it comes after painstaking efforts that have come to nothing.

The invention of basketball followed the second pattern. You may have thought that Dr. James Naismith just grabbed two peach baskets in a sudden fit of insight and nailed them up at either end of the gym. But it didn't happen that way.

Naismith did set out to invent a game. He wanted an indoor sport that would rival baseball and football in popularity and keep students from disliking physical education indoors. He first tried to modify an existing game. But his indoor rugby was a flop with the boys, and his indoor soccer was a disaster. His indoor lacrosse was no better.

What should he do? He decided to look at the nature of games in general. Most of them used a ball. Naismith, after some thought, settled on a soccer ball. Some games used sticks, but these usually required more space. So sticks were out. Next, he had to figure some way to move the ball. Naismith decided on passing.

This left only the question of goals. It seemed like a good idea to prevent defending players from massing in front of a goal. But how could that be accomplished? Ah, ha! thought Naismith. By raising the goals off the floor.

The following morning, Naismith asked the building superintendent if he had two boxes 18 inches square. (You see, the game could have become "boxball.") The super said no, but he did have two old peach baskets. He brought them in, and Naismith nailed one to the lower rail of the balcony at each end of the gym.

Naismith wrote years later of the boys' reactions. "The game was a success from the time the first ball was tossed up," he said. Yes, it was an instant hit, but only after repeated failures.

INNOVATION

Basketball

Purists may consider the rules in sports to be sacred, but sometimes there is simply no choice but to make change. A case in point is the 24-second rule in basketball. The game prospered for more than half a century without it, yet the time finally came when the new rule seemed to be essential.

By the late 1940s, both the pros and the colleges had discovered the strategic virtues of stalling on occasion. This was not always bad. But one dismal game on November 22, 1950, between the Fort Wayne Pistons and the Minneapolis Lakers, made even the sleepiest owners sit up and take notice of the abuses.

When the Pistons met the Lakers in the historic game, the Minneapolis team had a 29-game win streak going on their home court. The court, which was smaller than standard size, gave the slow-footed home team a distinct advantage. The Lakers also used what Piston coach Murray Mendenhall regarded as an illegal zone defense.

To dramatize his complaints, Mendenhall had his players pass the ball back and forth at midcourt. The object of this stall was to draw the Lakers out of their zone. But the Lakers refused to move. Time passed. Nothing happened. The ball sailed back and forth far away from the basket. The Pistons led 8 to 7 at the end of the first quarter. The Lakers led 13 to 11 at the half.

By this time the Laker fans were going bananas. They were screaming for action, and some demanded their money back. They were pelting the Fort Wayne players with whatever was handy.

But coach Mendenhall was as every bit as determined as the Lakers' defense was unyielding. Nothing changed in the second half. With four minutes to go, the Lakers led by a single point. The Pistons went into a four-minute freeze, determined to take—and make—the final shot.

You have to give them credit. They made it work. With ten seconds left, the Pistons' Larry Foust dropped in a hook shot to give his team the lead. The Lakers' final desperation shot missed, and the Fort Wayne Pistons won 19 to 18. It was the lowest scoring game in NBA history.

Loud were the wails of the Lakers' partisans after the game. But Fort Wayne had done nothing illegal. There was no rule to prevent a game-long freeze. And although the league directors hoped that moral persuasion would prevent the same thing from happening again, it didn't.

The directors finally adopted a rule—a time limit on how long a team could hold the ball before shooting. The figure chosen—24 seconds—was based on fairly casual research. But it was needed, and it worked. There were no more 19 to 18 games in the NBA.

INNOVATION

Football

Innovation is a fine thing, but it can sometimes be carried too far. In 1965, Cornell's Big Red football team tried a ploy against Princeton that was spectacular—and even legal at the time—but maybe a bit ill-conceived.

They were playing the Princeton Tigers, whose field-goal kicker was the talented and later famous Charlie Gogolak. Since Gogolak was so good, the Big Red decided to use extraordinary means to try to stop him.

When the Tigers went for their first field-goal attempt, Gogolak found himself facing a defense that no one had ever seen before. Two defensive backs had climbed onto the shoulders of two tackles. In theory there was no way Gogolak could get the kick past them.

But Gogolak noticed that they were lined up perfectly with the goal posts. He thought he could boot it by them to the left. When his kick went wide, it looked for the moment as if the twin-tower defense might have a future.

It didn't. Later in the game Gogolak kicked two field goals—44 and 54 yards—right over the tower. Princeton went on to win, 36 to 27. And after the season, the Rules Committee outlawed the twin-tower defense.

INNOVATION

Football

Once upon a time, back during the Depression, the Washington Redskins had a full-blooded Indian coach named Will "Lone Star" Dietz. He lasted only a couple of seasons, possibly because of his assortment of trick plays that didn't work.

He did have one trick play, though, that succeeded now and then, and the players got a charge out of trying it. Lone Star called it the Squirrel Cage.

The play was used on a kickoff return. Back in those days, no one kicked from a tee, so the kickoff would usually come in on a line. That gave the receiving team time to set up the Squirrel Cage.

After the kickoff reception, every player would race into a huddle at about the ten-yard line. The player who had caught the ball would hand it to another player. Then the team would break sharply from the huddle, with each player pretending to carry the ball behind his back.

Turk Edwards, the biggest man on the team at 250 pounds, often got the ball. No one suspected him, and a couple of times he gained 50 yards or more. The crowd loved it.

The Squirrel Cage wouldn't work today, but back in those more innocent times, it sometimes did. At least it worked a lot better than Lone Star's fake fumbles and triple reverses.

INNOVATION

Football

As Pop Warner grew older, he became more and more set in his ways. The innovations that had made Temple University a great football power were copied by other coaches. As time went by, some of these coaches made innovations of their own. Warner's teams had trouble with certain new methods of attack, especially the passing game. Sportswriters, fans, and alumni could see that Warner's pass defense had become outmoded. But not Pop.

"I don't see what's wrong with it," he said sadly. "It's worked for forty years."

INNOVATION

Football

Every coach wants to befuddle the opposing team. In the early days of football, Pop Warner was one of the great innovators. And nothing caused greater confusion among the guys at the other end of the field than Warner's hidden ball trick.

Warner coached at half a dozen colleges in his long career. In 1903 he was at Carlisle, and his Indians were taking the opening kickoff from Harvard. The ball sailed all the way to Carlisle's five-yard line, where quarterback Jimmie Johnson gathered it in.

Now, in those days, there was no huddle as there is today, but the Indians immediately converged in what looked like a huddle. Johnson quickly slipped the ball under the back of guard Charlie Dillon's jersey. Pop Warner reasoned that the hump would be visible from the stands, but would be invisible to the charging Harvard players.

When Jimmie Johnson yelled "Go!" the players fanned out and headed downfield. Oh, yes, each of the backs had removed his helmet and was hugging it to his chest like a football.

Talk about confusion!

The Harvard players zeroed in on the backs and tackled them one by one. But no one paid much attention to Charlie Dillon, the guard, whose hands were empty. When Dillon raced toward Harvard's safetyman, Carl Marshall, the safety sidestepped what he thought was a block and took off after someone else.

Dillon waltzed across the goal line, untouched.

The crowd had been going crazy ever since the huddle broke. They'd seen the guilty hunchback for the entire 95-yard run. So they weren't surprised to see a teammate grab the ball from underneath Dillon's jersey and plop it to the ground for a touchdown.

Pop Warner, canny coach that he was, had tipped off the referee about the play. It came as no surprise, then, when the ref ruled the play perfectly legal.

INNOVATION

Hockey

One of the true innovators in sports broadcasting was a modest young Canadian reporter by the name of Foster Hewitt. He began his work behind the mike in the late 1920s, when radio was in its infancy. Long before sports programming became popular in the United States, Hewitt was broadcasting hockey games north of the border.

He started doing play-by-play for the Toronto Maple Leafs in 1931. It's no exaggeration to say that his electrifying broadcasts made hockey fans of thousands upon thousands of people across Canada. Hockey stars gained the celebrity of movie stars.

Saturday night became hockey night on Canadian radio. Hewitt was heard from coast to coast. His weekly play-by-play attracted more listeners than any other program originating in Canada.

Like many radio and TV sportscasters since, Hewitt developed a standard expression that thousands, if not millions, of Canadians were fond of quoting. It was simple and effective: "He shoots! He scores!"

INNOVATION

Hockey

The first time you heard an announcer going on about a "hat trick" in hockey, you probably wondered what he was talking about. You still may not know. Is it three consecutive goals by one player in a game? Or is it simply three goals—consecutive or not—by one player? According to the National Hockey League Guide, the goals have to be consecutive—with neither team scoring in between.

But where did that term come from? The hat trick—why?

It seems to have originated in cricket more than a hundred years ago. When a bowler took three wickets on successive balls—if you know what *that* means—his cricket club awarded him a new hat. No doubt the hat was a bowler.

The term found its way into hockey in the early 1900s. The hat trick is not uncommon, although the double hat trick is. Only one player—Joe Malone of the Quebec Bulldogs—ever achieved the double hat trick. On January 31, 1920, Malone scored seven straight goals against the Toronto St. Pats.

INSTRUCTION

Baseball

Charley Lau was a journeyman major league catcher and a lifetime .255 hitter. He was also a close student of the art of hitting. Eventually he became the best known batting instructor in baseball. Many players, including super-star George Brett, were disciples of the Lau method.

Yet Charley Lau didn't claim to have all the answers. On hitting the knuckleball, for instance, he said: "There are two theories on hitting the knuckleball. Unfortunately, neither of them works."

INSTRUCTION

Football

Like the baseball manager in the movie *Bull Durham*, Selby College's football coach couldn't believe how little his players knew about the game. He decided he'd have to start at the beginning.

At their usual Monday morning meeting, the coach held up a football.

"This," he said, "is a football. It's an inflated ellipsoid, according to the dictionary, but that's not important. Just try to get the general idea through your heads. You're looking at a football. I'll spell it for you. F-O-O-T-B . . . ."

He was interrupted by the puzzled voice of a lineman. "Slow down, Coach. You're going too fast."

INSTRUCTION

Football

The football coach was talking earnestly with his second-string quarterback on the sideline.

"Remember, son, football develops initiative."

"Yes, coach."

"It develops decision-making and leadership."

"Yes, coach."

"Now get in there and do exactly what I tell you."

INSTRUCTION

Football

Joe Don Looney, an all-too-aptly-named football player, bounced in and out of four colleges and on and off the rosters of five pro teams. He had an attitude problem, to say the least. He didn't take kindly to advice or instruction.

With the New York Giants, he ran the seven-hole in scrimmages when he was supposed to run the five-hole. He offered this unusual explanation: "Anyone can run where the holes are. A good football player makes his own holes."

INSTRUCTION

Football

Bum Phillips had a theory about coaching and about the players he coached: "Two kinds of football players ain't worth a damn," he said; "the one that never does what he's told, and the other that never does anything *except* what he's told."

INSTRUCTION

Golf

The price of learning can be steep. There are experts to teach you everything from birdwatching to sex. But it costs money. Sometimes, big money.

Among teachers, golf pros have to be right up there in the high income brackets. I mean it. Never walk into a pro shop and ask about lessons unless you're thinking second mortgage.

A friend of mine asked about golf lessons not long ago. The pro looked him over carefully and watched his swing.

"You need work," he said with a frown. "I'd say a two-year course, which goes for $750 down and $150 a month for each lesson."

Now, my friend has other financial commitments, such as rent, gas, and alimony.

"I don't know," he said. "That sounds like buying a car."

The pro looked startled and a little embarrassed. "Well, yeah, you're right. I *am* buying a car. A Mercedes, but how did you know?"

INTELLIGENCE

Football

People sometimes think of football as a game for deadheads. Not so, says pro coach Chuck Noll. Intelligence is important in football—it helps a player "assimilate" quickly.

But you can't count just on thinking, he says. You have to react. Noll uses the familiar phrase for what you should avoid—the "paralysis of analysis."

INTELLIGENCE

Football

Joe Paterno, who has coached football successfully at all levels, said, "All coaches are thinking men, or else they wouldn't survive."

INTELLIGENCE

Football

Dixon Ryan Fox, a professor of history at Columbia, had a low opinion of football—and football coaches.

Said Fox, "I listened to a football coach who spoke straight from the shoulder—at least I could detect no higher origin in anything he said."

INTELLIGENCE

Horse Racing

Most people who have dealt with horses will say that equine intelligence varies as much as human intelligence. Some horses are smart, and some are not so smart.

Amagansett, trained by the famous Hirsch Jacobs, was one of the smart ones. Jacobs was pretty smart himself. Later in his career, he turned a claiming horse Stymie—which he obtained for $1,500—into the greatest money winner of his time.

But that's another story. This one is about Amagansett. According to a steeplechase expert, Amagansett, who was making his first start that day, had not even been trained over the jumps. It seemed incredible to him that Hirsch Jacobs would turn the horse loose in the steeplechase.

Well, Amagansett won, and won easily.

Jacobs explained why. "Amagansett is an intelligent horse," he said. "And he's a safe, sure jumper." The trainer had taken Amagansett to one of the jumps in the infield. He had let the horse put his nose against it.

Said Jacobs, "You just knew he understood."

Apparently he did.

INTELLIGENCE

Soccer

Soccer star Vladislav Bogicevic said, "Soccer is a game of thinking, not of running. I play with my head, not my feet."

INTENSITY

Baseball

Hall of Fame pitcher Early Wynn had the reputation of being a mean competitor. He didn't deny it. He said, "You'll never be a big winner until you start hating the hitter. That guy with the bat is trying to take your bread and butter away from you. You've got to fight him every second."

INTENSITY

Baseball

Eddie Stanky played second base for a number of National League teams. He was a particular favorite of manager Leo Durocher. As The Lip liked to say, "Stanky can't hit, run, or throw, and I wouldn't trade him for a million dollars."

Eddie Stanky was out to win. So was Leo Durocher. The Lip appreciated a tough, smart, tricky player like Stanky—a guy who would find a way to beat you whether he had the skills or not.

INTENSITY

Baseball

Leo Durocher didn't like to lose. "Show me a good loser," he said, "and I'll show you an idiot."

INTENSITY

Baseball

John J. McGraw: They called him "The Little Napoleon." He guided the fortunes of the New York Giants for 31 years. Hard-bitten and intense, he said, "We'd spit tobacco juice on a spike wound, rub dirt in it, and get out there and play."

INTENSITY

Boxing

This is a sad story, as so many stories in boxing are. But it shows the kind of fire and drive it takes to be a world champion.

Davey Moore held the featherweight championship of the world for almost five years. He lost the title to Sugar Ramos in a fight that he seemed to be winning.

For nine rounds, Davey Moore was ahead on points. Then Ramos caught him with a solid right, and Moore fell backward, hitting his head on the bottom ring rope. His head pounding, he got up before the count of ten, but Sugar Ramos finished him off a few seconds later.

Moore regained consciousness in the ring and went over to Ramos's trainer, Angelo Dundee. His head was still pounding, and he was in a daze.

He said, "Angie, you're gonna give me a rematch, ain'tcha?"

Those were his last words. He collapsed, unconscious. He was carried from the ring and died three days later.

INTENSITY

Boxing

Two-Ton Tony Galento wasn't supposed to have any chance at all of taking the heavyweight title away from Joe Louis. Tony looked more like a beer barrel than a boxer, and most sportswriters thought the fight was a mismatch.

But to everyone's surprise, early in the bout Galento knocked Louis to the canvas with a solid left hook. Louis was startled, but unhurt. He jumped to his feet before the referee even began to count.

Joe's trainer, Jack Blackburn, took his fighter to task at the end of the round. "You're supposed to take a count when that happens, Joe. Why didn't you stay down for nine like I always told you?"

"What," said Louis, "and let him get all that rest?"

INTENSITY

Football

Football coaches talk a lot about intensity. If they're old-timers, the one player they're likely to mention is Ernie Nevers. He was intensity with a capital *I*.

Nevers was a versatile guy. He pitched for the St. Louis Browns for three seasons. He played some pro basketball. And on Thanksgiving Day, 1929, he set a football record that may never be broken. Playing for the Chicago Cardinals, he scored all six of the Chicago Cardinals' touchdowns and kicked four extra points. The final score was Cardinals 40, Bears 6. Ernie Nevers scored every one of those 40 winning points.

What really impressed people about Nevers was his intensity. He never quit—even when he was a standing ruin. He played the 1925 Rose Bowl game with two smashed ankles. He was knocked cold in a game against Brooklyn and, when he came to, he carried the ball 16 straight times on a scoring drive. In a game against the Packers, while suffering from acute appendicitis, he threw a 62-yard touchdown pass. The doctors removed his appendix that night.

Ernie Nevers just never quit.

INTENSITY

Football

Dan Reeves likes to tell this story about the time he and Mike Ditka played for the Dallas Cowboys.

One night they were playing gin rummy. Ditka lost a few hands in a row, and this naturally enraged him. He picked up a chair and slammed it into the wall. All four legs went through the wallboard. The chair stuck there.

Reeves watched calmly. He said, "God, this guy must hate to lose."

LEADERSHIP

Baseball

When a baseball manager takes his team to the World Series, you expect him to be honored by the press and given a new contract by his club. But consider the strange events of 1964.

The New York Yankees won the pennant in the American League. The St. Louis Cardinals won it in the National League. In a cliff-hanging World Series, the Cardinals nosed out the Yanks four games to three. An exciting season and a memorable Series.

Neither manager returned to his club in 1965. Why?

First, take Yogi Berra. Many people had been surprised when Berra was named Yankee manager in the first place. Some thought that Ralph Houk, expecting the Yanks to fade after three straight pennants, wanted the ax to fall on someone else. Houk had managed the three pennant winners and in 1964 moved up to general manager.

For much of the season, the cynics seemed to be right about Berra. The Yankees struggled. With 41 games to play, they were six games out of first place. Many sportswriters had counted them out of the race. So, apparently, had the Yankee front office, but they didn't bother to tell Yogi.

Suddenly in September, the Yankees came alive. They closed the gap; they went on an 11-game winning streak. When it was all over, the Yanks had won their fourth straight pennant—this time under Yogi Berra.

Over in the National League, Gussie Busch, St. Louis's king of beer, was unhappy with Johnny Keane as manager of the Cardinals. Like the Yankees, the Cardinals struggled early in the season. Gussie Busch refused to discuss a new contract with Keane, and he talked openly with Leo Durocher about the managerial job for 1965.

Then the Cardinals, like the Yankees, put on a late-season drive and won the pennant. Then they went on to win the World Series by a whisker. Then Gussie Busch decided he wanted to talk with Keane about a new contract after all. Keane didn't.

In one of the strangest managerial shakeups on record, Yogi Berra was dumped by the Yankees and became a coach for the New York Mets. Johnny Keane walked away from the pennant-winning Cardinals and became manager of the pennant-winning Yankees. Both were solid managers and proven winners.

The bottom line, of course, is that you have to have good ballplayers to win. And both clubs were about to fall on evil days. Keane's Yankees finished in sixth place in 1965. The Cardinals, under Red Schoendienst, slid all the way to seventh.

By any rational measure, Yogi Berra and Johnny Keane had managed well in 1964. The World Series proved it, and later events confirmed it. But the die had already been cast that season for both men. Their leadership went unrewarded.

LEADERSHIP

Baseball

As Casey Stengel said, "The secret of managing a club is to keep the five guys who hate you away from the five who are undecided."

LEADERSHIP

Basketball

One mark of a leader is a willingness to take responsibility. Coach Red Holzman singled out four of the outstanding leaders in his years with the New York Knicks. The four were Bill Bradley, Dave DeBusschere, Walt Frazier, and Willis Reed.

He said, "Those guys always wanted the ball when the game was on the line.   "

LEADERSHIP

Basketball

Wilt Chamberlain, seven feet and one inch tall, dominated pro basketball for many years. But his personal success didn't translate into success for his team, the Philadelphia 76ers. In 1967, however, his team finally won the championship. Someone asked him if he thought this title would rally everyone around him.

"No way," he said. "Nobody roots for Goliath."

LEADERSHIP

Football

When Jim Lee Howell was head coach of the New York Giants, he had plenty of critics. Most sportswriters thought he was too pleasant and passive. Jerry Izenberg said that he was not a head coach, but a "head smile."

Howell certainly had limitations, but he also had assets. One was his belief in organization; another was his willingness to delegate authority. Of course, delegation works well only when the assistants are competent.

It worked very well for Jim Lee Howell. His assistants were Tom Landry and Vince Lombardi.

LOGIC

Baseball

Yogi Berra went into a pizzeria by himself and ordered a small pizza. "Shall I slice it into four pieces or eight?" asked the counterman. "Make it four," Yogi said. "I don't think I can eat eight."

LOGIC

Baseball

Logic is logic, but Yogi Berra's logic is something special. It has a beauty all its own.

"Nobody goes to that restaurant anymore," Yogi says, "because it's crowded all the time."

LOGIC

Baseball

No one has ever denied that Casey Stengel knew a lot about baseball. But a good many people have questioned whether the early New York Mets knew much about it.

Casey, on the far side of 70, managed the Mets to a tenth-place finish in their first season. From the start of spring training, he seemed to doubt that he had a pennant winner.

At Huggins-Stengel Field in St. Petersburg, he assembled his team at home plate. He started to talk. As he talked, he ambled down toward first base. The boys tagged along, listening to his gems of wisdom.

Then Casey struck off for second, with the pack on his tail. He kept talking as he moved over to third. After a while, he strolled to home plate, still jabbering, with his players still following.

When he reached home, he said, "Them are the bases. We just went around them."

A guffaw sounded from his team.

"Well," Casey snapped, "show me a better way to score runs."

LOGIC

Baseball

Casey Stengel may or may not have said it. Experts differ. But whatever the source, it's a thought worth pondering: "Baseball is 90 percent mental. The other half is physical."

LOGIC

Baseball

For every miracle season the New York Mets have seen, they've suffered through half a dozen disasters. As late as 1980, the Mets players could hardly wait to finish that 162nd game. When it was over, pitcher Pat Zachry said, "You can get to the good stuff."

One player who couldn't even wait for that final game was Frank Taveras, the shortstop. He left the Mets five days before the scheduled end of the 1980 season. His reason: to attend the funeral of his grandmother. Trouble was, she had died the previous September, too.

LOGIC

Baseball

While covering the Mets in spring training, journalist Robert Lipsyte filed a story from the west coast of Florida. In it he described the sun as rising out of the Gulf of Mexico—in other words, from the west. A friend on the sports desk in New York couldn't let that pass without a quip. He wired back: "Forget about Mets, please cover irregularity of sun."

LOGIC

Baseball

Former umpire Ron Luciano, now a best-selling author, tells a host of funny baseball stories. In his third book, he reports on his interviews with some of the non-superstars of baseball. Among them are Marc Hill and John Wathan.

Luciano makes the point that there are some excellent players who go through their careers without attracting much attention. They're fine major league ballplayers, but they just aren't known.

He adds: "I don't know who they are, of course. But they're there, believe me."

LOGIC

Baseball

When Walt Alston was managing the Dodgers, there was a padded cushion along the top of the outfield fence. A ball hitting the cushion was a home run. A ball hitting the wood wall below it was in play.

The Dodgers' Ron Cey hit a deep drive that thudded off the cushion and bounced back on the field. The umpire called it in play.

Alston, who was not given to temper tantrums, came out of the dugout, furious. In the ensuing conversation, he yelled, "If you couldn't hear that, you've gotta be blind!"

LOGIC

Baseball

Danny Cater, a first-baseman/outfielder, played for seven different teams 'in his 12-year major league career. He had very little power at the plate, but a pretty fair sense of humor.

One day a Milwaukee Brewers pitcher nailed him in the helmet with a fast ball. It was a direct hit, and Cater dropped to the ground.

Several of his Boston teammates gathered around him. Also looking on was George Scott, formerly with the Red Sox, but now the Brewers' first baseman.

Cater began screaming, "I can't see! I can't see!"

That was enough to worry even the most hardened Bostonian, but George Scott semed merely amused.

As Cater continued to roll and scream, Scott said with a laugh, "Try opening your eyes."

He tried—and succeeded. That was the problem all right.

LOGIC

Baseball

From the very beginning, baseball has been dismissed by its critics as being a slow, boring game. These critics are wrong, of course, but baseball executives tend to listen worriedly to such complaints.

And occasionally they act, or at least they think about acting. Many years ago, Ban Johnson, founder and president of the American League, asked his umpires to recommend ways to cut down on the time the games were taking.

Then, as now, there were a lot of obvious suggestions. Impose various time limits, as in modern basketball. Allow automatic, no-pitch intentional walks. Limit the number of warm-up pitches to hardly any. The usual stuff.

It fell to umpire Tim Hurst to come up with the simple solution. Never mind the tinkering, he said. Never mind the clever refinements. Just cut the games to six innings.

LOGIC

Baseball

Willie Mays was hired to play himself in a television show. When he arrived for the filming, the director asked him how he planned to handle the role.

"I don't know," Willie said. "Just turn those cameras on, and if it ain't me, let me know."

LOGIC

Baseball

The rookie outfielder for the old New York Giants couldn't seem to catch anything. Left field was a disaster area. Easy flies were falling for doubles. Base hits were rolling through the rookie's legs to the fence.

At last, manager John McGraw decided he'd had enough. He replaced the rookie with a veteran left fielder. But the usually steady veteran did no better. He missed a couple of easy chances, too.

McGraw turned to the rookie on the bench and said, "See what you've done. You've screwed up left field, so now nobody can play it."

LOGIC

Basketball

Barrie Haynie, basketball player at Centenary College, commenting on his jump shot: "I sight down my nose to shoot, and now my nose isn't straight since I broke it. That's why my shooting has been off."

LOGIC

Basketball

Bones McKinney, a famous basketball coach of his day, refused to take airplanes. He was a fatalist, he told his players. He wouldn't mind being aboard a plane when his own number was up. But he was afraid of being up there when some other passenger's number was up.

LOGIC

Basketball

Marty loved the game of basketball, but he made the mistake of betting on it heavily and often. He almost never won. Day by day, week by week, he fell deeper and deeper in debt.

His bookie sympathized with Marty's plight.

"Marty," he said, "you just can't pick 'em in basketball. I figure you're losing at least five out of six bets. At this rate, you're gonna go broke."

"You're right," Marty said. "But I don't know what to do."

"You could quit gambling," the bookie said, surprising even himself.

"Forget it."

"Okay, then, why not switch to some other sport? Maybe hockey."

"You've got to be kidding," Marty exploded. "What the hell do I know about hockey?"

LOGIC

Boxing

When Rocky Graziano was making the changeover from boxing to show business, someone suggested that he could improve his English by studying at a place like the Actors Studio.

"Why should I go to a place like that?" Graziano asked. "All they do is learn guys like Brando and Newman to talk like me."

LOGIC

Fishing

As the chambermaid went about her duties, she came across a guest in the bathroom.

The guy was standing in the bathtub. It was half full of water. The man was wearing waders, a wading jacket, a hat with colorful fishing flies, and he had a creel slung over his shoulder. He was casting a dry fly into the tub.

The chambermaid wanted nothing to do with this character. She went straight to the manager's office and said, "Look, there's a whacko in Room 718. If you want me to clean the room, you'll have to get him out of there."

The manager went to Room 718 to see for himself. Sure enough, there was the fisherman, still casting into the tub. Figuring it might be best to humor him, the manager said, "Catching any fish?"

The man in the bathtub looked at him with a startled expression. "Are you kidding?" he asked. "In a *bathtub*?"

LOYALTY

Basketball

The time was the late 1960s. Among professional athletes, money was fast replacing friendship, commitment, and other noble instincts. It was hard to resist the lure of bigger and bigger bucks, but John Havlicek of the Boston Celtics managed to do it.

People in the American Basketball Association were offering John a long-term two million dollar package. Boston, an NBA club, was offering him $105,000 a year, period. Negotiations between the ABA and Havlicek's agent soon reached the point when John had to make a decision.

Here is what he reportedly said:

"I've worked all my life and have always tried to do what was right. I never thought I'd earn more than $25,000. I just can't believe the money we're talking about, but to tell the truth, I love Boston . . . I value my reputation. I value what I think is right, so my answer is this. Even if they offered me another two-and-a-half million, I'd stay with the Celtics."

Idealistic? Sure. Dumb? You be the judge.

LOYALTY

Football

Call it loyalty to a memory.

Assistant football coach Chris Faros of Memphis State University had a saying written on the blackboard in the football office. It read: "We get what we ask for, and what we see is a reflection of what we demand."

The philosophy had yielded results. Memphis State was named as the second most improved football team in the nation in 1983.

On December 12 of that year, tragedy struck. Chris Faros, along with head coach Rex Dockery, a freshman defensive back, and the pilot of their light plane were killed in a crash.

Nothing can replace such a loss. But both coaches did leave a legacy to their players.

Dockery had a short prayer that the team repeated after each football game. His prayer is still repeated today.

And Chris Faros's saying, written in chalk, remains unerased on the blackboard.

LOYALTY

Football

The Big Ten football rivalry between Ohio State and Michigan goes back a long way. Both teams are powerhouses in the conference year after year. It's been suggested that the Big Ten should be called the Big Two and the Little Eight.

Naturally, the rivalry extends to the opposing coaches. For many years, Woody Hayes directed the Ohio State Buckeyes. Woody had a phenomenal record and a formidable temper. He was fiercely loyal to Ohio State and resentful of anything that suggested a liking for Michigan.

One day Robert Vare, an out-of-town reporter, managed to get an interview with Woody. That was never easy, but on this particular day the coach was expansive. He talked for more than four hours. It was an interviewer's dream, a real coup, because Hayes had a deep distrust of all but a few local sportswriters.

The reporter was ecstatic when he got up to go. But as he arose, Woody grabbed the end of his tie and flipped it in the air. The coach said, "If you come here again, you'd better not wear that."

The reporter was puzzled. He looked down at his two-color rep tie. "What's wrong with it?" he asked.

"The colors!" Woody roared. He pointed at the blue and yellow stripes. "Those are the Michigan colors!"

LUCK

Baseball

"Bob Gibson is the luckiest pitcher I ever saw," Tim McCarver used to say. "He always pitches when the other team doesn't score any runs."

LUCK

Baseball

Branch Rickey was the father of baseball's farm system and the executive who signed Jackie Robinson, thus breaking the color barrier. Rickey was a pioneer. He was also a planner. "Luck," he said, "is the residue of design."

LUCK

Boxing

There are perhaps half a dozen events in American sports history that everyone has heard about. One is the so-called "long count" in the heavyweight title fight between champion Gene Tunney and ex-champion Jack Dempsey. A hundred and five thousand fans were on hand in Chicago, many of them hoping to see the old Manassa Mauler regain the crown he had worn for so many years. It almost happened, but it didn't, because Gene Tunney brought more than boxing skill to the ring with him that day—he also brought along Lady Luck.

Paul Gallico, a young reporter, was on hand for the fight. He had a telephone wire to New York and a ringside view of the action. When Dempsey tagged Tunney with what looked like a knockout punch in the seventh round, Tunney hit the canvas directly in front of Gallico.

Dempsey stood over the fallen champ, paying no attention to referee Dave Berry's motion to send him to a neutral corner. The count couldn't start until Dempsey backed off. When Dempsey finally did, a number of seconds had elapsed. The question is, could Tunney have gotten to his feet before a normal ten-count gave the fight to Dempsey by a knockout? Gallico says no. The champ was stunned and glassy-eyed. Only luck—and Dempsey and the rattled referee—gave Tunney the time he needed to recover.

How long was the champ down? A little fellow with a bashed-in nose and a stopwatch was sitting next to Paul Gallico. His name was Battling Nelson, and his stopwatch told the tale. Said Nelson, "Why, he's been down for sixteen seconds!"

Tunney struggled to his feet before Berry's "long count" reached ten. He then backpedaled for the rest of the round, held off the old mauler's challenge through the rest of the fight, and kept his title.

Dempsey opened a bar in Times Square.

LUCK

Football

Nobody likes to lose, but on one occasion the Boston College football team had reason to be grateful for a big loss.

The year was 1942, and Boston College expected an invitation to the Sugar Bowl. All they had to do was get by a none-too-strong Holy Cross team. The game was played on November 28 at Fenway Park, Boston.

In an amazing upset, Holy Cross not only beat Boston College but massacred them. The final score was 55 to 12. Curiously, the numbers 55 and 12 were the numbers worn by Boston College's co-captains, Holovak and Naumutz. These were the two players pictured on the front of the game program.

That was eerie enough, but it's not the most memorable part of the story.

Boston College had scheduled a victory party that night at the Cocoanut Grove nightclub in Boston. Having lost the game—and along with it their Sugar Bowl hopes—they canceled the party.

That night the Cocoanut Grove burned to the ground with the loss of 491 lives.

LUCK

Football

Luck is seldom as dramatically evident as it was in the 1972 playoff game between the Pittsburgh Steelers and the Oakland Raiders. Football fans who saw the end of that game will never forget it.

The name: Franco Harris. The play: the much ballyhooed "immaculate reception." Even without that terrific name, it would be a play to remember. But with it, hey. . . .

The Raiders were leading 7 to 6 with 20 seconds remaining. The Steelers had possession on their own 40-yard line, and it was fourth-and-ten.

Quarterback Terry Bradshaw dropped back to pass. Although he was rushed, he managed to throw deep to Frenchy Fuqua, a halfback. Oakland's free safety, Jim Tatum, had Frenchy covered perfectly, and the ball bounced off one or the other of them. No one is quite sure which.

That should have ended the game, but no. The unsnared football floated straight toward Pittsburgh's running back Franco Harris. Franco the Fortunate plucked it from the air and raced all alone into the end zone.

Sixty yards for a touchdown. Five seconds left on the clock. The extra point was good, and Pittsburgh seized victory from what looked like certain defeat.

They'll probably talk about the "immaculate reception" as long as football is played. It's the kind of stunning finish that's always possible in a close game but is hardly ever so spectacular.

LUCK

Golf

Luck is a part of every sport, but only a top player gets certain kinds of luck.

Take Lew Worsham. In 1953 in the world's championship tournament at the Tam O'Shanter golf course in Chicago, Lew needed a birdie 3 on the last hole to tie.

Charley Harper had just finished the 72 holes with a 279, and he looked like the sure winner. Television cameras caught his pleased expression.

On the 18th hole, Worsham got off an excellent drive, straight down the fairway. It stopped 104 feet short of the pin. That gave him a 277. If he parred the hole, which most spectators expected him to, he would finish the tournament one stroke behind Charley Harper.

Lew's second shot, a wedge shot, rose over a brook that fronted the green. It cleared a small ridge on one bounce about 25 feet from the cup. Then it rolled . . . and rolled . . . and rolled right into the cup.

The spectators gasped. With that eagle-deuce, Worsham's score was 278. He won the tournament.

Was it luck? Up to a point, certainly. But Lew Worsham was a high-ranking pro. His odds against making that incredible wedge shot were a lot lower than those against your Uncle Duffer, say, who plays twice a year. Within limits, you make your own luck.

LUCK

Horse Racing

Allan Sherman, a comedian best known for his funny songs, also told some good jokes. On betting the horses, he said, "Finally I had a streak of luck. For three races in a row, I didn't get to the window in time to bet."

LUCK

Marathoning

One of the best-known hoaxes in sports history began with a stroke of good luck. Or at least Rosie Ruiz must have thought it was good luck.

Ruiz, a Cuban-born New Yorker, 26 years old, had managed to talk her way into the 1979 New York Marathon as a late entrant. She received her number, along with its bar code for finishers, and started the race. At some point, no one knows where, she injured her foot or ankle. She boarded a subway, where she fell into conversation with a woman photographer who was headed for the finish-line area to take some pictures. Rosie said she was going there, too.

When they got there, Ruiz went through the barricades behind the finish line. Limping, she told the officials about her injury. They assumed she was a finisher. They removed the bar code from her number and took her directly for treatment.

Fred Lebow, the man who staged the New York Marathon, guessed that Rosie was probably surprised when she received her certificate for completing the race. The bar code made her a finisher. And she must have been very pleased with her time—two hours, 56 minutes, and 29 seconds. Her own predicted time for New York, her first marathon, had been four hours and ten minutes, about right for a beginner.

Rosie's brief marathoning career had begun. Her outstanding New York time automatically qualified her for the Boston Marathon, and in 1980 she was ready to take on Beantown.

Wearing number W50, Rosie Ruiz, who looked about as much like a marathoner as Jody Foster, dashed across the Boston finish line in an apparent time of two hours, 31 minutes, and 56 seconds. She had missed the American women's record by only half a minute.

But hold the applause. She had also missed most of the race. It was Fred Lebow in New York who blew the whistle. He knew most of the world's good marathoners, but not Rosie Ruiz. He investigated and discovered that while Rosie's bar code had been turned in, the videotape of all 1979 finishers in New York showed no Rosie Ruiz anywhere in sight.

Witnesses later confirmed that Rosie had jumped into the Boston Marathon about half a mile from the finish—no 26-mile ordeal for her. Just a subway ride in New York and a half-mile trot in Boston, and she had two impressive finishes. Of course, both were soon taken away from her.

If Fred Lebow was right (for Ruiz has never gone public), it was simply a stroke of luck in New York that helped make Rosie Ruiz a marathoning legend . . . of sorts.

MATURITY

Baseball

When one thinks of common sense and maturity in baseball, one thinks first of Billy Martin. Take that with a grain of salt.

Back in 1982, Martin showed up at the ballpark with a splint on one finger and bandages on two others. For some reason, he had locked himself in his Oakland office the night before and punched it out with his furniture and walls. The office couldn't fight back, but it won anyway.

The battered Martin said, "I'm getting smarter as I get older. I finally punched something that couldn't sue me."

MATURITY

Football

Businessmen are forever trying to apply business principles to professional sports. It seems so logical. After all, pro basketball is a business, isn't it? Or pro football?

Most owners learn to their sorrow that it isn't. Not exactly.

Gene Klein, who had made more than a few million dollars in used cars, real estate, and other ventures, decided to buy the San Diego Chargers of the National Football League.

From the outset, he made no bones about his intentions: He expected to apply the principles of good business management to the running of his team. He had succeeded in the corporate world. He would now succeed in the world of pro football.

It was a happy time—for a while. "There was also a time," he later wrote sadly, "when I believed in Santa Claus, the Easter Bunny, and the Tooth Fairy."

Pro football turned out to be more of a game in the business office than it was on the field. He discovered that he could lose money faster on the Chargers' franchise than he had ever dreamed of losing it on his Minnie Pearl Chicken franchise—and the fried-chicken deal had cost him 31 million.

MATURITY

Hockey

Ken Dryden, who was NHL Rookie of the Year in 1972, went on to have a fine career with the Montreal Canadiens. In retirement, he took a thoughtful look back. He said, "Nothing is as good as it used to be, and it never was. The 'golden age of sports,' the golden age of anything, is the age of everyone's childhood."

MATURITY

Tennis

Billie Jean King felt that the childish behavior of some athletes—she was probably thinking of tennis players—is understandable.

"It's really impossible for athletes to grow up," she said. "As long as you're playing, no one will let you. On the one hand, you're a child, still playing a game . . . but on the other hand, you're a superhuman hero that everybody dreams of being."

MEMORY

Baseball

What is it that's so special about baseball? Bill Veeck had a pretty good answer: "Baseball's unique possession," he said, "the real source of our strength is the fan's memory of the times his daddy took him to the game to see the great players of his youth."

MEMORY

Baseball

The catchers on the early New York Mets teams were a pleasant bunch, though not really All-Star material. Choo Choo Coleman had a smile and hello for everyone. But like Casey Stengel, the Mets manager, Choo Choo couldn't remember people's names.

Charlie Neal, one of the better Mets ballplayers, roomed with Choo Choo Coleman the first season. At spring training the next year, Neal said to a group of ballplayers, "I'm going over to say hello to Choo Choo." He predicted that Coleman wouldn't know his name.

Nobody believed him, but they listened in as Neal said, "Choo Choo, it's good to see you."

Choo Choo said "Hi."

"You know my name, Choo Choo?" Neal asked.

Choo Choo assured him that he did.

Neal said, "I'll bet you don't."

"I do," Choo Choo insisted. "You're number four."

MEMORY

Boxing

Jimmy Jacobs, a producer and collector of films on boxing, once lived in Los Angeles, around the corner from a memory school. He learned the name of the director, and one day he decided to stop in at the school.

Approaching the director, he chirped, "George, how are you?" The director, nonplussed, stared at this perfect stranger, trying to come up with a reply.

"George!" chided Jacobs. "You've forgotten!" He turned on his heel and left.

MISINFORMATION

Baseball

When Gerry Coleman was the play-by-play announcer for the San Diego Padres, it seemed to many like the second coming of Dizzy Dean. Coleman's grammar was better than Dean's, but his message was often just as garbled. Here are three Colemanisms:

"We're all sad to see Glenn Beckert leave. Before he goes, though, I hope he stops by so we can kiss him good-bye. He's that kind of guy."

"There's a fly to deep center! Winfield is going back, back! He hits his head against the wall! It's rolling toward second base!"

"He slides into second base with a stand-up double."

MISINFORMATION

Basketball

Nat Holman spent 37 years as head basketball coach at CCNY—City College of New York. Over those years, his teams won 421 games and lost 190. His 1949–50 squad was the only team ever to take both the NIT and NCAA championships in a single season.

When Holman first started coaching at City College, he was also playing for the famed Original New York Celtics basketball team. He was a star forward for the Celtics.

Slightly older than his CCNY players, Holman got into every practice with them, showing his college squad exactly what he wanted done. On one occasion, a scout for a team on the CCNY schedule slipped into the gym, saw Holman practicing, and was highly impressed.

He wired the opposing coach that City College was going to be tough. As he explained, "They have the greatest forward I've ever seen on a college team."

MISINFORMATION

Football

Vince Lombardi was always looking for ways to motivate his football players. He was not above using deception if he thought that would work.

As head coach at St. Cecilia's High School in Englewood, New Jersey, he used the postcard trick. In the week before the game with Brooklyn Tech, each St. Cecilia's player received a postcard signed by a Brooklyn Prep player. It contained insulting remarks about the St. Cecilia player and his team.

Today the St. Cecilia players might be sophisticated enough to realize that no coach would permit his players to write such postcards to their opponents. It was sure to backfire, and of course it did. St. Cecilia's team, all fired up, rolled over Brooklyn Tech that Saturday.

Later the players learned that Coach Lombardi had written the cards himself and driven to Brooklyn to mail them.

MISINFORMATION

Football

Coach Mike Ditka of the Chicago Bears sometimes had his differences with star quarterback Jim McMahon. When McMahon was sidelined for a few games with tendinitis, a sportswriter asked Ditka why he wasn't talking to his quarterback on the bench.

Ditka said the questioner was mistaken. "Remember the game against Dallas?" he asked. "I told him to shut up. That's talking to him, isn't it?"

MISINFORMATION

Hockey

When Americans hear the word "national," they assume it applies to the United States. Usually it does.

But how about the National Hockey League? As a matter of fact, "national" in this case refers to Canada. The NHL goes back to 1917, and at that time every city in the league was Canadian—Montreal, Ottawa, Quebec, and Toronto.

Not until 1924 did the National Hockey League go international. That year the Boston Bruins became the first U.S. entry.

MISINFORMATION

Hunting

Misinformation can be costly, but it isn't usually fatal. It almost was for Napier Shelton, though, a young botanist doing research on plant life in the wilds of Alaska.

Shelton remembered reading a book called *Lives of North American Game Animals*. "The full-grown grizzly bear never climbs," the writer had written. "The hunter who succeeds in getting up a tree is safe." That was what all the experts said.

Still, Shelton didn't want to meet a grizzly bear. He was hunting for plants, not animals, and he had no gun. But he figured that if he did meet one, he could always scramble up a tree.

Suddenly, without warning, as he was examining a spruce tree near the edge of a forest, he heard a loud, angry "Warf!" behind him.

Without looking back, he grabbed for the low-hanging branches of the spruce and started to climb. When he was about ten feet up, he looked down. A huge grizzly loomed below him. It was snarling viciously.

And it was climbing! It was climbing fast!

Shelton started to go higher, but it was too late. The bear's teeth closed on the calf of his left leg. He felt no pain at the time, but he had been badly bitten.

He scrambled higher. So did the bear.

The bear's teeth caught the heel of his boot. The bear tried to drag him down. Then, suddenly, the grip loosened, and Shelton heard a crash. The grizzly had fallen heavily to the ground.

At this point, the botanist was 15 feet above the ground. The tree was only about 20 feet high.

Would the bear try again? Indeed it would.

Up it came, huge and awkward, its teeth bared. It growled angrily as it climbed. Shelton, terrified, smashed his heel against the bear's head. It had no effect. The grizzly kept coming. It bit down hard, slashing Shelton's right thigh.

At the instant it bit his thigh, it lost its footing. The bear crashed to the ground again.

For a while the grizzly prowled beneath the tree. But at last it moved off and disappeared in the forest.

Shelton's car was parked about 300 feet from the tree. After a long, fearful wait, the botanist worked his way down the tree. He couldn't run on his mangled legs, but he finally managed to get to his car. He slammed the door, breathing, "Thank God."

He then drove to safety, swearing never again to believe the conventional wisdom.

Full-grown grizzly bears *can* climb trees.

MISTAKE

Baseball

Casey Stengel, after he was fired from the New York Yankees in 1960 for being too old: "I'll never make the mistake of being 70 again."

MISTAKE

Baseball

Anybody can make a mistake, but Hack Wilson made one at Baker Bowl in Philadelphia that became a legend.

Walter Beck was pitching for the Dodgers. He was the notorious "Boom-Boom" Beck, so named because the ball went "boom" off the bats of opposing hitters—and then "boom" again as it ricocheted off the outfield wall. On this particular day against the Phillies, he was pitching in his boom-boom mode, and manager Casey Stengel went out to relieve him.

Beck asked Casey for one more chance. Casey gave it to him. But the next Phillie hitter showed Beck no mercy and lined a "Boom-Boom" offering over the fence.

This time Stengel went out to the mound and asked for the ball. Beck, furious at his failure, whirled and fired it nearly out of the park. The ball hit the tin facing of the right-field wall and caromed down to the playing field.

Hack Wilson, the Dodger right-fielder, had been paying very little attention to the game. Head down, he may have been meditating on the summer game. He may have been recovering from a hangover.

Whatever he was doing, he was alert enough to hear the ball rattle against the tin. And he was fast enough to grab the ball on the bounce and rifle it back to the infield. In fact, he threw a strike to second base. If there had been a runner trying for a double, Hack would have had a good shot at gunning him down. But, of course, there wasn't.

Tony Cuccinello, the Dodger second baseman, called it "a hell of a play," which, when you come right down to it, it was.

MISTAKE

Baseball

Babe Herman is one of baseball's legendary characters. He played 13 years in the majors, and he left the game with a lifetime batting average of .324. One year, 1930, he hit .393 for the Brooklyn Dodgers and cracked 35 home runs.

But Herman just couldn't shake the reputation of being a catastrophe in the outfield. Despite the rap, he was pretty good at catching flies and had a strong throwing arm, although there was some doubt about where the ball would end up. A wag said, "Baseball wouldn't be any fun if they had only one base and he couldn't throw to the wrong one."

MISTAKE

Baseball

According to the columnist who called himself F.P.A., the saddest of possible words were "Tinker to Evers to Chance." But a good runner-up for that honor appeared in a Midwestern newspaper.

The reporter noted that a local baseball game in a cow pasture was temporarily suspended when a galloping baserunner slid into what he thought was third base.

MISTAKE

Basketball

John Wooden, the famous basketball coach at UCLA, filled his speech with little nuggets of wisdom. One writer called him a reincarnated Ben Franklin.

About mistakes on the basketball court, Wooden said, "If you're not making mistakes, then you're not doing anything. I'm positive that a doer makes mistakes."

MISTAKE

Boxing

Jack Roper's name isn't much remembered anymore. But on the night of April 17, 1939, Roper had a chance to become boxing's heavyweight champion of the world.

Well, maybe not, considering that his opponent was Joe Louis, the Brown Bomber. Louis, to no one's surprise, bombed Roper out in one round.

The challenger, thus dispatched, might be forgotten entirely, but after recovering from the knockout he delivered a line that is quoted to this day:

"I zigged when I should have zagged."

MISTAKE

Fishing

It can be painful to make a mistake. Sometimes it can be even more painful to learn about a mistake you didn't know you'd made.

Red Smith, the famous sportswriter, tells a story about a friend of his who had a phenomenal day of fishing on Lake Stocco, Ontario. He landed a 24-pound muskie within minutes. He brought in a number of walleyes averaging six pounds each. But his best catch of all was a five-and-a-half-pound smallmouth bass.

That's far from a record, but it's a good-sized fish. It was also a good eating fish. Nick—that was the friend's name—filleted it, cooked it, and ate it.

The next day Nick went into a nearby village to buy supplies. He got to talking with the owner of the general store, and he told him about the smallmouth bass he'd caught and how delicious it was.

The man stared at Nick. "Five and a half pounds—and you ate it?"

Nick probably looked puzzled. As it happened, there was a fishing contest going on, and so far nobody was doing especially well with smallmouth bass.

The owner seemed as sympathetic as he was surprised. "You've just eaten two thousand dollars worth of prizes," he said.

And he was right. When the contest closed, the winner claimed his bundle of prizes with a smallmouth bass that weighed just four and a quarter pounds.

Nick could never get over that savory smallmouth bass. "Most expensive meal I ever had," he said.

MISTAKE

Football

Sometimes a small oversight can lead to trouble. Consider the bed check. From time immemorial, athletes have tried to figure out ways to beat the bed check—to make it appear they're sound asleep when, in fact, they're out on the town.

One football player thought he had the perfect answer. It was an easy answer. All he had to do was slip the old standup lamp in his motel room under the covers. The bulge of the base could pass for feet, and the shade, up near the pillow, would stand in for his head. At a quick glance, even he was fooled.

Thus covered, he took off for the pleasures of the night.

Some time later, an assistant coach came by, checking each room. He opened the door to our hero's room. By now it was dark, so he flipped the light switch.

You guessed it. The phony head under the blanket lit up with a hundred watts of incriminating evidence. Our hero had forgotten to unplug the lamp.

MISTAKE

Football

Everyone has missed an important appointment now and then. But few have missed one as publicly as Pittsburgh Steelers' coach Johnny Blood.

Sportswriters noticed Blood watching a Sunday game at Wrigley Field between the Chicago Bears and Green Bay Packers. They approached him and asked him why he wasn't with the Steelers.

Blood explained that the Steelers weren't playing that week.

He then settled back comfortably, just as the public address announcer said, "Here's a final score—Philadelphia 14, Pittsburgh 7."

MISTAKE

Football

University of Delaware football coach and athletic director Dave Nelson served as a color man on ABC Sports telecasts for four years in the early 1970s. He tells this story.

"I'm glad nobody makes much mention of my four years as an ABC color man, analyst, expert commentator, or whatever they call them. My career ended at a ho-hum thriller called the Grantland Rice Bowl around 1972.

"The score at halftime left little doubt that Louisiana Tech would win easily over Tennessee Tech. Then, on the first play of the second half, Louisiana Tech scored again to make the score 44 to 0.

"Geoff Mason, the director in the ABC truck, said, 'Shorty, say something smart or funny, because we're losing our audience.' "

So Nelson said, "We wish to say goodbye to our viewers who are leaving to watch the Dallas-Washington game. . . ."

Mason agreed it was funny, but said it wasn't too smart.

"Needless to say," Nelson added, "ABC never picked up my option."

MISTAKE

Golf

Golfer Lee Trevino was commenting on Ben Crenshaw's driving and putting. He admitted that Ben was a great putter, but he added that Ben had trouble keeping his ball on the fairway.

"I've told him he might have a tan like mine," Trevino said, "if he didn't spend so much time in the trees "

MISTAKE

Hockey

Every professional sport has its familiar tales of dumb trades. In hockey one of the dumbest trades of all-time was made by Jack Adams of the Detroit Red Wings, usually a shrewd bargainer.

A Canadian sportswriter, Trent Frayne, had discovered by accident that Jack Adams had asked Red Kelly, the Red Wings' all-star defenseman, to play the last few games of the previous season with a broken ankle. Kelly had done so. The club kept it quiet. Kelly, taped from his ankle to his knee, played poorly, was booed by the fans, and, incredibly, was fined $100 for lack of effort.

Frayne, the sportswriter, wrote up this story, sent it off to a magazine, and forgot about it.

When the article appeared, Jack Adams blew his cork. He threatened to sue Frayne. He threatened to trade Kelly. In fact, he did more than threaten to trade Kelly. He did trade Kelly—hastily.

Act in haste, repent at leisure.

In the trade, the Wings got a journeyman defenseman from Toronto named Marc Reaume in exchange for their all-star Red Kelly.

Marc Reaume was no Red Kelly. In two and a half seasons, Reaume recorded two goals and 13 assists. For the Red Wings, he played 47 games, with no goals and two assists. Off he went to Hershey, a minor-league team, and never came back.

Red Kelly, on the other hand, spent the next seven and a half years with the Toronto Maple Leafs. Switching from defense to center, he contributed 119 goals and 232 assists. Kelly helped lead the Leafs to four Stanley Cup titles.

You'd think Jack Adams might have had second thoughts about this terrible trade. But Jack, or Jolly Jawn as he was called, never had second thoughts about anything. He didn't repent in leisure, or at all. He defended the trade. Reaume was seven years younger than Kelly, he pointed out.

MISTAKE

Horse Racing

A horseplayer looks for any advantage he can find. So when Briscoe saw a priest bless a particular horse, he paid attention. When he saw that horse breeze across the finish line in first place, he thought he'd found an angle

Next race, he kept an eye on the priest. The priest blessed Oatmuncher's Uncle. The sorry-looking nag was 30 to 1, but Briscoe figured, why not? He put down his money—and Oatmuncher's Uncle won by half a length.

He tried again. The priest blessed Gray Monday, another long shot, and that horse, too, romped home in front.

This went on all afternoon. Briscoe's winnings grew beyond his wildest dreams. He told himself he should quit. But how could he? The priest's picks were running first every time.

On the final race of the day, Briscoe put his whole stack on Dusteater, a 25 to 1 shot that the priest had visited. The horse broke in front, but soon began to droop like a wilted lily. Dusteater finished dead last.

Briscoe ran up to the priest. He was furious. "What happened in the last race?" he shouted. "That horse you blessed was worthless."

The priest sighed. "That's the trouble with you Protestants," he said. "You can't tell the difference between blessings and last rites."

MISTAKE

Horse Racing

Gravel-voiced Clem McCarthy was the ultimate pro when it came to broadcasting horse races. On May 10, 1947, he was at the microphone on network radio to cover the Preakness, the second leg of thoroughbred racing's Triple Crown.

There were four horses to watch. Two of them were Jet Pilot and Phalanx, which had finished first and second in the Kentucky Derby. The other two were Faultless and On Trust, which had finished third and fourth. You could forget about the other horses in the race: they went off at odds ranging from 24 to 1 up to 90 to 1. It seemed certain to be a four-horse affair.

And it was. As the horses approached the three-quarter pole, On Trust was in the lead, with Jet Pilot second. Faultless had moved into third on the rail, while Phalanx was moving up fast on the outside.

That was the situation when McCarthy said, "And the crowd blocks me for a moment." It was true. His vision shouldn't have been obstructed, but it was. After the starting gate was pulled off to the inside of the track, hundreds of people had clambered onto it for a better view. So, for about 70 yards, the horses disappeared from Clem McCarthy's line of vision.

What happened during those few critical seconds almost defies belief. Jet Pilot slanted toward the outside and began to fade. Faultless, moving up, plugged the spot Jet Pilot had just vacated. The silks of the two horses were of a similar color.

As soon as McCarthy picked up the horses again, he still had On Trust in the lead. And he still had—or thought he had—Jet Pilot in the same spot as when the fans blocked his view. But, of course, he didn't. He had Faultless there, coming up hard, challenging for the lead. It was now a two-horse race between On Trust and Faultless. In the foreground, clearly visible to McCarthy, was On Trust. Behind the leader on the rail was . . . was. . . .

Clem's voice growled it out: "Jet Pilot has got him . . . Jet Pilot by a neck . . . Jet Pilot by half a length . . . Jet Pilot by a length . . . Jet Pilot the winner!"

There was a three-second pause before Clem McCarthy spoke again. He said: "What am I talking about? . . . Ladies and gentlemen, I've made a terrific mistake . . . I've mixed my horses, and I've given you the winner as Jet Pilot . . . and it is Faultless . . . the winner of the race is Faultless."

And so it was. McCarthy had lost sight of the field for 70 yards. He called what he thought he saw. But something had changed quickly behind that wall of people, something important. And as sharp and as skillful as Clem McCarthy was, he missed it.

MISUNDERSTANDING

Auto Racing

Over the years, the Indianapolis Speedway became almost the private fiefdom of Tony Hulman, who had purchased the track from Eddie Rickenbacker. Even so, Hulman's name was much better known than his face.

One race day, many years ago, he and Wilbur Shaw, the Speedway's president and general manager, were checking their ticket-taking system. Shaw had won the Indy three times in the past and was a well-known figure at the Speedway.

The two men didn't see anyone taking tickets at first. They climbed the stairs in the grandstand and finally came across a lone ticket taker, who asked them for their tickets.

Wilbur Shaw smiled. He told the man that his companion was Tony Hulman, the owner of the track. The ticket taker looked unconvinced.

He said, "I recognize you, Mr. Shaw, from your racing days. But don't expect me to believe the man with you is Mr. Hulman. I've already had 14 people today tell me they're Tony Hulman."

MISUNDERSTANDING

Auto Racing

At one time, not so many years ago, two of the top racing drivers in the world were Graham Hill of Great Britain and Phil Hill of the United States. Sports reporters of the time were assumed to know such elementary facts, but one reporter from a Scottish newspaper obviously didn't.

Jim Clark, a great racing driver of that time, got a phone call from the Scottish journalist. The Scot asked a number of questions, which Clark answered as best he could.

Near the end of the interview, the Scot said, "And tell me, Mr. Clark, what is your greatest opposition?"

Clark, a bit surprised, assumed that he meant for the upcoming South African race, and he answered, "Oh, Hill."

After a moment of dead air, the Scot asked, "What Hill?"

Well, Clark figured, maybe a Graham-or-Phil-Hill question was bothering the reporter, so he replied, "Graham Hill."

This time the pause was longer and the puzzlement more pronounced. The Scot ventured a timid question. "Is that a particularly difficult one?"

MISUNDERSTANDING

Baseball

When Yogi Berra returned to hometown St. Louis after a great career in the majors, he was interviewed by Jack Buck, a local broadcaster.

At the end of the show, he received a check for his appearance. The check said, "Pay to Bearer."

Yogi looked hurt. "Jack," he said sadly, "you know me all these years, and you still can't spell my name right?"

MISUNDERSTANDING

Baseball

The manager was a little surprised when a horse trotted up to him in the dugout and asked for a tryout. He'd never seen a horse that was worth a damn in the outfield, but he figured what the hell.

"Okay, let's see if you can hit," the manager says, trotting out to the mound.

The horse grabs a bat between his teeth, stands in, and pummels the first three pitches into the stands. All of a sudden, the nag looks like Lou Gehrig in a horse costume.

Impressed, the manager says, "Hey, not bad. Can you field?"

The horse whinnies, canters off to the outfield, and begins snaring long fly balls with his teeth. Now he looks like a four-legged Willie Mays.

The manager is paying very close attention at this point. After all, his regular left fielder is batting .190 and misjudging every tenth fly.

"You know," the manager says thoughtfully. "You're pretty good. Best horse I've ever seen when it comes to hitting and fielding. But there's one other thing, and it's important. Can you run?"

The horse gives the manager a look of patient disbelief. "Run? If I could run," he says, "do you think I'd be looking for a job in baseball? I'd be up at Saratoga."

MISUNDERSTANDING

Baseball

A co-ed was trying out to be a bat girl for the University of Washington baseball team.

"How much do you know about baseball?" the interviewer asked her. "Have you ever seen a major league game?"

She thought about it. "I know baseball pretty well," she said. "But major league baseball—no. I've just seen the Seattle Mariners play a few times."

MISUNDERSTANDING

Baseball

When Mickey Mantle, the New York Yankee star, was new to the big city, he was shy and uncertain at interviews.

One day a reporter complimented him on a television appearance. He asked Mantle whether he had used a script or ad-libbed.

"Gee," Mantle replied, "I don't know."

MISUNDERSTANDING

Baseball

Most of Joey Bishop's sports stories have to do with golf. This one has to do with baseball, but you may have to think about the punch line for a while. The comedian himself claimed that no one except a resident of Chicago ever understood it—and that plenty of Chicagoans missed the point, too.

It concerns a German immigrant getting off the train in Chicago. He doesn't speak English, and his conversation with a porter is getting nowhere. Finally, the German says, "Was sags du?" [vas sogs doo]

The porter, thinking that at last they're communicating on a primitive level, says, "I heard they lost five to three."

MISUNDERSTANDING

Baseball

Dizzy Dean, the St. Louis Cardinals' eccentric pitcher, was being interviewed by a British reporter. The reporter asked him, "Mr. Dean, don't you know the king's English?"

Diz thought for a moment. "Sure I do," he said. "And so's the queen."

MISUNDERSTANDING

Basketball

One summer the St. Louis University basketball team was touring Europe. Most of the players had never been out of the Midwest, let alone out of the country.

On the way to practice one day, the team bus was stopped by a border-patrol officer. As the policeman looked around the bus, he casually asked, "Are you all Americans?"

To this, a point guard named Darryl "Pee Wee" Lenard popped up and responded, "No, but our center was All-Conference last season."

MISUNDERSTANDING

Basketball

Brad had once played guard for his college basketball team, and he remained a dedicated fan. When he took his new girlfriend out on a date, they headed straight for the bleachers to watch a basketball game.

It was near the end of the season, and Brad studied the team closely. He was sorry to see them losing the game, but encouraged to see the brilliant play of a sophomore center named Sam Horton.

"You know," the fan said thoughtfully to his girlfriend, "I think Sam Horton's going to be our best man next year."

The girl moved closer to him and squeezed his arm. "Darling," she said, "this is so sudden."

MISUNDERSTANDING

Curling

The sport of curling is better known in the United States than it used to be. Curling originated in Scotland, and because it's played on ice, it caught on in Canada many years ago.

This story concerns a Minneapolis lawyer who was attending a dinner dance. He'd been on the ice all day and, having passed the age of 30, was feeling the effects of all those hours of pushing the stone toward the tee.

Another man at the table noticed that the lawyer hadn't been dancing. He asked about it.

"I don't think I'm up to it," the lawyer said. "I'm a little stiff from curling."

"Hey," the other man said, "so what? I'm just a little guy myself." He held out his hand in a friendly manner. "Bill Engels from International Falls."

MISUNDERSTANDING

Football

A Chicago Bears fan arrived home after the start of the big game with the Detroit Lions. The television set was tuned to the game, and his wife was watching it.

"What's the score?" he asked.
"Ten to seven," she replied.
"Who's winning?"
She hesitated. "Ten, I think."

MISUNDERSTANDING

Football

The great football player Red Grange recalls the time that Senator McKinley of Illinois introduced him to President Calvin Coolidge.

The senator said, "Mr. President, I'd like you to meet Red Grange, who plays with the Bears."

Coolidge shook his hand and said, "Nice to meet you, young man. I've always liked animal acts."

MISUNDERSTANDING

Football

As head coach of the Pittsburgh Steelers, Buddy Parker was in complete charge of wheeling and dealing. The trouble was that he liked to make his moves the night after a loss and sometimes after one drink too many.

One time Parker waived linebacker Dick Hayes and another player to the Chicago Bears. The Bears waived two players to the Steelers, with the understanding that after the Bears and Steelers played, all four players would be waived back to their original teams.

However, in the Bears-Steelers game, Dick Hayes made a tackle that won the game for the Bears.

Parker was furious. He wanted no part of this traitorous linebacker. So when Hayes climbed on board the Steelers' plane at the Houston airport, Parker shouted, "What are you doing here?"

Hayes looked bewildered. "They said I was a Steeler."

"No," shouted Parker, "you're not!"

But when Hayes tried to board the Chicago Bears' plane, he got no better a reception. "You're not a Bear anymore," they told him. "Get back on that other plane"

What was he to do? He sneaked back on the Steelers' plane, where some friends hid him in the restroom. After takeoff, he rejoined his team.

MISUNDERSTANDING

Football

Philby had put in a long Sunday watching pro football on television. When he went to bed, visions of sacks and spikes and beer commercials danced in his head.

He slept so soundly that he failed to hear the alarm go off at 6:30. His wife shook him awake 20 minutes later.

"Honey," she said. "It's ten to seven."

He sat up and shook his head groggily. "Whose favor?" he asked.

MISUNDERSTANDING

Football

The football coach paced the sidelines angrily. His players weren't showing the drive he'd tried so hard to instill in them. They were going through the motions. He decided to put in a big, rugged nose tackle who was known for having a mean streak.

"Okay, Murdock," he snapped. "I want you to get in there and get ferocious."

"You got it, coach!" boomed Murdock, leaping off the bench. "What's his number?"

MISUNDERSTANDING

Hockey

The sixth grade teacher was surprised when her slowest student raised his hand. Her question had been, "Can anyone tell me where Winnipeg is?"

A tough question, she thought, but the little guy was smiling. He looked confident

"Yes, Jason, where is Winnipeg?"

"Second place in the Smythe Division," he said. "Calgary's in first."

MISUNDERSTANDING

Hockey

Perhaps the funniest man in ice hockey—an unfunny game for the most part—was Jean Baptiste Pusie. He wasn't a great player, but he kept the guys laughing.

While playing for London, Ontario, Pusie pulled off a stunt he had been practicing. In a game against Buffalo, he checked an opponent lightly, then fell back as if he had been poleaxed. The idea was to draw a penalty call.

Pusie's execution was perfect, or so he thought. He lay on the ice, apparently hurt by the bad guy he had checked. The referee ignored Pusie's act completely. No penalty.

He was furious. He rose in righteous anger. "You knock Pusie down," he screamed at the Buffalo player, who had done nothing at all. Pusie took a swing. The bewildered guy from Buffalo swung back. They went at it.

Recognizing injustice when they saw it, the crowd swarmed onto the ice, more than 400 strong. Fists were flying everywhere. In hockey that's just part of the fun, of course, but it can get out of hand. And it did. The police had to be called in to quell the riot.

MISUNDERSTANDING

Horse Racing

He went to a dealer to buy a racehorse.

"The horse I'm looking for has to be fast," he said. "I mean fast. Do you have a horse like that?"

The dealer pointed to a fine-looking animal and said, "That horse is fast—and its endurance is unbelievable. If you start from St. Louis at midnight, he'll have you in Rolla at three in the morning."

The buyer had to think about it for a while. When he finally turned it down, he said, "I just can't think of any reason why I'd want to be in Rolla at three in the morning "

MISUNDERSTANDING

Hunting

The story goes that Alfred, Lord Tennyson had invited a Russian nobleman to spend some time at his home on the Isle of Wight. One morning the nobleman set off on a hunting trip. When he returned, Tennyson asked him if he had had any luck.

"I shot two peasants," the nobleman replied.

"Ah, you mean two 'pheasants,' " Tennyson said gently. "The pronunciation is 'pheasants.' "

"No," insisted the Russian. "Two peasants. They were insolent, so I shot them."

MOTIVATION

Auto Racing

Bobby Unser took the checkered flag in first place at Indianapolis in 1975. Although he won fewer races over the years than his brother Al, he was no less competitive. He said: "Desire! That's the one secret of every man's career. Not education. Not being born with hidden talents. Desire."

MOTIVATION

Baseball

A manager has to be a motivator, and L.A.'s skipper Tommy Lasorda was one of the best in baseball. He had a gift for it, a gift that was evident from the outset. For three years Lasorda managed L.A. rookie farm teams in the Pioneer League. His teams won the pennant every year.

Lasorda, above all else, instilled confidence in players who lacked it. The question is, how? There's no precise answer, because he did it on a player-by-player basis. He was a born psychologist. He had no magic formula, but he got magical results.

Take the case of Freddie Katawich. A tall, left-handed pitcher from Pennsylvania, Katawich was showing very little promise as a rookie at Ogden in the Pioneer League. Lasorda was told to release him.

Releasing rookies was a painful but common experience for Tommy. It was part of his job. However, in the case of Freddie Katawich, he thought the decision was premature. He felt that Freddie could pitch better than he had shown.

Up in the big leagues, the Los Angeles Dodgers' ace reliever that year was Phil Regan, nicknamed The Vulture. The idea behind the nickname was that Regan swooped down and snatched up saves in relief.

Lasorda told Katawich that henceforth he, Freddie Katawich, would be known as The Vulture of the Ogden Dodgers. And Tommy pushed it. He would tell his infielders that The Vulture, sniffing a save, was now coming in. Local sportswriters picked it up, and before long Katawich was The Vulture of northern Utah.

He improved. He started to get those saves. He began to refer to himself as The Vulture. His confidence rose, and he became what he hadn't been before—an effective relief pitcher. Lasorda advised the front office not to release him. The kid was on his way.

At the end of the season, Freddie Katawich was drafted by Indianapolis, a Triple-A farm club of the Cincinnati Reds, for something in the neighborhood of $12,000. A year later he was drafted from Indianapolis by the San Diego Padres for more than ten times that amount—$125,000.

There's no perfect ending to the story. Katawich never pitched in the majors. Motivation carried him only so far. But he made spectacular progress for a kid who was supposed to have been dropped from the very lowest level of professional baseball.

MOTIVATION

Baseball

Finley Peter Dunne was one of America's great humorists. As the fictional Mr. Dooley, an Irish saloon-keeper, he commented on all aspects of American life. Dooley's rich brogue is a bit hard to understand—and even harder to pronounce—but it carries a lot of worldly wisdom, as you'll see from this example·

"In me younger days, 'twas not considhered rayspictable f'r to be an athlete. An athlete was always a man that was not sthrong enough f'r wurruk. Fractions dhruv him fr'm school, an' th' vagrancy laws dhruv him to base-ball."

MOTIVATION
Basketball

Getting people to give you their best efforts—it isn't easy. Whole books have been written on motivation. Nearly every book on business management has at least one chapter on the subject. In sports, motivation is vital.

Red Auerbach of the Boston Celtics has a chapter about motivation in his book *On and Off the Court*. He makes the point that a coach has to motivate players for the *easy* games. The big games are self-motivating; they take care of themselves. The sure things are the ones that sometimes even the great teams lose.

Why is it that in UCLA's or Kentucky's 21 and 3 or 23 and 2 seasons, one of the losses is to an inferior team? Overconfidence. Complacency. The team is sure it won't be beat—and then it's beaten.

Auerbach's solution is to come up with a good reason why the team *must* win *this* game now. He says, "I'll bet I came up with 2,000 reasons why we *had* to win."

It worked for him. He was one of the greatest motivators who ever coached: eight NBA championships in a row; and 11 out of 13 at one stretch. Auerbach's Celtics played every game to win. And they won—even the easy ones. Especially the easy ones.

MOTIVATION
Basketball

Joe Turner played center for the University of Arizona's basketball team from 1984 through 1988. He was the sixth man on the Wildcats' 1988 team, which posted a 35 and 3 record and reached the Final Four.

During the team's tour of Europe in 1985, the Wildcats arrived at the town of Dieppe, France, to play in a tournament. When assistant coach Scott Thompson casually asked who was favored before the tournament began, a French host replied, "Oh, I would say the Soviet Union National Team, with Arvidas Sabonis."

The Wildcats reached the tournament's semifinals, where the Soviets defeated them, 70 to 50. However, Joe Turner had the best game of his career, with 20 points and 10 rebounds against the best Soviet player, Sabonis.

From Dieppe, Arizona went to the Netherlands, where it played a series of four games against the Dutch National Team. Turner hardly figured at all in the games. Playing at least 12 minutes in each game, he scored either one point or no points each time.

Finally, Wildcat coach Lute Olson approached Turner, "Joe," he said, "you ripped apart the best team in the world, and then didn't do anything against the Netherlands. What gives?"

"Coach," Joe replied, "I just can't get fired up for the Dutchess."

MOTIVATION

Football

"Win one for the Gipper" has become a cliché—a common expression even among people who never saw the Pat O'Brien movie version of Knute Rockne's life. There are probably many people today who don't know who the Gipper was. Sportswriters have called the Gipper tale the most mangled of all the Rockne stories. And it is.

First, about the Gipper. He was George Gipp. From 1916 to 1919, he starred for Knute Rockne's Notre Dame football teams. At the end of his senior year, he left the team banquet, feeling ill. His illness developed into pneumonia, and within a month of his last game he was dead. Gipp had just been named to the first-string All-America team, the first Notre Dame player to make it.

Now ... jump forward to the 1928 season—eight years after Gipp's death. Notre Dame, plagued by bad luck and injuries, has lost four games under coach Rockne. That was almost unheard of for a Rockne team. When Notre Dame went to Yankee Stadium to play Army, the Fighting Irish were given little chance of winning

Knute Rockne, as you know, was famous for his motivational talks In the locker room before the Army game, he gave the talk of his life. He paid homage to George Gipp. He told of Gipp's great ability and competitiveness. He described his tragic death.

He said that George Gipp had made two requests on his deathbed. One was that he become a Catholic. The other was that someday, when defeat for the Irish seemed certain, he hoped coach Rockne would ask the team to win one for him. Rockne spoke of the incident in a soft, choked voice.

His final words were, "This is that game."

The Fighting Irish won the game, 12 to 6.

MOTIVATION

Football

One of Vince Lombardi's motivational devices was persistent and vehement criticism. It usually worked. Most players took it in stride and vowed to try harder. But occasionally there would be a flareup. One of the players who objected to Lombardi's browbeating was fullback Mel Triplett.

Although Triplett was a bonafide star, Vince thought he lacked motivation. At a Tuesday film session, the head coach ran the same film sequence over and over. It showed Triplett missing a key block.

Each time he ran it, Lombardi growled, "Look at yourself, Triplett! Triplett! Hear me? Triplett! Triplett!" On and on.

Finally, Triplett snapped, "Get off my back or get yourself another fullback!"

The room went quiet, including Lombardi. Without a word he pushed the forward button the projector and went on with the film.

After the session, as the players were leaving, Vince confided to one of his players, "I meant to make him mad, but I didn't mean to make him *that* mad."

MOTIVATION

Football

When it comes to motivation, praise has its uses, but it also has its drawbacks. As coach Wallace Wade said, "Nobody ever got backslapped into winning anything."

MOTIVATION

Skiing

Skiing is the national sport of Austria. Back in the 1930s, Christian Pravda, who would become an Olympic medalist, showed great promise as a young Austrian skier. The government sent him to an Alpine camp for special training.

The training methods at camp were thorough, efficient, and not exactly subtle. Each trainer carried an air rifle to shoot pellets into the rear end of slackers. The rifle was no toy. It had power enough to deliver pellets that required surgery for extraction.

Pravda had no fond memories of this severe training—but it did get results.

MYSTERY

Horse Racing

Great Britain's Grand National at Aintree is the premier steeplechase in the world. The race has been run ever since 1837, often with members of the British royal family in the stands.

Without a doubt, the most amazing finish in the long history of the Grand National occurred in 1956. What made it amazing was the odd behavior of a horse named Devon Loch, owned by Queen Mary, the queen mother. She was on hand for the finish, along with her two daughters, Queen Elizabeth II and Princess Margaret.

Devon Loch was being ridden that day by Dick Francis, now a best-selling mystery author, and then one of England's finest steeplechase riders. Devon Loch, a superb horse with a fine record, was the popular favorite, partly because a horse owned by the royal family had not won the Grand National since 1900.

Against this spectacular backdrop came a race in which it looked as if the crowd's wishes would come true. Devon Loch, after four miles and 30 fences, thundered down the homestretch leading by six lengths. He had already cleared the last fence and was on his way to victory.

And then it happened. No one could explain it then; no one can explain it now.

A mere hundred feet from the finish line, with the crowd roaring its approval, Devon Loch suddenly broke stride and appeared to be trying to jump a phantom fence. Up in the air he went. Then, as if realizing his mistake, he seemed to put on the brakes. He thudded down on his belly, his forelegs stuck out in front and his hind legs trailing behind.

Dick Francis, riding perfectly, stayed on for the unexpected takeoff and the rough landing. He had lost his whip and had to grab Devon Loch around the neck. But he was still aboard, still ready to go—if Devon Loch was.

Of course, by this time the other horses were coming abreast. Devon Loch struggled up, forelegs first. He stood there, unmoving. His right hind leg appeared to be paralyzed. At that point, Francis knew the race was lost. He dismounted, fearing that the royal horse had broken a leg.

When Devon Loch was examined an hour later, he was found to be uninjured.

From that day to this, no one has been able to explain the "ghost jump." Dick Francis thought the horse was frightened into a reflex action by the tremendous roar of the crowd. Maybe so. He should know as well as anyone, but no one knows for sure.

There are clear frame-by-frame photos of Devon Loch's strange leap, but they solve nothing. The mystery remains.

MYSTERY

Horse Racing

There are plenty of arguments in sports, but very few unsolved mysteries. One intriguing mystery, unsolved and apparently insoluble, is the death of the magnificent racehorse Swale.

This dark bay colt, winner of the 1984 Kentucky Derby and Belmont Stakes, a thoroughbred with a bright future, had never been sick, never taken so much as an aspirin. The three-year-old from Claiborne Farms had already won more than a million and a half dollars.

Then one morning, just nine days after winning the Belmont Stakes, Swale collapsed. The colt had just come back from a light gallop, and his exercise rider had noticed nothing unusual. As he was being led into a yard beside the barn for his warm-water washing, Swale fell over.

When trainer Woody Stephens reached him, Swale was hunched down on the ground. He struggled to get up, but floundered and dropped to his side. His breath came in gasps, and his eyes were rolling.

Bob Fritz, Swale's regular veterinarian, arrived within four minutes. But the great racehorse was already dead.

There were three possible causes of death, according to Dr. Fritz—heart failure, a stroke, or a toxic substance. The autopsy ruled out all three. As far as could be determined, Swale was in perfect health.

The toxic-substance theory gained support when heart or circulatory reasons were ruled out. But what could the motive have been? A grudge? No one was aware of any grudge. Insurance? Swale was insured for 15 million dollars, true, but the horse would have been worth three to six times that amount if alive and syndicated as a stallion. Besides, no evidence of a toxic substance was found.

Few horses are ever autopsied, so it's possible that the vets missed something. If so, maybe the answer will be revealed in the future. Swale's brain was ordered frozen, so that when veterinary knowledge expands, there will be evidence to examine in trying to figure out what struck down this great thoroughbred at the age of three.

MYSTERY

Hunting

Four dedicated wild turkey hunters from different parts of the country decided to form the Piney Ridge Hunt Club. They leased 5,000 acres of prime turkey country in the foothills of Virginia's Blue Ridge Mountains and converted an old farmhouse into a lodge. They hired a mountain guide, Lem Shifflet, to act as the caretaker for the club.

As Havilah Babcock tells the story, these four members seldom invited outsiders to hunt with them. Since one small mistake in a turkey shoot could ruin a day's hunting, they saw no reason to take the chance.

However, a member one day happened to come across a youngster from Seattle, Washington—Buck McCord, by name—who had won the trapshooting championship of his state at age 19. Buck was exceptional. He looked as if he might be a natural-born turkey hunter, and the members agreed to invite him for the second week of their hunt.

Young McCord lived up to his billing. He was personable and skillful. Near the middle of the week, he brought down a gigantic turkey. Lem Shifflet, mouth agape, said it was the finest bird he had ever seen—said it was, in fact, old Three Toes, a sagacious wild gobbler that local hunters had been after for years.

They measured the turkey's beard. An eight-inch beard is impressive; a ten-inch beard is a prized trophy. Old Three Toe's beard came in at 13 inches. None of the four Piney Ridge members had ever brought back a trophy to match Buck McCord's.

At this point, Havilah Babcock is careful to point out that turkey hunters are not people consumed with envy at another's success. They are not likely to plot ways to make off with a friend's prize trophy. Indeed, that day and night they praised Buck's feat and toasted it loudly with peach brandy.

During the celebration, Buck removed the turkey's beard and placed it on the mantel.

Next morning it was gone. Buck figured at first he was the victim of a practical joke. The four members, for their part, assumed that Buck had already packed the trophy with his gear and was kidding them. No one believed that the beard had truly and mysteriously vanished.

But it had. When Buck left Piney Ridge, he tried hard to hide his distress, but each member could see it clearly. And the members felt at least as bad as he did. They had searched high and low, but in vain, for the beard. The four members, who had been close friends for years, began to view one another with a trace of sad suspicion.

Upon returning home, each man decided on roughly the same plan to replace Buck's missing turkey beard. Each one scoured the country for the largest beard obtainable—price, no object—and mailed the beard he purchased to Buck, along with a lame explanation of how he had found it unexpectedly in his belongings.

Four long turkey beards reached Buck within a few days of each other. Buck, furious, never acknowledged their receipt or responded to the accompanying letters or separate telegrams. He could hardly imagine his former hunting companions carrying out such a monstrous joke.

The event threw a pall over the Piney Ridge Hunt Club. The members skipped their next year's hunting entirely and thereafter gave up the lease on the 5,000 acres. They drifted apart.

A more puzzling mystery could hardly be invented. Where had the beard gone? It was rather like an English manor-house mystery with four, or perhaps five, suspects. And no solution.

Buck McCord became a fighter pilot for a Canadian unit in the First World War. He was a superb pilot. He became officially an ace just a week before he was killed in action.

In 1923, five years after the war had ended, one of the four members of the former Piney Ridge Hunt Club received a letter and a package from Lem

Shifflet. The owners of the old farmhouse-lodge were having it rebuilt. Construction workers had found an abandoned squirrel's nest in a corner of the attic. In the nest was a 13-inch turkey's beard, intact and undamaged. Shifflet's package yielded the beard, and Shifflet supposed the member would give it to "that fine young fellow" to whom it belonged.

A week later the four members of the Piney Ridge Hunt Club assembled at the cemetery where Buck McCord was buried. They talked nostalgically about their young hunting guest, about old times in the Blue Ridge, and about what to do with the turkey's beard that had finally turned up.

They decided to put it in an airtight glass oval at the base of Buck McCord's tombstone. It was too little and too late, but it was the best they could do. And that is where it is today.

MYSTERY

Wrestling

Professional wrestling is often dismissed as a joke. But what's wrong with a joke?

Besides, wrestling is a good subject for jokes. Joey Adams, the comedian, offered this one-liner: "The wrestler couldn't understand why he lost the bout—he won the rehearsal."

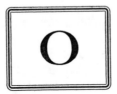

OBJECTIVE

Auto Racing

If you're a Grand Prix auto racer, it's axiomatic that you want to win the World Championship. It goes with the territory.

But at least one of the Grand Prix winners captured the championship by a single point—over Stirling Moss who wanted it desperately—and regarded the whole thing as a lark.

The driver was England's Mike Hawthorn. Mike's overriding goal in life was enjoyment. He was colorful and fun-loving, a handsome blond-haired playboy with remarkable driving skill, but with a greater interest in pranks than in serious racing.

His partner in practical jokes was Peter Collins, also a top driver. There is little doubt that some of the fun went out of auto racing for Mike Hawthorn when Collins died before his eyes at the German Grand Prix in 1958. The accident sent Collins flying out of his cockpit and crashing against a tree.

There were still three races to go in the season, and Hawthorn finished them reluctantly. He just barely managed to win the World Championship as Phil Hill, backing off, gave him the second-place finish he needed at Casablanca, the final race of the season.

After that Mike Hawthorn retired. Because of his amateurism, he had not been a particularly popular driver on the circuit. And despite the tragic loss of his friend, his carefree attitude toward life had not really changed. His aim in retirement would be to have fun

Unlike most racing drivers, Mike Hawthorn often drove fast and aggressively on public highways—which is what he was doing at about noon on a wet and windy January day in 1959. On the A3 highway from Portsmouth to

London, Mike entered into a friendly contest with racing driver Rob Walker. They had met on the road by accident and had begun the good-natured race on the spur of the moment.

Hawthorn's Jaguar and Walker's Mercedes stayed neck and neck until Walker prudently backed off.

As he did, he saw the Jaguar skid once, twice. Neither skid looked serious, but on the second skid the Jaguar struck a curb, spun around, grazed an oncoming truck, and disappeared from the shoulder in a blinding sheet of mud.

When Rob Walker reached the scene, Mike Hawthorn was dead. The coroner's inquiry found that he had died of a fractured skull and that speeding was the cause of the accident.

He was 29 years old.

OBJECTIVE

Fishing

A small boy asked his father if he could go fishing. His father asked what he would use for bait, and the boy opened his fist to display three squiggling worms.

The father had some reservations. He was a dry-fly fisherman himself, although he wasn't violently opposed to worms. Also, he doubted that there were any fish left in the brook after a recent flood. Both of those reasons were academic anyway because the fishing season had closed.

But his son seemed so eager that finally, thinking no harm could come of it, he said, "Okay, try your luck," The boy left happily.

His father thought no more about it until noon, when his son returned from the stream carrying a 12-inch brown trout. This posed a problem. He knew he should say something, but what? He explained that fishing is a sport. He said that a fisherman will often release a trout unharmed. He pointed out that the hook on a dry-fly is usually easier to get out than a hook baited with a worm.

His son listened in glum silence. Then he said, "Can I go fishing this afternoon?"

His father thought about it. Catching the brown trout was a fluke, after all. His son wouldn't catch any more fish. Still, taking that brown trout had been against the law. He told his son that. He explained about fishing seasons and conservation.

The boy listened, close to tears. He wanted to go fishing, and none of these reasonable objections had any effect. Perhaps he was too young to understand. "And, anyway, isn't fishing supposed to be fun?," his father asked himself. "Why not let the boy try again?"

So his father relented. "All right," he said. "There are no more fish there, I'm sure, but if you want to fish some more, go ahead."

His son left promptly for the brook. He never reported anything directly to his father, but an older brother brought back the news. The boy landed a 16-inch brown trout that afternoon—and released it.

OBJECTIVE

Fishing

Mort's Fish Market was conveniently located between Jerry's favorite trout stream and his home.

After fishing all one day without a nibble, Jerry stopped in at the market and said, "Hey, Mort, throw me three of your brook trout."

"Throw 'em?"

"Yeah," Jerry said. "I want to be able to tell the wife I caught 'em."

OBJECTIVE

Football

A good football coach never forgets the objective of the game. Coach Jess Neely of Rice University was a stern man with a gentle Southern drawl, but with a steely bite to it.

When the Rice Owls were getting ready to play Alabama in the 1954 Cotton Bowl game, Houston *Post* sportswriter Mickey Herskowitz asked, "Jess, you have a whole lot of seniors on this squad. Do you think you'll start an all-senior lineup tomorrow since this is their last game for the Owls?"

Neely didn't hesitate. "Mickey," he said, "this is no time to get sentimental."

OBJECTIVE

Golf

John Cunningham, the New Jersey journalist and historian, defined golf in this somewhat pessimistic way: "Golf: A game in which a ball 1½ inches in diameter is placed on a ball 8,000 miles in diameter. Object of the game is to knock the small ball off the large ball."

OUTCOME

Baseball

As Casey Stengel said, "You have to have a catcher, because if you don't, you're likely to have a lot of passed balls."

OUTCOME

Baseball

In his major league career, Al Rosen hit 192 home runs for the Cleveland Indians. He led the American League in homers twice. So he knew what he was talking about when he observed: "The greatest thrill in the world is to end the game with a home run and watch everybody else walk off the field while you're running the bases on air."

OUTCOME

Baseball

Bill Guthrie was an umpire, and like all umpires he had to deal with the temper tantrums of ballplayers.

One day after Guthrie had barked, "Strike three," a player stepped back from the plate and tossed his bat high in the air.

Guthrie took off his mask and watched the hickory go soaring.

"Son," he said, "if that bat comes down, you're out of the game."

OUTCOME

Boxing

Early in the Roaring Twenties, they struck oil out in Shelby, Montana. This caused some of the leading citizens of Shelby to lose their heads. They decided to promote a boxing match for the heavyweight championship of the world right in their own home town.

Talk about chutzpah! This meant getting the world-renowned Jack Dempsey and a contender to come to an isolated little town that, prior to the oil strike, was home to about 500 people. It meant guaranteeing a lot of money and spending a lot of money.

Shelby forged ahead. The fund-raising efforts were led by a mixed cadre—the mayor, a horse salesman, the owner of an army-navy store, the state commander of the American Legion, and the publisher of a boxing magazine.

Jack Dempsey signed on the dotted line. So did the challenger, Tom Gibbons. Dempsey was to receive 300,000 dollars. Gibbons would get 50 percent of any gate receipts above that amount.

The date for the match was set: July 4, 1923.

At this juncture, there was no arena in Shelby and no money subscribed for one. The promoters went to work. Within 20 days, the town had an arena for 40,000 spectators. It wasn't paid for—any more than Dempsey's 300,000-dollar guarantee was in the bank yet—but there it stood.

And, right on schedule, the biggest event in Shelby's history came to pass. Jack Dempsey, the Manassa Mauler, won a 15-round decision over the shrewd but overmatched Tom Gibbons.

And what about Shelby? Ah, Shelby. Enough money came in to cover Dempsey's guarantee. But Gibbons never got a nickel for his valiant 15-round effort. And the locals fared even worse. Three banks failed. The big shots of the town emerged dead broke.

It was a perfect promotion for the Roaring Twenties—all smoke and mirrors, no substance, and ultimately no money. For the town of Shelby, the great title fight brought on the Great Depression almost a decade early.

OUTCOME

Golf

As Fred Beck tells it in his book, *89 Years in a Sand Trap*, each one of the players in a foursome got off a good tee shot All but one of them hit a good second shot, too. The hero of our story, however, sent his ball flying into the rough, about 35 feet from the green.

We can assume he was annoyed, but he addressed the ball and manfully applied his wedge to the bad lie. The ball went nowhere. Actually, it went about ten feet.

The luckless player found this anything but amusing. His temper got the better of him. He took aim and threw his club in the direction of the ball.

Now, you have to suspend disbelief, because this incident really happened. The head of his whirling club struck the ball perfectly, lifted it up, and dumped it onto the green less than a foot from the cup.

The golfer made his putt. He marked down a par four.

There must be a moral here, but it's probably best to ignore it.

OUTCOME

Golf

Moses and St. Peter were playing golf in heaven, as they sometimes did in their spare time.

Moses teed off with a smooth, practiced swing and sent the ball rocketing down the fairway and onto the green. He smiled inwardly, knowing that St. Peter would have a hard time matching that first shot.

When St. Peter addressed the ball, he did so a bit hastily, and his drive hooked sharply toward the trees. Moses could barely conceal his amusement. The first hole was going to be his by a number of strokes.

But then, from out of nowhere, an eagle swooped down above the fairway, reached the hooking ball just as it was about to disappear in the greenery, and snatched it in its beak. The eagle then flew off toward the green, circled above it, and dropped the ball neatly in the cup.

"All right, Pete," said Moses grimly, "are we going to play golf, or are we going to fool around?"

OUTCOME

Hunting

Natural athletes should seldom stop to analyze what they're doing. If they do, their performance is likely to fall apart.

Coaches at all levels stress this well-known psychological fact. The more natural the athlete, the better he will perform. Thinkers are clinkers. If you analyze your tennis serve while in the act of serving, you'll double fault every time.

A long-time friend of Havilah Babcock, the *Field and Stream* writer, put the paralysis of analysis to use on a hunting trip. The "athlete" in this case was an incredible sure-shot by the name of Slim Boggins, a local hero from the Low Country of South Carolina.

Boggins, a natural if ever there was one, used an ancient pump repeater, and he could drop four quail on a rise. He demonstrated his dazzling skill while the writer and his friend Cliff watched in awe. As the exhibition wore on, both hunters began to wonder how many birds would be left when the gangling, untutored marksman was done.

Cliff stepped into the breach. He congratulated the Low Country native on his brilliant shooting. Then he asked, "Do you shoot with one eye closed, or with both open?"

Think about that. What's the secret of the natural athlete? The natural athlete doesn't *know* the secret. He just has it.

And Slim Boggins didn't know the answer. He said, "Funny thing, I ain't never noticed." But he promised that henceforth he would notice, and when he did, he'd let the two hunters know.

On the very next shot, Slim missed. "Shucks," he said "Had my left eye closed that time. That ain't the way I been doing it."

Well, you can guess the rest. Slim Boggins didn't bring down another bird all day. Left eye, right eye, both eyes, it didn't matter. Before long he slunk away from his once-triumphant demonstration without even trying to give Cliff an answer to his question.

The two hunters later heard Slim banging away at a single bird, which apparently dodged the volleys and went winging on its way.

Cliff's explanation for Slim Boggins's disgrace could have come from any high school or college coach. He said, "Our Mr. Boggins made the mistake of thinking."

PERFECTION

Auto Racing

You're heard it before—about perfection being dull. The player is so good, so mechanically perfect, that nobody wants to watch the performance.

It hardly seems as if you'd hear that criticism in auto racing. Since auto racing is far and away the most dangerous big-time sport, you might think the danger alone would rescue it from dullness.

Yet many people felt that Jim Clark, the World Champion in the mid-60s, was a great but boring driver. Clark had superb reactions and judgment. He had total confidence in his cars and in his ability to control a race. He would jump off to an early lead, build it up, and then adjust his pace to stay at the head of the pack.

To ordinary auto-racing fans, these tactics meant a dull race. It never occurred to them that at the speeds Clark was driving, he was forever flirting with disaster. Perfection looks easy, but in Jim Clark's perilous world it was something that could be shattered by any one of a thousand details going wrong.

For Clark it happened in an unimportant race in Germany. On a gentle right-hand turn—one that could be taken at full speed—his Lotus 48 suddenly plowed off the track and disappeared into a stand of trees. When they reached him, he was dead.

The most perfect of all race drivers, possibly the greatest of all, had met the same fate as so many of his talented peers.

PERFECTION

Auto Racing

Peter Revson was one of the great racing drivers of recent years. He finished second to Al Unser in the 1971 Indianapolis 500. "Racing," he said, "is a game of inches and tenths of seconds. It's not any one thing you do better than the other guy. It's just that you may have mastered each little thing a little better, so you go through the corner a tenth of a second quicker."

PERFECTION

Baseball

Roger Clemens of the Boston Red Sox struck out 20 batters in a nine-inning game in 1986. It's tempting to say that no one will ever do better than that. But it isn't wise.

Perfection demands 27 strikeouts in a nine-inning game—and, believe it or not, it's been done. Not at the major-league level, though. Not even in the high minors. But it was done in professional baseball—down in the old Class D Appalachian League.

The pitcher who did it was a young Pennsylvanian named Ron Necciai. He played for Bristol, Tennessee, and on May 13, 1952, he hurled a no-hitter against Welch, West Virginia. Bristol won the game 7 to 0. In the Appalachian League record book, there is this notation in parentheses: "(27 strikeouts)."

Perfection? Not quite, even though it sounds like it, because Bristol retired one batter on a ground out. The total of 27 resulted from the fact that Bristol's catcher dropped one of Necciai's third strikes. Ron had to fan four batters that inning.

The Pittsburgh Pirates were impressed enough to bring Necciai all the way to the majors in '52. Big-league hitters proved a lot tougher than the fellows down in Class D. Ron did win a major-league game that year, but he lost six. His ERA was 7.03, and he never made it back to the big time.

Still, he struck out 27 batters in a nine-inning professional game. No other pitcher in the history of baseball can make that claim.

PERFECTION

Baseball

Bill (Spaceman) Lee played college baseball at the University of Southern California. His coach there was Rod Dedeaux, a perfectionist. In fact, Dedeaux advised his players: "Don't be concerned with winning. That's not good enough. Play to achieve perfection."

PERFECTION

Baseball

Steve Bilko, a hulking first baseman, played a few seasons for Rochester in the International League. While he was there, he made the acquaintance of Angelo Guglielmo, a tiny umpire with a flair for the dramatic.

On a strike-two call, Bilko stepped out of the batter's box, turned to Guglielmo, and asked him how long he'd been umpiring.

It had all the earmarks of a loaded question, but the ump answered, "Twenty-six years."

Bilko said that he'd been around quite a while himself. He added that in all his time in the league he'd never seen Guglielmo miss a call before. That strike-two call was the first one.

The little ump called time and looked up toward the official scorer in the press box. He shouted, "That's ball two." After the count had been changed on the scoreboard, the ump moved back behind the plate.

As Bilko stepped into the batter's box, Guglielmo said, "Now I'm perfect."

PERFECTION

Basketball

"Practice makes perfect" is a proverb that goes back thousands of years. But the saying ignores something important. It's possible to practice a flaw until you master it—and that's not the aim at all.

Red Holzman, former coach of the New York Knicks, made the point this way: "Practice doesn't make perfect," he said. "Perfect practice does."

PERFECTION

Bowling

A 300 game in bowling occurs once in every 450,000 or so games. Of course, if you're a top pro, you'll do better than that. Elvin Mesger of Sullivan, Missouri, has bowled 27 perfect games. Among women bowlers, Jeanne Maiden of Solon, Ohio, has bowled 11. Dick Weber once rolled three perfect games in one tournament. A few others have done the same.

But the 300 bowler you have to admire most is Diane Ponza of Santa Cruz, California. During the season in which she bowled her perfect game, her average was—get this—112.

PERFECTION

Boxing

Greasy Johnson was a professional boxer. To the delight of his opponents, he spent much of his time on the canvas. In fact, he spent so much time there that he had to get a job at a parking lot to make ends meet.

Alas, for Greasy, one day a woman driver mashed his hand at the lot in a freak accident. He needed that hand to box, and he could no longer use it. He sued.

When Greasy got on the witness stand, the woman's lawyer noted that the plaintiff claimed to be a professional boxer. He claimed he could no longer earn his living in the ring. The lawyer then went over Greasy Johnson's won-lost record. It was mostly a dismal string of losses. Greasy had nothing to say. He couldn't argue with *The Ring Record Book*.

But the implication was serious—the implication that, with his record, Greasy had no business being in the ring.

Greasy's trainer, Angelo Dundee, knew how to handle the implication. Obviously, the defendant's lawyer didn't understand how boxing careers are built.

Dundee, who knew all too well, put it this way on the witness stand: "Greasy—I mean, Mr. Johnson—is what you call a perfect opponent. And there's a market for perfect opponents."

Now, that's not the kind of perfection that makes world champions. But it's the kind that for years had made Greasy Johnson a popular boxer. He helped to build other boxers' reputations.

Greasy, the perfect loser, won his case.

PERFECTION

Football

Vince Lombardi was the ultimate perfectionist. "You don't do things right once in a while," he said. "You do them right all the time."

PERFECTION

Horse Racing

The sportswriter Heywood Hale Broun has said that golfer Jack Nicklaus will never be completely satisfied until he hands in a scorecard that reads eighteen—in other words, until he achieves perfection.

But, as Broun points out, Nicklaus once observed perfection in another arena. As he sat alone in his living room in 1973, he watched Secretariat, one of the great racehorses of all time, romp home 31 lengths in front of Twice A Prince, the second-place finisher in the Belmont Stakes.

Nicklaus, like many others who watched the Belmont that year, could hardly believe it. He could hardly believe the awesome performance of the big chestnut horse. The great golfer wept, literally, as Secretariat swept across the finish line.

Broun suggested a reason: "The sight of perfection achieved by another is painful," he said. And that may be true—even if the other is a horse.

PERFECTION

Tennis

As a young player on the pro tennis tour, Mary Carillo used to get annoyed by people who objected to Chris Evert's perfection on the court.

"It drives me crazy when people say they get bored watching Chris," she said. "I find it dazzling. It's beautiful. What in the world is boring about perfection?"

PERSEVERANCE

Boxing

Stanley Ketchel, an early middleweight boxing champion, was shot and killed many years ago. When a sportswriter of the day heard about it, he said, "Start counting ten over him He'll get up "

PERSEVERANCE

Hunting

At one time, California employed full-time hunters of mountain lions. One such hunter was Jay Bruce, a hard-as-nails character who killed hundreds of mountain lions over the years.

The mountain lion is known by various names—puma, cougar, panther. By any name, he is a vicious predator. Don't believe the lie that all wild animals kill only for food. The cougar—let's call him that—will also kill for the joy of killing. In other words, the cougar is plenty mean.

Jay Bruce was paid by the state to track down and shoot cougars. But while he was doing his job, he was often accompanied by Sidney Snow. Snow's job was to photograph cougars in the wild, and he brought along the ponderous motion picture equipment of that era.

Jay Bruce, intrepid hunter, often found himself in the position of trying to set up good movie shots for Sidney Snow. He took the assignment seriously. So did Snow.

One day they had a big cougar treed on a steep hill. Snow set up his camera on the up side of the hill beneath the tree. To Snow's surprise, the cougar marched straight out on a limb toward him and leaped. If Snow hadn't ducked behind his camera, the cougar would have clipped his head.

Jay Bruce owned hunting dogs, and one of them, named Duke, pounced on the cougar as it landed. Together Duke and the cougar rolled down the steep hill. At the bottom, the big cat escaped and bolted up a second tree.

Sidney Snow got some fine movie footage of all this. He added more when the cougar went up a third tree.

Bruce thought the picture-taking had gone far enough, but Snow wanted more. Some running shots, he said. So after the equipment was set up—once more on a hill—Bruce began to throw rocks at the tree. The cougar wouldn't budge. Finally, Bruce fired a pistol shot in the general direction of the cougar.

Startled, the cougar hung down from a branch and dropped to the ground. Once again he just missed the camera, as Snow quickly pulled it aside.

Duke was on top of the cougar again. Bruce, for some reason, now tackled both the cougar and the dog. Two other dogs leapt to the attack, and all five bodies began rolling down the hill.

Make that six bodies. Snow had lost his footing when the cougar jumped. Clutching his camera and tripod, he slid down after them. He thought wildly of trying to spear the cougar with the sharp legs of the tripod, but the mixup was too great.

All six of them landed in a shallow pool at the bottom of the incline. The cougar was dead. Somehow Jay Bruce had managed, on that headlong descent, to press his pistol to the cougar's body and fire.

Snow hadn't even heard the shot.

PERSEVERANCE

Marathoning

There are not many shortcuts to success. As Grete Waitz, the superb marathoner notes, "For every finish-line tape a runner breaks—complete with the cheers of the crowd and the clicking of hundreds of cameras—there are all the hours of hard and often lonely work that rarely gets talked about."

PERSEVERANCE

Track and Field

"He has more determination than four mules."

That's what Parry O'Brien's father used to say about his shot-putting son. And he had stories to back it up.

In a meet at Fresno, California, O'Brien reached 53 feet and 6⅞ inches. That wouldn't be impressive today, but back then it was good for second place in the meet.

O'Brien was disappointed. While the meet continued under the lights, he stayed there and practiced steadily for two hours. He barely made his plane home to Santa Monica at 1:30 a.m.

At about 3:00 a.m., Parry's father was awakened by the sound of heavy thuds. He got up and found his son in the asphalt alley by the house. Parry had drawn a chalk circle and was putting the shot under the street light.

He said to his father, "I think I've discovered something." And he went on practicing until four in the morning.

O'Brien got better and better. He changed the style of his delivery and began to close in on the magic 60-foot mark. Eventually, he became the first shot-putter to reach the goal. He did it with a 60 foot 5¼ inch put.

Whatever Parry could do to better his performance, he tried. He was an early believer in weight training. He drank honey for instant energy. He studied physics, Yoga, and self-hypnosis. But most of all, he practiced. He found the time, or he made the time. "I don't quit until my hands are bleeding," he said.

POTENTIAL

Baseball

Casey Stengel was a shrewd judge of potential. He once said, "See that fella over there? He's 20 years old. In 10 years, he's got a chance to be a star. Now, that other fella over there, he's 20 years old, too. In 10 years, he's got a chance to be 30."

POTENTIAL

Basketball

Even before he became coach of the Boston Celtics, Red Auerbach was teaching his Potential Limit Theory. It deals with the question of natural ability versus training.

Let's say (according to Auerbach) a man has the potential to jump 20 feet. With no training at all, he'll jump 15 feet or so. But if the man gets proper guidance, and if he works hard, he may get up to 19 feet. He'll probably never jump the theoretically possible 20, because almost no one reaches his or her full potential.

Now take another guy. He has a potential limit of 15 feet. He's born that way. With training and hard work—ten times as much work as the first man, perhaps—he'll jump 14 feet. That's it. He'll never hit 15. The natural athlete will beat him every time, with or without instruction.

This theory, Auerbach suggests, applies to other fields besides athletics. One of Red's students became a successful TV writer. He'd been a fair student, but an indifferent basketball player. And he'd clearly succeeded off the court. When Auerbach met him on a New York street years later, the writer told him:

"You know, you taught me something in one of your classes that I've never forgot."

"What was that?" Red asked.

"You once gave a lecture on the Theory of Limited Potential. . . . "

POTENTIAL

Boxing

John L. Sullivan was the first heavyweight champion of the world to become an American institution. In John L.'s heyday, virtually every schoolboy in the United States knew his name and could recite his feats.

But John L. Sullivan didn't start out at the top. He attended Boston College, but he dropped out. He became a plumber, but he was fired for breaking his foreman's jaw. He turned to tinsmithing, but he found semipro baseball more to his liking than the routine of the smithy.

Then one night he went to a boxing benefit performance at the opera house in Boston Highlands. The featured boxer was Tom Scannel, a local hero who offered to take on anyone in the house and stop him in three rounds.

Sullivan sat in the front row. Some of the Boston sports knew John L. as a tough brawler, and they began to shout, "Sullivan!"

John L. obliged. He took off his coat, took off his collar and tie, and rolled up his sleeves. As he climbed onto the platform, he looked very dandified beside Scannel in green tights.

Scannel moved in quickly on the rugged challenger, his guard up. Sullivan had seen amateur boxing matches and expected to touch gloves with his opponent. He tried. But Scannel had no interest in such niceties. He uncorked a left hook that caught Sullivan on the neck and sent him reeling.

It was a big mistake. So was Scannel's mocking smile.

John L. charged Tom S. like an enraged bull. He threw a right to the jaw that blasted Scannel straight backward off the platform. Scannel, birds tweeting in his brain, lay sprawled in the orchestra circle, his performance ruined.

No one who saw Sullivan's one-punch demolition of the evening's featured attraction doubted that John the Great had a bright future in boxing.

POTENTIAL

Hockey

Hockey, like winter, begins early in Canada. There are leagues for Tykes, Novices, Pee Wees, Bantams, and Midgets. The next step up—to Junior hockey—is a big one. And even then, it's a long step to the National Hockey League.

"In Quebec," says a Canadian businessman, "you aspire to be either a priest or a hockey player."

With that much riding on a single sport, it's not surprising that people get carried away. Marcel Dionne of Drummondville, Quebec, got his first skates at the age of two. Seven years later, Dionne, who would one day star for the Detroit Red Wings, went to Quebec City for a Pee Wee tournament. There were 117 teams competing during the Winter Carnival.

A fan—or maybe it was a scout—called the nine-year-old Dionne over and asked him for his autograph. An autograph at nine. They can spot future NHL talent young in Canada.

POTENTIAL

Tennis

George Parma, who once played on the Czech Davis Cup team, heard about Martina Navratilova when Martina was nine years old. He decided to take a look at her to see if the reports were accurate. At the time, Parma was the leading tennis coach in Czechoslovakia, employed by the government to train future champions. He said that he could tell in a few minutes whether this small, wiry girl had any potential.

Martina used the second-hand wooden racket her father had given her. She wore a little burgundy warmup suit for the test, which she later called the most important of her life. Loose and confident, she "showed off," as she described it. She returned many of the tough shots Parma gave her to handle, and felt she was doing well. The session went on much longer than Martina and her father had expected.

Finally, Parma walked over to her father. "I think we can do something with her," he said.

POWER

Baseball

The man who writes the checks may not be able to hit a fastball over the center-field fence, but he has some power all the same.

When Billy Martin managed the New York Yankees, he had a sign in his office that read:

1. The boss is always right.
2. If the boss is wrong, see No. 1.

Billy Martin's boss at the time was meddlesome Yankee owner George Steinbrenner.

POWER

Boxing

Rocky Marciano looked crude and awkward in the ring, but when he retired as heavyweight champion of the world, no one had ever beaten him as a pro. He'd won 49 bouts in a row, 43 of them by knockouts.

The secret of his success was not his grace but his power. Yet his power was deceptive to the ringside crowd. As veteran trainer Freddie Brown put it, "He hits you with something that looks like a little tap . . . but the guy who gets hit shakes right down to his legs."

POWER

Football

In a crucial game between the New York Giants and the Washington Redskins, the Giants' Lawrence Taylor sacked the Redskins' quarterback Jay Schroeder three times.

"When he hits you," Schroeder said, "you have to take inventory."

POWER

Football

The very name of Bronko Nagurski was enough to instill fear in opposing football players. In his rookie year with the Chicago Bears, Nagurski took a handoff on the two-yard line and rammed into the line, head down. Two would-be tacklers bounced away like dust devils. Nagurski plowed on, into the end zone and through it.

As it happened, the Bears were playing that day at Wrigley Field, and just beyond the end zone stood Wrigley's red brick wall. Nagurski crashed into the wall and went down. He got up dazed, shook his head to clear the cobwebs, and trotted toward the sideline.

The Bears' coach, George Halas, met him near the bench, looking worried.

Nagurski said, "That last guy really gave me a good lick, coach."

PREDICTION

Baseball

One winter when Tommy Lasorda was coaching Caracas in the Venezuelan League, he invited shortstop Bill Russell to lunch. They walked to a cafe that was popular with local sportswriters. While they were eating, one of the writers asked Lasorda in Spanish how he thought the Caracas team would do the next day against the opposing pitcher, Milt Wilcox.

Bill Russell, who didn't understand Spanish and didn't realize that a question had been asked, said, "Hey, Tom, whenever you're ready to start back, I'm ready to go."

"What did he say?" asked one of the sportswriters in Spanish.

Lasorda, who spoke the native language fluently, responded in Spanish: "Bill Russell, the outstanding shortstop of Caracas, said to tell you that Milt Wilcox will not last five innings and that he will personally knock him out of the game."

The quote appeared in the Caracas newspapers the next morning.

In the first inning of the game that day, Russell singled in two runs. Then, with two men on in the fifth inning, Bill Russell, the outstanding shortstop of Caracas, drove a Milt Wilcox pitch out of the ballpark for three more runs. It knocked Wilcox out of the box.

After the game, the Caracas sportswriters crowded around Russell's locker. They were wide-eyed and excited. They wanted to know how he could make such an amazingly accurate prediction.

Russell was confused. At first he didn't know what they were saying. And when he finally learned what they were talking about, he said he didn't know anything about the prediction.

PREDICTION

Baseball

We all know the scenario. It's Wrigley Field, Chicago, October the first, 1932. The Cubs are behind in the World Series, having lost their first two games to the mighty New York Yankees.

The score is tied 4 to 4 in the top of the fifth inning. The bases are empty. Babe Ruth steps to the plate. He has already hit one home run in the game. The embattled Cubs have been riding him brutally from the bench, but the Babe is unmoved. He has a single goal.

Charlie Root is pitching for the Cubs. He throws a perfect strike, and the Sultan of Swat raises an index finger even before the ump calls it.

The same thing happens again. Two Ruthian fingers stab the charged air. Strike two.

Does this begin to sound a little like "Casey at the Bat?" You bet. But, as you know, there's a happy ending coming—at least for New York Yankee fans.

The Babe now steps out of the batter's box, waits for the proper moment, and points toward the flagpole in center field. Could any stranger in the crowd doubt that Ruth is about to crash a mighty homer into the center-field bleachers?

No indeed! Root pitches—and there it goes! Up, up, and out! It misses the flagpole by inches!

The Babe has hit the ball exactly where he said he would. He has called his shot. The Cub fans are speechless. Undone. The Babe is smiling as he rounds the bases. The Yanks are on their way to a World Series sweep.

Ah . . . but did it really happen that way? The truth is that it probably didn't. But the incredible thing is that no one knows for sure. With all those fans, all those players and umpires, and all those sportswriters, there's still a question of what really happened on that October day in 1932 at Wrigley Field.

Joe Williams of the New York *World-Telegram*, the only sportswriter who flatly claimed the next day that Ruth "called his shot," said years later he was probably wrong. But by then the myth was firmly established as the most electrifying prediction in the annals of sports.

And Williams himself admitted, in his words, that "the thunderous drama still lives in my memory, and no amount of testimony is ever going to change it in the slightest. I always was a pushover for wonderful fairy tales. . . ."

PREDICTION

Basketball

For seven seasons the varsity basketball coach of Calais College led his team to losing records. This year, with three returning seniors, it looked as if the record might improve slightly over the 4–17 mark of the previous year.

A local sportswriter approached him before the first game. "Looks like a different story this year, eh, coach? According to the preseason dope, your boys might make it all the way to the NCAA tournament."

The coach gritted his teeth and snapped, "Could you give me the name of the preseason dope who told you that?"

PREDICTION

Basketball

When gamblers determine the point spread in a basketball game, they often do it in half points.

One night as Wilt Chamberlain was walking through the lobby of Madison Square Garden, a young fan asked him, "Hey, Wilt, how many you gonna win by tonight?"

Chamberlain smiled and said, "Three and a half."

PREDICTION

Basketball

They have a ritual at Fairfield University for welcoming rookies to their basketball team. It takes place at the pregame meal before the first game on the schedule. While dessert is being served, a crescendo of clinking glasses heralds the introduction of a predetermined rookie. This rookie has to sing a song of his choice before his teammates. He can't lip-sync it, and he can't involve anyone else or use electronic aids.

The most memorable performance came from six-foot-ten freshman Alex Forbes, who delivered a fine a cappella rendition of "Taps."

The Fairfield Stags had just come off back-to-back league championships and were preparing to do something that no other team in the league had ever done—win a third straight crown.

As it turned out, Forbes's musical selection was appropriate for the Stags' ensuing season. They won only 8 games while losing 20, for the worst finish in the school's history

Fairfield's coach said, "I'll never forget how Alex got up and sang the words to 'Taps,' which most of us never heard before. . . . But if I knew that his song was going to be an indication of the season—I might have cut him."

PREDICTION

Boxing

One of the most emotionally charged boxing matches of all time was the return bout between Joe Louis and Max Schmeling. Louis had lost the earlier match to the German boxer.

Schmeling was a good fighter, but feeling in the United States ran high against him. Adolph Hitler was using Schmeling and other German athletes to push his master race theory. That didn't go over very well at New York's Yankee Stadium, where Louis and Schmeling were to fight.

As Joe Louis made his way toward the ring, the actor George Raft raised his finger and shouted, "One round!"

Louis remembered saying to him, "What's the matter? You in a hurry?"

But everyone who saw that fight agreed that Louis was in a hurry, too. He went after Schmeling from the opening bell. It was never a contest.

Louis knocked out the German champion in two minutes and four seconds of round one.

PREDICTION

Football

The conventional wisdom is that Joe Namath fashioned a career out of one Super Bowl game. Like most conventional wisdom, there's a grain of truth in this—but only a grain. Namath made the Pro Football Hall of Fame, and he didn't get there because of a single big game.

Still, the publicity surrounding that game was, and still is, enormous. Broadway Joe, the quarterback of the New York Jets in the upstart American Football League, was predicting a Super Bowl win against the mighty Baltimore Colts. The odds-makers picked the Colts by 17 points.

For the first half, it looked as if Joe was right and the Las Vegas boys were wrong. The Jet defense shut down Baltimore completely, while Namath directed the Jet offense to the only touchdown of the half. It was 7 to 0 at halftime.

Most experts expected the Colts to come roaring back in the second half.

They didn't. Instead, the Jets' Jim Turner got three chances to kick field goals—and made all three. As the game began winding down, the Jets led 16 to 0.

Baltimore's great quarterback, Johnny Unitas, finally directed the Colts to one touchdown. But it was too little and too late. When the gun sounded, Joe Namath's New York Jets were Super Bowl champions, 16 to 7.

Namath's predictions—some called them boasts—had proved accurate. The American Football League could no longer be dismissed by the National Football League as a bush-league operation. Broadway Joe and his talented Jet teammates had seen to that.

PREDICTION

Hockey

A Toronto columnist, Jim Coleman, created the so-called "Muldoon jinx" in pro hockey. According to the jinx, the Chicago Black Hawks would never finish first in their division. Here's how it began.

When the Black Hawks, who had finished third, lost their Stanley Cup playoff series to the Boston Bruins, the Hawks' owner, Major Frederick McLaughlin, was unhappy. He called the Hawks' coach, Pete Muldoon, into his office. Hot words passed between them. Major McLaughlin thought the Black Hawks should have won, and that in losing they were disgraced.

"You're crazy!" shouted Muldoon.

"You're fired!" shouted the owner.

According to Coleman, the Toronto columnist, as Muldoon turned to walk away, he said, "I'm not through with you. I'll hoodoo you. This club will *never* finish in first place."

There's some doubt that Muldoon ever said it. But whether he did or not, *something* hoodooed the Chicago Black Hawks. Try as they would, the Black Hawks could finish no higher than second in their division for the next 45 years.

PREDICTION

Mountaineering

The first mountaineers who make it to the top of a difficult peak tend to think that no one else will ever match their feat. They know how tough it was for them. So they write something foolish, such as this: "It's doubtful that others will ever climb Mount Whatever "

Big mistake. Many others will probably do it. Once a peak has been conquered, there are other climbers waiting in line. They may even find it easier. For instance, the first person to climb one of Yosemite's peaks wrote, "It is difficult to conceive of an ascent . . . being completed in less than two days." The second ascent took eight hours. Later ascents took four hours.

You've got to be careful with these predictions. The first climber of Charlotte Dome in Kings Canyon National Park fell into the old trap: "The difficult climb," he wrote, "will probably remain unknown."

Hardly. Within the next eight years there were at least 60 ascents of Charlotte Dome, and climbing parties had begun to meet on the way up and down. Proving—if proof is needed—that what's been done once can be done again . . . and again . . . and again.

PREPARATION

Baseball

An umpire who tangles with Billy Martin had better know the rules of baseball. Martin proved that time and time again in his stormy managerial career. One of the most famous examples was the pine-tar incident involving George Brett of the Kansas City Royals. Brett, you'll recall, had a home run taken away from him by umpire Tim McClelland, a decision that gave Martin's Yankees a win they didn't seem to deserve.

The league overruled McClelland, allowed Brett's home run, but decided that the game had to be resumed from that point. Twenty-five days later, with a new crew of umpires, the teams resumed play.

Billy Martin saw a new opening. As soon as play began, George Frazier, the Yankee pitcher, threw the ball to first base. Martin strode out of the dugout to claim that Brett, in circling the bases, had failed to touch first base. The ball then went to second, where Martin made the same claim, and to third.

Clever Billy. How could the new crew of umpires know whether Brett had touched all the bases or not?

Enter Bob Fishel, public relations director of the American League. Fishel had watched the action from the press box. He had a smile on his face. He knew what was coming.

Dave Phillips, the crew chief of the umpires, pulled a piece of paper from his pocket. It was a notarized affidavit signed by all four of the original umpires. It stated that George Brett had touched all the bases while running out his home run. It further stated that U.L. Washington, who scored ahead of him, had done the same.

Fischel took the press-box microphone and explained what was happening on the field.

After that, play resumed. It took the Royals just 12 minutes to defeat the Yankees. The always-clever Billy Martin had been one-upped and then beaten.

PREPARATION

Baseball

Managers come and go in baseball, but few depart with the clever touch of Birdie Tebbets of the Milwaukee Braves.

When Bobby Bragan took over after Tebbets' departure, he found two sealed envelopes in his desk. They were marked "No. 1" and "No. 2." Both carried the warning, "Open in emergency only."

Bragan didn't open either envelope during his first year. But in his second year he started to run into trouble. He opened envelope number one. The message read: "Blame it on me."

Things got worse the next season, and Bragan began to wonder seriously about his future with the club. He decided the time had come to look at message number two. He opened the envelope and read Tebbets' advice. The note said: "Prepare two letters."

PREPARATION

Football

Lindsey Nelson, the sportscaster, is a great believer in preparation. And he has quite a story—almost an eerie story—to support his belief. It goes back to the 1954 Cotton Bowl: Alabama versus Rice.

On New Year's Eve, the night before the game, Nelson and Red Grange, who was to handle the color, met to talk about their next day's telecast. They went over a recent NFL play in which the quarterback, Bobby Layne, had taken a forward pass from halfback Doak Walker after having handed the ball off to Walker. It was a weird play, one that reminded Nelson and Grange of the importance of reviewing the rules.

Here is the strange part. The only other rule they reviewed that night (the quarterback was an ineligible receiver, by the way) was the one dealing with a tackle made by a player coming off the bench. You've heard about its happening, of course, but it's a rare occurrence. Nonetheless, that's the one specific rule they discussed.

Next day, early in the second period, Rice led Alabama 7 to 6. Rice had possession deep in its own territory. The handoff went to the Owls' right halfback Dick Moegle, who sliced through the right side of the Alabama line. Free at the 20-yard line, Moegle broke into the clear at the 35. Prancing down the far side of the field from Nelson and Grange, he looked unstoppable.

He was unstoppable. But wait.

All of a sudden Dick Moegle crashed to the ground at the Alabama 38. Getting up, he looked around, dazed. And no wonder. He'd been blindsided, tackled hard by an unexpected twelfth Alabamian, Tommy Lewis, the Crimson Tide's hard-driving fullback. Lewis had come off the bench like a mad avenger, unhelmeted but hell for leather.

Red Grange, grinning, turned to Lindsey Nelson and said, "Lindsey, what about this play?"

Lindsey Nelson spelled out the rule carefully for the TV audience while the officials discussed it on the field. Finally, the referee in charge, Cliff Shaw, began to walk. He carried the ball over the goal line and held his hands aloft. Touchdown, Rice, just as Nelson had told the fans it would be.

Years later Red Grange autographed his autobiography for his telecast partner of that day. "To Lindsey Nelson," he wrote. "The first guy who knows the rules."

PREPARATION

Football

Everyone knows about Monday morning quarterbacks. There are probably a lot more Monday morning head coaches. Coaching looks so easy on the magic tube.

When Joe Robbie founded the Miami Dolphins, he received head-coaching applications from a trash collector, a hotel clerk, and a traveling evangelist.

The general manager of the New England Patriots once said that the most impressive application he got came from an 11-year-old girl in Swampscott.

People who have watched pro football for years on television often think they're ready for a pro coaching job. Many wives recommend their husbands as head coaches. Usually these women are sincere, although one admitted to Gene Klein of the San Diego Chargers that her real aim was to get her husband out of the house on weekends.

PREPARATION

Football

Jack Kemp, for many years a Congressman from western New York State, once played for the Buffalo Bills and the San Diego Chargers.

On the campaign trail, Kemp said, "Pro football gave me a good sense of perspective when I entered the political arena. I had already been booed, cheered, cut, sold, traded, and hanged in effigy."

PREPARATION

Football

Talent alone isn't enough. As Ohio State's Woody Hayes used to say, "Give me enough of a head start, and I can beat Jesse Owens in a hundred-yard dash."

PREPARATION

Golf

The Boy Scouts have a motto, "Be prepared." One of the legendary golf hustlers and gamblers had the same motto.

Titanic Thompson, as he was called, was no Boy Scout. When Titanic made a bet, he intended to win. And he worked out some clever ways to do it.

One of his favorite tricks was the long putt—a 30-footer. He would bet that he could sink three out of five shots at the 30-foot distance.

The mark would smile and accept the bet.

Titanic Thompson would then putt three straight balls into the cup.

Jack Nicklaus himself couldn't do that. How could Titanic Thompson? Easy.

The day before the bet, he would lay a water hose on a green that had just been watered. The hose would run from the cup to whatever position Titanic intended to take the following day.

The next day he would move the hose. When the green was mowed, there would be an all-but-invisible trough leading into the cup.

Titanic Thompson then moved to his predetermined position and started to putt. It took almost no skill at all. One ball after another would roll straight down that pathway and into the cup.

PREPARATION

Hockey

When Canadian mothers tell their three-year-old boys not to fight, they're likely to get the defiant answer: "Hockey players fight."

They sure do.

And what better way to prepare for fighting than to practice it? Keith Magnuson of the Chicago Black Hawks took lessons in judo. Next he worked his way up to a brown belt in karate. But he found that karate didn't help much.

He said: "The secret, you see, is using your feet to kick somebody. And when your feet are in skates it's not exactly legal. It's not very easy either."

So he took up boxing. His instructor was a former featherweight champion of the world.

"Boxing helped me," Magnuson noted. "It helped me to block and throw punches better on skates."

The moral is, if you want to play professional hockey, don't bother with judo or karate. Train yourself to box.

PREPARATION

Rugby and Cricket

Every schoolboy knows that the Battle of Waterloo was won on the playing fields of Eton, where youthful athletes, all unaware, prepared for war. Did the Duke of Wellington really say that? Yes, he did, but not on the morning of the battle, not when his ex-rugby and cricket players were facing the mighty army of Napoleon Bonaparte. That morning he was not so philosophical. Looking out on the field, Wellington noticed a number of his young gentlemen officers, their commissions purchased for them by their fathers. Many of them were struggling to put up umbrellas against a June shower.

Wellington turned to an aide and snapped, "I don't know if they frighten Napoleon, but by God, they frighten me!"

PREPARATION

Soccer

Soccer is an international game, and styles of play vary from country to country. In Brazil the goalie traditionally used what was called the carioca style for a save. The carioca depended on footwork.

The result was that in international play the Brazilian goalies were at a disadvantage. They had little experience in stopping the cross—a ball passed laterally from the corner to a teammate who takes the shot.

Brazil had lost a few key matches in World Cup competition because of its inability to defend against the cross. A new goalie using a new style of defense was needed.

The task fell to Gilmar, who spent almost three years getting ready for the 1958 World Cup. He traveled throughout Europe to watch the style of play. He studied movies of European games and had his Brazilian teammates practice European moves.

When the World Cup games began in Sweden, Gilmar was ready. In the opening round, he shut out Austria, England, and the USSR. In seven games he allowed only four goals.

European spectators watched in amazement as Gilmar plucked opponents' crosses out of the air. The world-class soccer player had learned a new skill, and his knowledge paid off handsomely.

PRESSURE

Baseball

There's no tougher job in baseball than pitching in relief. The reliever is usually there because the pitcher before him got into a jam. He often inherits runners on base.

How do pitchers react to this pressure? Lefty Gomez, the great Yankee pitcher, sometimes had to relieve. He said, "There are a lot of things that go through your head when you're coming in to relieve in a troubled spot. One of them is 'Should I spike myself?' "

PRESSURE

Baseball

Satchel Paige had a number of remedies for pressure and other ailments. One of them was, "If your stomach disputes you, lie down and pacify it with cool thoughts."

PRESSURE

Baseball

As Joe Garagiola said, "Baseball gives you every chance to be great. Then it puts every pressure on you to prove that you haven't got what it takes. It never takes away the chance, and it never eases up on the pressure."

PRESSURE

Baseball

It depends on how you define pressure. George Brett, the nearest thing to a .400 hitter in a long time, said, "There's no pressure playing baseball. . . . Pressure is when you have to go to the unemployment office to pick up a check to support four people."

PRESSURE

Basketball

Everyone has seen film clips of a high school basketball star sinking an incredibly long shot at the buzzer. It's good for a few "oohs" and "aahs."

But it was just such a shot by the Los Angeles Lakers' Jerry West that coach Red Holzman remembers as one of the most remarkable performances he ever saw.

The occasion was a championship series between the Lakers and the

New York Knicks. With the series tied at one game apiece, New York was leading 102 to 100 a second or so before the final buzzer in the third game.

Enter Jerry West. He took a pass-in under his own basket and dribbled briefly before running out of time. He then fired a two-handed shot from well behind midcourt. The ball swished through the net, tying the score. (There were no three-point shots in those days.)

The Knicks' Dave DeBusschere dropped to his knees in despair and disbelief. "My heart dropped into my stomach," he said later. "It was just an impossible shot."

New York went on to win the game in overtime, but the memory of West's shot lingered on.

In the case of the high school shot, everyone knows it was incredible luck—somewhat like one out of a billion chimpanzees tapping out *Hamlet* on a typewriter.

In the case of West's shot, it was different. He was known as a clutch player and one of the game's great shooters. He might have missed that fantastic shot, of course.

But he didn't.

PRESSURE

Football

In college and pro football, Mike Ditka did it all—All-American end at Pitt, all-pro tight end with the Chicago Bears, head coach of the 1986 Super Bowl champion Bears. And he did it all with a kind of controlled—well, not always controlled—ferocity.

As a rookie player for the Chicago Bears, Mike was really psyched up for a game against the Colts. He'd heard that Colts' linebacker Bill Pellington was going to play rough with him. The rumors were right. On the first play, Pellington bashed him in the mouth.

You didn't do something like that to Ditka and get away with it. On the next play, Mike got off a shot of his own. It went on like that for a while, and then things settled down.

But later in the game Ditka was a few yards downfield on a running play. He felt a thump on his elbow. He looked back. On the ground he saw a white cloth with a piece of lead in it.

His first thought was that Pellington was out to blackjack him. Or white-jack him.

Mike grabbed the cloth and and ran over to an official. He was scream-ing. "There's a piece of lead in here, and he's throwing it at me."

The official gave him a strange look. "Give me that damn thing," he said. "It's my flag."

In those days, the flags were white. The face of an embarrassed rookie, though, was the still-familiar red.

Ditka had been so fired up he didn't know an official's flag from a UFO.

PRESSURE

Golf

Professional golf sometimes seems dull to people who watch it on televi-sion. It isn't one of the really electrifying media sports. A few of the greatest golfers look paunchy and unathletic.

Yet golf is one of the most demanding games there is. A winning golfer is often under intense pressure. Only a few strokes separate the stars from the also-rans. Every tournament is a study in coolness under mental and emotion-al strain.

If you're five shots behind the leaders with ten holes to play—as Jack Nicklaus was in the 1986 Masters—you might wonder if even those deep reserves of poise, judgment, and class will be enough to close the gap.

They were for Jack Nicklaus in 1986. The 46-year-old Nicklaus startled the golfing world with a blazing finish, ending with a 65 on the final round. Almost no one thought he could do it. Many thought he would never win another big tournament. Rumors of retirement were circulating. He had earned less than $4,500 on the tour that spring.

Jack Nicklaus's son, Jack Jr., caddied for him on that amazing April day in Augusta. As he approached the final ten holes, still far back, Jack Sr. turned to his son and said, "If I'm going to do anything, I better start doing it."

Whether that was a prayer or a promise, probably not even Jack Nicklaus knows for sure. What he does know is that he came out of the depths of disappointment with a performance that is celebrated as one of the greatest comebacks in golf history.

PRESSURE

Horse Racing

Elizabeth Arden Graham, better known as plain Elizabeth Arden, owned a string of racehorses. One of her colts from Maine Chance Farm, Jet Pilot, won the Kentucky Derby in 1947. But on the whole she was not too successful as a sportswoman-owner.

Part of her difficulty stemmed from the fact that she fired trainers faster than George Steinbrenner fired managers. When Eddie Neloy took over as trainer, she had dismissed 45 previous trainers.

At the time Eddie Neloy was hired, Mrs. Graham hoped to win the Kentucky Derby with a horse named Black Metal.

On the night before the Derby, there is a big event called the Derby Trainers' Dinner. Eddie Neloy was there; Mrs. Graham was at home in New York.

The MC introduced Eddie as the current trainer at Maine Chance—and then added, as a joke, "at least he was at seven o'clock, when we got started."

Eddie fell into the spirit of things and said, "I've just called New York, and as of eight-forty-five, I'm still her trainer."

A nice guip, but Mrs. Graham had no sense of humor. She'd once fired a trainer for chewing gum during a conversation with her. Still, Eddie Neloy might have survived for a while if Black Metal had romped home the next day with the roses.

Instead Black Metal finished 13th in the Derby, and Eddie Neloy became the 46th Maine Chance trainer to go down the tube.

PRIDE

Boxing

Every champion has his own pride, but not every champion attracts the pride of a whole city.

Rocky Marciano did. His home town of Brockton, Massachusetts, admired and backed him from the very beginning, from the time he was still fighting four-round preliminary bouts in Providence. The Brockton fans showed up for those fights. Later they poured into New York to watch him in the main events.

After Marciano won the heavyweight championship of the world in 1952, he was usually greeted by crowds of 25,000 to 40,000 on his return to Brockton. For a city of 95,000, that's quite a show of support. To the people of Brockton, Rocky wasn't just a hero, he was *their* hero.

Some of it probably had to do with the fact that Brockton is a fairly small city, and Marciano put it on the map. But a lot had to do with Rocky himself. He was modest, warmhearted, decent, and sensible—the kind of heavyweight champion who's often celebrated in boxing myth but seldom exists in boxing fact.

Marciano, the pride of Brockton, existed in both fact and myth. He deserved all the accolades he received in his too-brief lifetime.

PRIDE

Football

Never insult an old pro. That was one of the lessons Bill Bergey learned as a rookie middle linebacker for the Cincinnati Bengels.

Coach John Madden of the Oakland Raiders watched from the sideline as Bergey smashed past the Raiders' veteran center Jim Otto and tackled the Oakland ballcarrier right in front of Madden.

Madden was mad. "You gotta block Bergey!" he yelled. "We can't run if you don't block Bergey!"

Jim Otto didn't say a word, but the Bengals' Bill Bergey did. He said, "Otto can't block me. He's too old. I'm too fast for him."

Madden says he knew right there that Bergey had made a mistake. You don't taunt an old pro like that and get away with it.

Bill Bergey didn't make another tackle for the rest of the game. And in one pileup, Jim Otto sailed headfirst into Bergey—a helmet-to-helmet collision that echoed across the field. Bergey said later that he played the rest of the game in a daze and didn't fully recover from the encounter for about five days.

PRIDE

Track

The press is fickle. It loves a winner and will manufacture all kinds of explanations to explain defeat.

In 1980 Sebastian Coe of Great Britain held the world record for 800 meters. But at the Moscow Olympics in 1980, his fellow countryman Steve Ovett raced home the winner. Coe had to settle for a silver medal.

The two of them would also be running the 1,500-meter race, and Coe was determined to win it. In the semifinal, though, he allowed himself to be boxed in and had to drop back and then sprint around the cluster. The move worked. He won the race.

But he knew he had made an error, one that might have been disastrous. It could prove fatal in the final race.

By now the British press was a bit down on Sebastian Coe. A nice guy, they said. Maybe too nice. It's all well and good to be a gentlemen, but Ovett was tough. A fighter.

Ovett had won the 800. Who would win the 1,500?

Going back to May of 1977, Steve Ovett had won 45 straight 1,500-meter or mile races. It was his specialty. Coe's specialty, as sportswriters knew, was the 800. So the press had a pretty good idea of what to expect when nice-guy Coe went up against hard-as-nails Ovett.

None of this journalistic guff made much impression on Sebastian Coe. He knew what he had to do. He had no intention of making either of his earlier mistakes this time. He intended to win the 1,500. Maybe he was a nice guy, but he was also tough.

Coe ran his race just as he had planned it, staying wide, staying back, and then moving up fast from seventh place. East Germany's Jurgen Straub held the lead, setting a furious pace. But Coe moved quickly into second, with Steve Ovett off his shoulder.

In the last turn, Straub faltered. Coe passed him. Ovett tried to move up, made a desperate final effort, but couldn't close the gap. Coe sprinted to victory. Straub finished second and Ovett third.

Sebastian Coe, not usually one to show emotion, fell to his knees and touched his forehead to the track. The gold was his.

The press could now try to explain what had happened to Steve Ovett. Only a bronze medal? Hey, Seb Coe had won a silver in the 800, and he was just a Goody Twoshoes, wasn't he?

PRIORITIES

Baseball

One of the greatest of all sports legends ran a bar on West 52nd Street, New York City. His name was Toots Shor, and Toots was a friend to heavy-weight champs and green rookies. He was a sports fan above all else

Toots liked to sit at the table with his customers. One night the group included Sir Alexander Fleming, the discoverer of penicillin. Fleming had just won the Nobel Prize for medicine.

Halfway through a conversation, Mel Ott came through the front door. Ott, a great power hitter for the Giants, was nearing the end of his playing career.

"Pardon me," Toots said, getting up, "but I have to go. Somebody important just came in."

PRIORITIES

Baseball

Pat Kelly, a major league outfielder in the '70s, was a born-again Christian.

One day Pat said to his manager, Earl Weaver: "Aren't you glad I walk with the Lord, Earl?"

Weaver replied: "I'd rather you walked with the bases loaded."

PRIORITIES

Baseball

Not many people in or out of sports would presume to question God, but Kenesaw Mountain Landis was no ordinary man. As Commissioner of Baseball after the Black Sox scandal, his grim visage and harsh judgments reminded many of the Old Testament prophets.

When Christy Mathewson died at an early age, Landis wondered about the Lord's selection process. "Why," he asked, "should God wish to take a thoroughbred like Matty so soon, and leave some others down here that could well be spared?"

PRIORITIES

Baseball

Jim Bouton, the Yankee pitcher who wrote *Ball Four*, had no illusions about the priorities of Yankee management. Said Bouton, "They'd find room for Charles Manson if he could hit .300."

PRIORITIES

Baseball

A scout for the Chicago Cubs phoned from a small town in Nebraska and asked to speak to Charlie Grimm, the Cubs' manager.

When Grimm came on the line, the scout began talking excitedly. "Boss," he said, "I've just seen a pitcher who's amazing. This afternoon the kid pitched a no-hitter. And not your usual no-hitter—he threw 27 strikeouts in a row. Nobody touched the ball until the last inning when some guy hit a foul. I've got the pitcher right here with me. Shall I sign him up?"

"No," Grimm said. "Sign the guy who got the foul. We need hitters."

PRIORITIES

Baseball

Dan Quisenberry, Kansas City's ace reliever, felt that maybe too much religion was creeping into the national game.

"I don't think God really cares about baseball," Quinsenberry said. "He's got more important things on His mind."

PRIORITIES

Bowling

Fred bowled every Monday night. His average was nothing much, but his devotion to the game was fierce. Sick or well, he would keep his Monday night appointment. He thought of himself as the iron man of bowling.

Then one Monday night he went out for bowling and disappeared. His wife called the police and the local hospitals. Nothing. He had simply vanished.

A year later to the day, he reappeared. He gave no explanation for his absence, and his wife didn't press him for one. Instead, she began phoning their friends.

"What are you doing?" he demanded suspiciously.

"I'm arranging a party," she said, "to celebrate your return."

"Not for tonight you're not," he growled. "This is my bowling night."

PRIORITIES

Fencing

However important sports may be in the Soviet bloc, they have usually taken second place to politics. Take the case of Jerzy Pawlowski, Poland's great Olympic fencer.

Pawlowski finished second in the 1956 Melbourne games. He slipped to sixth at the 1960 Rome Olympics. Then in 1968, at Mexico City, he bounced back to win the gold medal. By that time he was a 35-year-old Polish army major.

In addition to his Olympic fencing victories, Pawlowski won the world sabre championship three times and was runner-up four times.

None of this meant much when, in 1981, the Polish government asked him to become a spy. He refused.

The Polish government, unhappy with their fencing and sabre star, accused him of *being* a spy. He wasn't, of course, but it made no difference. He received a sentence of 25 years in prison.

His name and exploits were ordered removed from all Polish books about the Olympics.

PRIORITIES

Football

The Harvard-Yale rivalry goes back a long way. It has always been intense. An early Yale coach, Tad Jones, caught the spirit of it when he said, "Gentlemen, you are now going out to play football against Harvard. Never again in your whole life will you do anything so important."

PRIORITIES

Football

Many sports fans wagged their heads sadly when Herschel Walker passed up his last year, and his degree, at the University of Georgia and signed a pro football contract instead. They saw it as another example of greed winning out over education.

But consider the facts: Herschel Walker was one of eight children whose father worked in a chalk mine in Wrightsville, Georgia. His mother worked in a garment factory. They were people to whom a dollar meant a great deal. And Herschel was being offered millions of dollars—literally, not figuratively—to forego that last year as a Georgia Bulldog.

Suppose he had turned down the pro offer and returned to Georgia. Suppose he had broken a leg or smashed a knee in his senior year. No pro career. What kind of a future? An education for what?

It's hard to imagine even the most dedicated student from an impoverished background refusing the kind of offer Herschel Walker received. College running backs may be bright and conscientious, but they're not philosopher-princes.

PRIORITIES

Football

You could guess Vince Lombardi's philosophy of life from one quotation—and not the one about winning being the only thing. He always felt that people judged the meaning of that statement too harshly.

He never disclaimed the following sentiment, though. "There are three important things in life," he said, "—family, religion, and the Green Bay Packers."

PRIORITIES

Football

According to Vince Lombardi, Max McGee was one of the greatest ends of all time. But according to Jerry Kramer, McGee was not entirely dependable.

In *Instant Replay*, Kramer tells about the time Max McGee disappeared for almost two months. It seems that Max and Fuzzy Thurston, a Green Bay guard, had gone into partnership to run a restaurant in Manitowoc, Wisconsin.

Not long after the place opened, Max vanished. He didn't get in touch with anyone, and his partner Fuzzy began to suspect foul play. He put tracers on the missing Max. He heard nothing at first. But in seven weeks or so, some of McGee's checks began arriving at his bank. They had been cashed at the Racquet Club in Miami.

Naturally, Fuzzy phoned the club and had McGee paged. When the missing end came to the phone, Fuzzy shouted, "Max, where the hell have you been?"

Max cut him short. "Hold it, Fuzz," he said. "I'm in the middle of a set. I'll call you back later."

PRIORITIES

Football

Notre Dame head football coach Frank Leahy used to ask his former players three basic questions: How do you feel? How's your mother? What's your weight?

He spoke to a former star of the Fighting Irish.

"How do you feel?" he asked.

The old-timer shrugged. "A little better," he said, "since my major operation. I wasn't getting around too good, but now I can move some."

"Great," Leahy said. "How's your mother?"

The ex-player said, "Well, my mother died a couple of months ago."

"Great," Leahy said. "What's your weight?"

"Uh, let's see," the player thought. "About 240."

Leahy gave him a disapproving look. "No wonder you don't look so good," he said. "You're five pounds overweight."

PRIORITIES

Golf

The golfer was telling his buddies that his wife had threatened to leave him if he didn't give up golf.

"That's terrible," said one of them. "What are you going to do?"

He thought for a moment and said. "I'm going to miss her."

PRIORITIES

Golf

Most stories about golf have to do with the game's supreme importance. Here's one that puts it in perspective. It's from Joey Adams, who says, "He plays golf in the low 70s—When it gets colder, he quits."

PUBLICITY

Auto Racing

Almost from the invention of the automobile, manufacturers felt that people expected a first-class car to be fast enough to beat the competition.

Early in the 20th century, a number of auto makers promoted their cars through racing. Three of these owner-racers were Frank Duryea, Alexander Winton, and Ransom Olds.

At the Detroit Edison Company, there was another young man who intended to build his own gasoline-powered cars. To do so, he resigned from his job as Detroit Edison's general superintendent. He started with two racing cars, which he called *999* and *Arrow*.

It was 1904, and the land speed record was 84.73 miles per hour. In a test run on Michigan's ice-covered Lake St. Clair, the *Arrow* seemed ready for its race against the record.

AAA officials were on hand as the car made its way onto the ice covering the lake. Spider Huff rode at the side of the young automaker as he revved up the *Arrow*, spun its wheels, and raced away. The car bounced wildly as it hit cracks, but it kept going, picking up speed.

The *Arrow* took the measured mile at 91.37 miles per hour, a new world record. The owner was exultant. The fame of the four-cylinder 70-horsepower machine—and of the man who made it—spread from coast to coast and around the world.

This convinced the *Arrow*'s owner-driver that speed was indeed good advertising. His name was Henry Ford.

PUBLICITY

Auto Racing

If anyone ever deserved a prize for self-promotion, it was Andy Granatelli. He started as a kid on the back streets of Chicago, offering to start stalled motorists' cars for a dime. He ended as the multimillionaire who owned STP and put that familiar red oval on every piece of racing equipment in sight.

Granatelli was always getting into trouble with the racing establishment. He put a turbine engine into an Indy race car. It infuriated the other drivers and owners, and it would have infuriated them even more if Parnelli Jones, his driver, had won the race. With only four laps to go—and miles in the lead—

Granatelli's big orange car rolled to a stop with a failed bearing in the gear case.

Undaunted, Granatelli published his autobiography a year or so later. Its title: *They Call Me Mister 500.* Well, they didn't call him any such thing. One disgusted reader said *"They Call Him Horatio Hornblower"* would have been more like it."

But maybe he was writing prophecy instead of history. Granatelli came back to Indy the next year with a more or less ordinary Lotus driven by Mario Andretti. Granatelli had ten other cars in the race too, but he didn't need them. Andretti took the checkered flag in the first place.

That might have been triumph enough for an ordinary ego. But Andy Granatelli needed more. He kissed his winning driver joyfully in Victory Lane—and the photo of it made the front page of many American newspapers. Later, he would use the picture as a centerpiece of his STP ads.

For the moment, though, his driver, Mario Andretti, had to carry the publicity ball. On the Speedway's PA system, he explained his victory: "I guess we just had more STP in our Ford engine than the other guy."

Sure, Mario. Sure, Andy. Thanks for the tip.

PUBLICITY

Baseball

When Mickey Mantle first came to the big leagues, he was tough to interview. He was wary and suspicious. Because of his potential, and because he played in New York, he got a tremendous amount of publicity. But he didn't help the reporters much. He seldom gave them good quotes.

That changed as Mantle matured. In 1962 he went to Florida early, before spring training, to act in a baseball movie called *Safe at Home.*

When the filming was done, a reporter asked him if he was glad it was over.

Mantle said, yes, he was. He added: "And I told them my next movie has to be a musical. I don't want to be typecast."

PUBLICITY

Basketball

Like most young basketball players, six-foot four-inch Nova Madison dreamed of playing before a national television audience.

But in college he had little chance of doing so. He played for Fairleigh Dickinson University in Madison, New Jersey, a Division III school. His audience was strictly local.

Then one night the freshman forward went up for a slam dunk. He took off too early and sailed over two defenders from Muhlenberg. Said Madison, "I think I panicked. . . . I thought they were going to cut my legs out from under me.'

Suddenly there was a thunderous shower of glass. No sooner had he taken his shot than the Plexiglas backboard exploded. His Darryl Dawkins imitation was as spectacular as any glass cloudburst ever filmed.

And it was filmed. Not by a cameraman from ABC or NBC, but by a student operating FDU's videotape recorder. Sports Information Director Tom Bonerbo took one look at the film and called the local media and national wire services.

Nova Madison wasn't hurt much, but he did have to have pieces of glass removed from his back. It was worth it. As he relaxed later, he watched the play on nationwide television and read about it in Associated Press dispatches.

It was a dream come true.

PUBLICITY

Boxing

Now for another side of Muhammad Ali. You'll recall that the ex-heavyweight champion was one of the great self-promoters of all time. The Greatest, by his own admission. His poetry is still quoted.

But back when Muhammad Ali was still Cassius Clay—back when he was 19 years old—he hadn't really developed his gift.

He was scheduled to fight the first main event of his career in Los Angeles, and ticket sales were dragging. The promoter of the fight decided to send the young boxer downtown to publicize the fight himself.

"Just tell them you're the greatest," the promoter said.

Clay started off downtown as instructed, but he soon returned to the promoter's office.

"I can't do it," he confessed. "It's embarrassing."

PUBLICITY

Boxing

Jake LaMotta, the Raging Bull of boxing, became quite a showbiz personality in his later years. Like a number of other boxers—Rocky Graziano, Sugar Ray Robinson, and Sugar Ray Leonard—he found the glare of the spotlight to his liking.

His one-liners are classics:

"My first wife divorced me because I clashed with the drapes."

"My wife used to ignore me all the time. And if there's one thing I can't stand, it's ignorance."

"I fought Sugar Ray Robinson so many times it's a wonder I don't have diabetes."

Not many boxers have had a movie made about their lives, but LaMotta did: *Raging Bull*. Robert DiNiro, playing the part of Jake LaMotta, won an Academy Award for Best Actor. If you've seen the movie, you'll agree with one of Jake's not-so-funny lines—"I fought like I didn't deserve to live."

PUBLICITY

Boxing

"Float like a butterfly, sting like a bee."

When Muhammad Ali broke into pro boxing under his birth name of Cassius Clay, he drew good crowds in Louisville, his hometown. But despite having won an Olympic gold medal, he drew very poorly in Las Vegas for a ten-round bout with Duke Sabedong. The arena was only a quarter full as Clay won on a decision.

At that point, the young boxer had won all ten of his pro matches, but he was no poet yet. That wrinkle would come later. He was still unknown except for the brief flurry of publicity surrounding the Olympics. Although he sometimes shouted "I'm the greatest!," not too many people were listening.

Red Greb, the Las Vegas promoter of the Sabedong fight, told young Clay that being an amateur champ just didn't sell tickets. "If you want to pack them in, Cassius," he said, "you gotta have a name."

Greb then mentioned that Gorgeous George, the wrestler, would be performing in the same arena the next night. Clay and his trainer, Angelo

Dundee, stayed for the wrestling match. At that moment in history, Gorgeous George had a big-box-office name, and the arena was full to overflowing when the wrestler made his gaudy entrance, robe glittering, golden locks gleaming.

After the match, Clay, Dundee, and Greb met Gorgeous George in the wrestler's dressing room. George was smart, articulate, and fully aware of the power of his outrageous image.

"It's my gimmick," he said. "I suppose without it this place would have been empty tonight—right, Red?"

Red agreed.

Gorgeous George added that you have to have the talent, too. Image alone isn't enough. But image is very, very important.

Cassius Clay listened intently as the famous wrestler talked about name recognition and how he had achieved it. Clay definitely felt he was the greatest—he wasn't just kidding about that—but now he also realized the immense value of publicity.

Years later, Angelo Dundee wrote: "George can never have dreamed of the effect his words were having, and that the young, polite black man would become the most famous human being in the whole darn world."

PUBLICITY

Football

The name Jimmy Snyder was known around Las Vegas before the 1969 Super Bowl game between the Baltimore Colts and the New York Jets. But Jimmy was just another oddsmaker and PR guy.

Jets' quarterback Joe Namath boldly guaranteed a victory for his team in 1969. Snyder, better known as Jimmy the Greek, didn't buy that prediction. The Greek told Dave Anderson of *The New York Times*, "It's the Colts by 17."

People believed the *Times* and the Greek. In fact, they bet the point margin up to 19 and a half.

Jimmy the Greek, like almost everyone else, was wrong. Namath was right. The Jets won the Super Bowl game 16 to 7. Even so, if you had put down your money and stuck with the Greek's 17 point spread, you would have won your bet.

People forgot that. All they remembered—and laughed about—was the Greek's idea of an easy Colts' victory. Shame on Jimmy! Sportswriters and fans talked about him. His name and his advice were on everyone's lips. Next year at the Super Bowl, there were signs making fun of him.

The Greek didn't care. What did it matter to him? By then he was a celebrity. He signed fourteen advertising endorsements and a network contract.

PUBLICITY

Football

Sportswriters are always looking for quotes and interesting angles. That puts a burden on the coaches and players. How many clever sayings or amusing anecdotes can the average linebacker come up with?

Carl Banks tossed the press a bombshell not long ago. At the age of four, he said, he'd murdered an aunt with a horseshoe. They gave him three years in prison. That didn't sound quite right, so the reporters kept after him.

Well, all right, Banks finally admitted. "I was just trying to entertain you guys."

PUBLICITY

Football

One of the most electrifying plays in college football history occurred when Tommy Lewis of Alabama came off the bench—literally—to tackle Rice's Dick Moegle as he roared by on what would have been a 95-yard touchdown run.

There's a sidelight to that play. As Moegle lay stunned after getting hit, the Rice Owls' trainer, Eddie Wojecki, rushed out to tend him.

"Are you okay, Dick?" the trainer asked.

"Yeah, I'm okay," said Moegle, more startled than hurt. "Let me just get up."

"No, no!" Wojecki said quickly. "Stay down a little more, Dick. We're on national TV, and I got a bunch of relatives back in Erie watching! This is the best chance we've ever had for national pub!"

So Dick Moegle rested another minute or so before he got up and let Wojecki lead him off the field.

PUBLICITY

Football/Boxing

Glynn (Bull) Rogers, a football player at Texas Christian University, was struck by the priorities of the media.

He said: "For three years I work and sweat at holding down a guard hole on the football team. Once in the great while, my name gets in the paper—usually when I do something wrong. Then I enter the Golden Gloves boxing tournament and score a technical knockout in the first round of my first fight. I get about a dozen pictures in the paper and columns and columns of comment. There just ain't no sense to it!"

PUBLICITY

Skiing

Any grand opening requires grand publicity.

The Union Pacific Railroad picked up the tab for developing the world-famous Sun Valley resort in Idaho. But it was Steve Hannagan, publicity dynamo, who sold Sun Valley to high society by getting a breathless article in *Life* magazine . . . some glamorous, widely circulated photos showing celebrities on the ski slopes . . . East Coast tie-ins with Sachs, Macy's, and Wanamaker's . . . and a Paramount movie about which everyone heard early and often that the gorgeous Alpine settings were really filmed in Sun Valley.

All this success came after an opening night fiasco—or something that could have been a fiasco except for the lemon-to-lemonade magic of Steve Hannagan.

Plenty of celebrities were on hand for the December grand opening banquet at Sun Valley. They included movie producer David O. Selznick and box-office stars Joan Bennett and Claudette Colbert. They didn't include Steve Hannagan, who hated snow.

Among the guests was one Charles F. Gore of Chicago. A young investment banker, Gore possessed good looks and lots of money, but no particular status. So when he barged in on a table with the stars of Hollywood—and presumed to ask one of the lovelies to dance—David O. Selznick put a quick stop to it.

He decked Mr. Gore with one solid punch to the eye.

Management at the elegant new resort was in despair The sophisticated opening dinner had been disgraced with fisticuffs. Someone thought to call Steve Hannagan with the bad news.

Bad news? Hannagan thought not. The press might downplay an uneventful opening, an ordinary press release. But how could it pass up a celebrity knockout? He wrote the headline himself:

"Sun Valley Opens with a Bang."

QUICK-THINKING

Auto Racing

Juan Manuel Fangio, son of a house painter in Argentina, became one of the world's greatest racing car drivers. He won the World Championship of auto racing in 1951, 1954, 1955, 1956, and 1957.

Remarkably enough, he retired from competition while still in good health. Most of his closest competitors in this dangerous sport died at the wheel. They died because of a fatal miscalculation, or another driver's error, or mechanical failure, or for no apparent reason at all.

Auto racing demands quick decisions and lightning-fast reflexes. Fangio had them. In the first Monaco Grand Prix after World War Two, he got a chance to demonstrate both.

He started the race brilliantly and was well in the lead when behind him, near the harbor, there was a bad pile-up.

He didn't know about the problem until he roared out of a tunnel and saw the yellow flag. A similar accident at this spot in 1936 flashed into his mind as he braked hard and watched for the marshal's directions.

The marshal for some reason sent him to the wrong side of the pile-up, and Fangio found his Alfa-Romeo completely blocked in.

Without a moment's hesitation, he jumped out of the car and ran to the rear. With his powerful arms he heaved the back wheels of the Alfa around—there is no reverse gear in these cars—and aimed it back the other way.

He jumped in, gunned the Alfa forward, and bore out around the wrecks. He still had 98 laps to go. Pouring it on, he far outdistanced the field, winning the Monaco Grand Prix with ease.

QUICK-THINKING

Baseball

Bill Mazer, sports broadcaster and trivia expert, was talking on the air with a young baseball fan. The kid mentioned that he had recently met Ralph Branca, a Brooklyn Dodger pitcher for many years. On some matter of opinion, he had told Branca, "That's what Bill Mazer says."

Branca's response was, "What does he know about sports?"

Mazer was stung when he heard about Branca's remark and snapped back: "I may not know much about sports, but I do know who threw the home-run ball to Bobby Thomson in the 1951 Dodgers-Giants playoff."

QUICK-THINKING

Baseball

When Rocky Bridges was managing the Giants' Triple-A farm club at Phoenix, his shortstop was Johnnie LeMaster. As a kid, LeMaster had lost the end of his little finger in an accident. The loss didn't affect his ability to play.

One night LeMaster was nicked by an inside pitch and started to trot down to first base. The umpire, Billy Lawson, called him back. He claimed the pitch had hit the bat.

Rocky Bridges came storming out of the dugout to argue. When he saw the argument was going nowhere, he turned to LeMaster and said, "Go ahead, show him your finger."

The shortstop help up his hand with the missing fingertip.

The umpire never missed a beat. He said, "Tell you what, Rocky. You find the rest of that finger—I'll give him first base."

QUICK-THINKING

Baseball

One night when Ron Luciano was umpiring a game in Pittsfield, Massachusetts, the badly scratched recording of "The Star-Spangled Banner" couldn't get past the first groove. It started out, "Oh, say can you see . . ."—then, "Oh, say can you see . . ." again. After four or five repetitions, a fan bellowed, "Well, I guess they know who's umpiring tonight!"

QUICK-THINKING

Baseball

Fran Healy, who caught for the Kansas City Royals in the 1970s, later moved on to the broadcasting booth. While covering a game between the Yankees and Blue Jays in Exhibition Stadium, Toronto, a flock of ducks landed on the field.

Healy seized the opportunity. "That's the first time I've ever seen a fowl in fair territory," he said.

QUICK-THINKING

Basketball

One of Bob Knight's habits as head basketball coach at Indiana University was to remind his players that Big Ten competition was a lot stiffer than what they'd seen in high school.

When Kreigh Smith was a sophomore at Indiana, Knight began calling the six-foot-seven kid "Tipton." The reason was that Smith came from the small town of Tipton in central Indiana. Knight's nickname was supposed to remind Smith that IU's schedule was tougher than the one he played at Tipton High School.

One day in practice, Kreigh Smith lost the player he was guarding. The player was Winston Morgan, who had gone to high school in the city of Anderson, Indiana, northeast of Indianapolis.

Knight jumped on Smith right away. He said, "Hey, Tipton, who are you supposed to be guarding?"

Kreigh Smith may have been lying in wait for the question. Without a moment's hesitation, he said, "Anderson."

QUICK-THINKING

Basketball

Mychal Thompson, a center on the Los Angeles Lakers, noticed the matchup of Seattle forward Xavier McDaniel with the Lakers' Orlando Woolridge. He said, "It's a coach's dream—X versus O."

QUICK-THINKING

Boxing

The airline flight attendant asked boxing champion Muhammad Ali to fasten his seat belt.

Ali said, "Superman don't need no seat belt."

The stewardess replied, "Superman don't need no airplane, either."

QUICK-THINKING

Golf

Lee Trevino tells a story about the golf course at Tenison Park in Dallas. It involves one of the big-money games in which thousands of dollars could change hands.

It seems that there were sometimes robberies on the more isolated holes. The thieves were aware that the players might be carrying large sums of money, and they laid their plans accordingly.

On this particular day, half a dozen gambling golfers had reached the far-off eighth hole when two men armed with shotguns appeared from the trees.

The golfers raised their hands. The robbers demanded money.

As the victims reached slowly into their pockets, one of them had an inspiration.

"Charlie," he said to one of his fellow golfers, "I owe you a thousand dollars. Here." He counted out the money and handed it to Charlie. "Now we're even."

QUICK-THINKING

Golf

The man was out hiking, and he wandered onto a golf course by mistake. As he was strolling along, a golf ball zoomed in and hit him on the head. He staggered around dazed, and then looked to see where the missile had come from. He saw a golfer in the distance.

"I'll sue you!" the man screamed. "I'll sue you for plenty! I'm thinking five million dollars right now."

The golfer shook his head disgustedly and shouted back: "Don't be ridiculous. Didn't you hear me say 'fore'?"

The man yelled, "I'll take it!"

QUICK-THINKING

Golf

A golfer who was having a bad time of it turned to his caddie and said. "You must be the worst caddie in the world."

"I doubt it," the caddie shot back. "That would be too much of a coincidence."

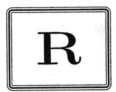

RELATIONSHIPS

Baseball

Jake Powell was an outfielder for the New York Yankees and Washington Senators. His greatest moments came in the 1936 World Series when his ten hits in 22 at-bats helped the Yankees overpower the New York Giants.

Unfortunately, Jake had a tendency to shoot from the lip. On a radio interview in Chicago, he made a thoughtless remark about blacks that outraged thousands of people across the country. There was talk of boycotting games in which he played.

Jake figured he had to do something to make up for what he'd said. When the Yankees returned to New York, he went to the northern edge of Harlem. It was nighttime, and Jake was alone. He began to work his way south, tavern by tavern, setting up drinks for the house along the way. In each place, he apologized for his remark. He said it was wrong, and he was sorry.

No one asked him to do it. He was taking a real risk in a section of town where he was anything but popular. Jake said and did some stupid things in his life. In one way, this late-night tour of Harlem was probably one of them. But in another way, it's hard not to admire what he did

RELATIONSHIPS

Baseball

Joe Pepitone, best known as a so-so Yankee first basemen, finished his career with the Chicago Cubs. One day his Cub teammates got into a brawl with the San Francisco Giants. Pepitone stood apart from the action, looking on

He felt a tap on his shoulder and turned to see the Giants' most imposing giant, Willie McCovey, at his elbow.

"Hey, Willie," Pepitone said quickly. "I'm on your side. I like the guys on your team better than the guys on mine."

RELATIONSHIPS

Basketball

Beano Cook, sports information director at Pitt, on why a star basketball player had quit college: "He got tired of his dad writing him for money."

RELATIONSHIPS

Football

Bart Starr, the Green Bay Packers' great quarterback, tells of the time he came home in a foul mood. He burst angrily into the house, yelled at one of his children, spanked another one, and snarled at his wife for not mailing some letters.

His wife asked him what was the matter.

He shouted that he was busy, busy, busy. "I've got a jillion things to do," he complained. And he wasn't getting them done. He told her he had to go to a banquet that night in Appleton.

She asked what kind of banquet.

Bart, still upset by his various commitments, barked irritably, "I'm receiving a nice-guy award."

RESOURCEFULNESS

Football

When Herman Hickman coached football at Yale, he had trouble getting his players to his 4:00 p.m. practice on time. At Yale, they took their studies seriously, and sometimes the whole squad wouldn't be on hand for practice until 4:30.

Hickman's solution was simple and effective. Whenever his entire squad was assembled—whether at 4:05 or 4:35—he would turn the clock back to 4:00 p.m and start the practice

RESOURCEFULNESS

Football

Clever deception is important in football. Of course, some forms of deception are more clever than others. Back in 1910, Kid Woodruff, quarterback of the Georgia Bulldogs, threw one of the more deceptive passes of all time.

The game was being played at Franklin, Tennessee, against the Sewanee Tigers. The Tigers were leading 15 to 6 in the final quarter. Disaster was closing in on the Georgia Bulldogs just as surely as a dense fog was settling in on the playing field.

Kid Woodruff decided to take advantage of the lowering clouds. On the snap from center, he dropped back to pass, all but disappearing in the gray mist. He cradled the ball in one arm, ripped off his brown-leather helmet, and fired it deep toward the left sideline—and the waiting arms of a Bulldog receiver.

The defensive backs tore off to the left.

Woodruff then took the football and tossed an easy pass to halfback Bob McWhorter, who raced 30 yards down the right sideline for a touchdown.

RESOURCEFULNESS

Hockey

Jacques Plante, goalie of the Montreal Canadiens for more than a decade, had plenty of chances to observe opponents trying to put the puck past him.

He said, "The difference between the great scorers and the average scorers is that the great ones can change their minds in the wink of an eye. . . . High scorers in hockey are always looking for new holes."

RESOURCEFULNESS

Hunting

The two hunters had struck off into the woods south of Forkston. By the time they had bagged their limit of rabbits, they knew they were lost.

"Now what do we do?" asked one of them worriedly. "We'll never find our way out of here by dark."

"No problem," said the other. "We'll just shoot one more rabbit, and the game warden'll find us within five minutes."

RETIREMENT

Baseball

When George Weiss retired from the Yankee front office, he spent most of his time at his home in Greenwich, Connecticut. His wife, Hazel, said, "I married George for better or for worse, but not for lunch."

RETIREMENT

Boxing

The championship boxing match between Gentleman Jim Corbett and the aging John L. Sullivan lasted 21 rounds. When it ended, John the Great lay on the canvas listening to the referee complete the ten count over him for the first time in his career. The heavyweight title went to Corbett.

When John L. got to his feet, he told the crowd what many other boxers might have admitted, but few ever did. He said, "I fought once too often."

RETIREMENT

Football

Fran Tarkenton, a brilliant quarterback of seasons past, wasn't talking about retirement when he made this remark. But it certainly fits. He said, "It's a lonesome walk to the sidelines, especially when thousands of people are cheering your replacement "

RETIREMENT

Golf

As Jack Nicklaus reached his forties, he found it increasingly hard to put in the time he needed to keep his golf fame at its peak. His five children and many business interests demanded countless hours that in earlier years would have gone into practice. The Golden Bear continued to compete in tournaments, but not with his earlier success.

Chi Chi Rodriguez was moved to remark that this made Jack Nicklaus "a legend in his spare time."

RETIREMENT

Golf

Our best-known golfing President prior to Jerry Ford was Dwight D. Eisenhower. Political cartoonists were forever showing Ike on the links.

After he left the White House, a reporter asked him if retirement from politics had affected his golf game.

"Yes," Ike replied. "A lot more people beat me now."

RETIREMENT

Hockey

Hockey star Ken Dryden said, "If it is true that a sports career prolongs adolescence, it is also true that when that career ends, it deposits a player into premature middle age."

RETIREMENT

Marathoning

"What do you do when the main thing in your life disappears?" asks Grete Waitz. "Competitive running has been my life for over 15 years. What will my life be like without it?"

RETIREMENT

Track

In the movie *Chariots of Fire*, one of the two main characters is track star Harold Abrahams of Great Britain. If you saw the movie, you'll recall that Abrahams won the 100-meter dash at the 1924 Paris Olympics. He wasn't expected to win.

Abrahams, running better than ever before in his life, tied the Olympic record of 10.6 seconds in the quarterfinals and semifinals. By that point, he realized he had a real shot at the Olympic gold.

He got off to a perfect start, stayed even for the first half of the race, and then pulled ahead to win by two feet.

Abrahams had never run so well before; he would never run so well again. A year later he injured his thigh while long-jumping and retired from competition. He wrote: "How many people find it almost impossible to retire at the right time? Would I have gone downhill, and tried to go on? That was the decision I never had to make; it was made for me. Rather painfully, but it was made."

Retirement for Abrahams hardly meant being put out to pasture. He became a lawyer, a writer, a radio commentator, and president of the British Amateur Athletic Association.

SARCASM

Baseball

About Don Buddin, an error-prone shortstop for the Red Sox, Cliff Keane of the *Boston Globe* wrote that he should be granted an "E-6" license plate.

SARCASM

Baseball

Ballplayers sometimes get annoyed with the questions asked them by sportswriters. They respond in various ways. Or they don't respond at all.

Spaceman Bill Lee, while pitching for the Boston Red Sox, was often good for a quotable comeback.

In the 1975 World Series between the Red Sox and Cincinnati's Big Red Machine, the Sox won the first game on Luis Tiant's 6 to 0 shutout. They were leading 2–1 in the ninth inning of the second game when a Johnny Bench double sparked a Cincinnati rally. The Reds went on to win the game 3 to 2.

After the game, a writer asked Bill Lee to sum up the Series so far.

Lee thought for a moment and replied, "It's tied."

SARCASM

Baseball

Gabby Hartnett, the Hall of Fame catcher, was behind the plate in his first professional game. The first baserunner for the other team, wanting to test Hartnett's arm, took off for second base.

Hartnett unleashed a throw that cleared the second baseman's head by a mile. The centerfielder took it on the first hop and threw it back in.

When the inning ended, Hartnett's manager motioned to him. "Come here, young man," he said. "I just want to let you know that they slide in this league—they don't fly."

SARCASM

Baseball

The humor of Don Rickles is the kind that roasts. In regard to the perennial L.A. Dodger manager, he said, "Tommy Lasorda figures that if the Dodgers blow the pennant again, he can tie a cord around his neck and work as a balloon."

SARCASM

Basketball

Phil Johnson, basketball coach at Weber State, commenting on his teams 18–5 record: "I don't think we've been beaten by officials more than five times this season."

SARCASM

Basketball

Walt Bellamy, the basketball star, had a habit of referring to himself in the third person. Instead of telling a referee, "I was fouled on that play," he would say, "Walter was fouled on that play."

This tended to annoy referees. One who was annoyed was Norm Drucker. In a game Drucker was refereeing, Bellamy kept saying, "Norm, Russell just fouled Walter." Or, "Hey, that was a foul on Walter." Or, "Walter just got fouled again."

Finally, the referee told him to shut up. If Bellamy complained one more time, Drucker said, he'd get a technical called on him.

The warning didn't help. A few plays later, Bellamy said. "Didn't you see that Walter was fouled?"

Drucker blew his whistle. He walked past Bellamy and said, "Bellamy, tell Walter that I just called a technical on Walter."

SARCASM

Fishing

The rowboat rocked gently in the drizzly gray dawn. The man and his wife had been there for an hour. The fish weren't biting, but the cold breeze was.

She said with a shiver, "Tell me again how much fun we're having. I keep forgetting."

SARCASM

Football

Knute Rockne, the great Notre Dame football coach, was known for his locker room pep talks. They could be sentimental, or they could be sarcastic.

Once after the team had taken a bad drubbing in the first half of a game, Rockne poked his head in the door of the locker room where the players awaited the worst.

Rockne said quietly, "Oh, excuse me, ladies! I thought this was the Notre Dame team."

SARCASM

Football

As a guard and linebacker for the Cleveland Browns, Chuck Noll did everything by the numbers. He was intense and competitive, but he was not one to innovate or break the rules. Later as a coach, he was just as inflexible.

Roy Blount, Jr., in his book about the Pittsburgh Steelers, wrote: "I can just see the movie ads for *The Chuck Noll Story*—'He came out of Cleveland, well-schooled in techniques.' "

SARCASM

Football

Gene Klein, the owner of the San Diego Chargers, had mixed feelings about his team from the very beginning.

"The first Chargers' roster," he would say, "included great names such as Royce Womble, Bobby Clatterburg, and Blanche Martin."

If the listener seemed a bit puzzled, he would add, "They weren't great *players*, just great *names*."

SARCASM

Football

Once when John Bodie was quarterbacking the San Francisco 49ers, he thought he'd been roughed by the Rams' Deacon Jones. He complained to referee Norm Schachter.

Schachter said he wasn't roughed and that Deacon Jones couldn't avoid the collision. But Bodie kept on complaining, waving, and pointing. Finally, Schachter told him to knock it off and play ball.

Bodie calmed down and said evenly, "No hard feelings, Norm. I still think you're the second best referee in the National Football League."

Schachter thought that one over. "I'm the second best?"

"That's right," Bodie said.

"So who do you think is the best?"

Bodie was lying in wait for the question. He said, "All the other referees are tied for first."

SARCASM

Golf

Charles Price, a golfer and golf writer who has seen golf courses through-out the world, makes a distinction between golf clubs and country clubs. Golf clubs he likes. Country clubs he doesn't.

He describes the typical American country club in various unflattering ways, mostly having to do with size. One distinctive feature of a country club, he says, is the dining room. It is "the size of an Elks hall" and "run by a *maitre d'* who used to be a mess sergeant and who thinks he's French."

If you can't tell the difference between a golf club (a place where members play golf) and a country club (a place where members hold wedding receptions), you probably belong to a country club.

SARCASM

Golf

Chi Chi Rodriguez, a tiny but personable golfer and a top pro in his day, was playing an exhibition match at West Point.

A beefy cadet shouted, "Hey, Chi Chi! How come a little squirt like you got to be a golf star?"

Now, Chi Chi Rodriguez came from a dirt-poor family on a sugar plantation in Puerto Rico, but he knew the origin of West Point cadets.

He smiled pleasantly and said. "My Congressman appointed me."

SARCASM

Hockey

Eddie Shore of the Boston Bruins was one of the best defensemen who ever played in the National Hockey League. Naturally, other teams were eager to obtain his services. One of them was Colonel John Hammond, the owner of the New York Rangers.

Now, Hammond, like many owners before and since, was none too shrewd about such things. He had a young defenseman named Myles Lane that he was willing to give up in a trade for Shore. It was a ridiculous idea—Shore was a superstar, and Lane was an average player.

But Hammond went ahead. He told his manager, Lester Patrick, to make the offer. Patrick knew it was silly, but he did as he was told. He wired the offer: Myles Lane for Eddie Shore.

Art Ross, the manager of the Bruins, couldn't believe it. Myles *Who?* For the great Eddie Shore?

He wired back an answer that has become a classic: "You are so many Myles from Shore you need a life preserver."

SARCASM

Hunting

Riding to the hounds held no fascination for Oscar Wilde, the Irish playwright. He defined fox hunting as "the pursuit of the uneatable by the unspeakable."

SECRECY

Baseball

Sports columnists, like other reporters, sometimes have to conceal the identity of their sources.

Mike McAlary of the *New York Daily News* was trying to do that, but only halfheartedly, when he reported the latest trouble for Billy Martin, famed manager, dirt-kicker, and marshmallow-salesman-basher.

Mike attributed his information to—quote—"an anonymous Yankee owner."

He conceded that this pretty much killed his relationship with Yankee owner George Steinbrenner

SECRECY

Sailing

Nathaniel Greene Herreshoff of Bristol, Rhode Island, designed and built six America's Cup defenders from 1893 and 1920. The well-heeled syndicates that paid for Herreshoff's boats included two Morgans, two Belmonts, and three Vanderbilts. This was before the days of federal income taxes, and private individuals controlled enormous wealth. Corporate sponsorship was a thing of the future.

Herreshoff, known as the Wizard of Bristol, was as strong an individualist as his wealthy clients. Herreshoff believed in secrecy. He built his boats under tight security, and he treated the press as his mortal enemy.

While building the *Reliance* for the 1903 race, a reporter from Boston asked Herreshoff for his opinion of the new boat.

The Wizard of Bristol replied, "I have nothing to say."

The reporter persisted. "Would the *Reliance* beat the *Constitution*?"

The great man said nothing

Well, continued the reporter, "What is your opinion of *Shamrock III?*" That was the new British entry.

Again the Wizard spoke not a word.

The reporter could tell that the interview was over. "Good day, Mr. Herreshoff," he said.

"Good day, sir," the designer said. Herreshoff began to walk away and then turned back. He had one request to make of the Boston reporter. "Please," he said, "do not print any more information than I have given you."

SELF-CONFIDENCE

Auto Racing

The Daytona 500 is the Indianapolis of stock car racing. Richard Petty won the race seven times.

But it was while talking about a lesser race—at Martinsville, Virginia—that he displayed his true champion's confidence. "When people go to Martinsville," he said, "they just figure on racing second. They don't go to win, because they know I'm going to win the race. And I know it, too."

SELF-CONFIDENCE

Baseball

Heinie Mueller was a pretty fair outfielder for the St. Louis Cardinals. He never made it to the Baseball Hall of Fame, but it wasn't for lack of confidence. As a rookie, he wanted manager Branch Rickey to look him over. Rickey agreed.

"I understand you're quite a ballplayer," Rickey said.

"Yes, Mr. Rickey."

"As good an outfielder as Tris Speaker?"

"Yes, Mr. Rickey."

"Can you run bases like Ty Cobb?"

"Yes, Mr. Rickey."

"I suppose you can hit like Home Run Baker?"

"Yes, Mr. Rickey."

The manager had never heard a better resume than that. "Judas Priest!" he exclaimed.

"I never seen him," said Heinie "but I'm just as good as he is "

SELF-CONFIDENCE

Baseball

Bill Klem, the umpire, is well known for his remark, "I never missed one in my heart." He had an unshakable faith in himself. He made his calls with authority and defended them with dignity.

One afternoon at Wrigley Field, he was behind the plate for a game between the Cubs and the Giants. A Giants' batter cracked a long drive down the left-field foul line, and the ball rattled off the scoreboard.

Now, this scoreboard had been installed after the foul line was marked. Consequently, the foul line stopped at the base of the scoreboard and resumed at the top. For a drive bouncing off it, fair or foul could only be guessed at.

"Foul ball!" Klem barked.

The Giants protested, but to no avail.

Next day a park attendant approached Klem. He told him that after the previous day's game the Giants' manager had asked him to examine the scoreboard to see where the ball had hit.

"You know," the attendant said, his voice filled with awe, "it was foul by two inches."

"Of course I know," Klem snapped. "That's why I called it that way."

SELF-CONFIDENCE

Golf

Walter Hagen was one of the great showmen of golf. He had a lofty ego and a taste for the good life. Once after winning the Canadian Open, he wired ahead to a Montreal hotel, "Fill one bathtub with champagne."

As a golfer Hagen was not in a class with Bobby Jones, but as a self-assured man about town he was in a class by himself. One morning a fan spotted him in front of a Long Island hotel. The golfer was wearing a tuxedo and was evidently returning from an all-night tour of Manhattan speakeasies.

That would have been common enough, but Hagen was scheduled to play in the final round of the PGA tournament that day. His opponent was Leo Diegel.

"Good morning," Hagen said cheerfully to the fan.

The fan was taken aback. How could this bon vivant expect to play championship golf in a few short hours? The fan blurted out what was on his mind. "Do you know that Diegel has been in bed since ten o'clock last night?"

Hagen shrugged. "He may have been in bed," he said. "But he hasn't been sleeping."

SELF-CONFIDENCE

Tennis

Bill Tilden, one of the great tennis stars of all-time, was an artist and a showman on the court. He seldom got angry at his rival or the crowd, but when he did he put on an act that no one has ever been able to match.

He would take five tennis balls in one hand—his hands were enormous—and then start to serve. The first ball—wham! Fifteen-love. The second ball—wham! Thirty-love. The third ball—wham! Forty-love. The fourth ball—Game. At that, he would toss the fifth ball aside.

Every top athlete has self-confidence, but it is hard to imagine any beyond that of a tennis player promising four straight aces.

SELF-IMAGE

Baseball

It pays to think well of yourself, but it's best not to overdo it. Harold Parrott, whose *Lords of Baseball* takes a few swipes at baseball owners and executives, tells this tale about a somewhat conceited publicity man, Red Patterson.

While Patterson was doing publicity for the New York Yankees, he started the practice of tape-measuring home runs. It was a clever gimmick. The resident Yankee slugger at the time was Mickey Mantle, and there's not much doubt that the tape measure helped to build Mantle's reputation. Patterson certainly felt that it did.

Following a fight with Yankee management, Red left the organization, joining the publicity department of the Dodgers.

Telegrams and letters of congratulation began to flow in from people who had known him with the Yanks. Red worked his way through the stack, but then voiced his despair.

"Can you imagine?" he said to Parrott. "Not a word from Mantle!"

Parrot wasn't surprised. In fact, he laughed, knowing that ballplayers are not very high on sentiment. At that Patterson began to sputter:

"But . . . but . . . ," the enormity of Mickey's insult blocked his speech. Then he got it out: "I *made* Mantle!" he said.

SELF-IMAGE

Baseball

Leon Wagner, known as Daddy Wags, was a journeyman outfielder for the Angels and Indians. In 1967 he was nearing the end of his playing career and having only a so-so season. Cleveland's manager, Joe Adcock, didn't have much sympathy for Daddy Wags.

Wagner explained to a reporter that Adcock liked to work on a player's weaknesses. "My problem," said Daddy Wags, "is I don't have a weakness. But I'm trying to develop one so Adcock can work on it."

SELF-IMAGE

Football

How large an ego does a coach at a major university need? Lou Holtz, head football coach at Notre Dame and before that at North Carolina State, tells a revealing story about himself.

"I was at a convention just after taking the job at North Carolina State," he says, "and I was talking to Wayne Hardin, who was coach at Temple.

He said, "Lou, do you think you're the best coach in the country?"

Holtz answered, "No way. I'm not even in the top ten."

"Well," Hardin said, "North Carolina State hired you because they think you are. If you don't act like you are, you shouldn't even be coaching."

SELF-IMAGE

Sailing

People who know Ted Turner as a broadcasting mogul sometimes tend to forget that he is also a noted yachtsman. Wearing his sportsman's cap, he has said, "If I just had some humility, I'd be perfect."

SELF-IMAGE

Soccer

If you have two of the greatest soccer players in the world on one team—
and if those players come from different countries—you may have problems.

Coach Gordon Bradley of the New York Cosmos faced such problems
when his team acquired Giorgio Chinaglia of Italy. The Cosmos already had the
incomparable Pele from Brazil.

How could coach Bradley use both players to best advantage? Well,
Bradley wanted Pele to lay back, allowing Chinaglia to get a clear shot at the
net. But Pele wouldn't do it—he insisted on moving in near the goal.

This precipitated a crisis, and, as is customary in such cases, the coach
was fired.

It didn't solve the problem, but Pele's retirement did.

The resentments lingered, though. Pele had once asked Chinaglia, "Why
do you shoot at such bad angles?"

The question was too much for the proud Italian. "Chinaglia has no bad
angles," he said.

SPORTSMANSHIP

Baseball

Most pitchers will admit that they occasionally throw at a batter. Some
are outspoken about it, claiming that intimidation is part of the game. The
batter, they say, is out to take the pitcher's job away from him. It's a tough
business, and losers don't last. These pitchers don't consider it a mark of poor
sportsmanship to aim at the hitter's head. It's a mark of good sense.

Walter Johnson didn't buy that view. He was well aware that a fast ball
could hurt a player seriously, and possibly even end his career. And since
Johnson had the most explosive fast ball in the game—some say his was the
fastest of all time—he never threw a duster on purpose.

Batters knew this about Johnson, but the knowledge did them precious
little good. "The Big Train," as he was called, won 416 games in his long
career, second only to Cy Young.

Could the batter afford to dig in on Johnson? Not really. Even though The
Big Train wouldn't hit a batter intentionally, he might hit him by mistake. In
fact, Johnson hit more batters—206—than anybody else in major league

history. He led the American League in wild pitches a number of times. And he once uncorked four wild pitches in a single inning.

Yet no one ever doubted that Walter Johnson was a true sportsman. He was soft-spoken. He never argued with umpires. He always seemed like the good-natured farm boy he had once been. And he certainly never planned on mowing down the man at the plate with a beanball.

SPORTSMANSHIP

General

When the One Great Scorer comes to write against your name—
He marks—not that you won or lost—but how you played the game.
—Grantland Rice

SUCCESS

Auto Racing

Jackie Stewart became a television celebrity. He was lucky. Most of the great auto racing drivers haven't lived long enough to do that.

Jackie was a terrific driver, three times World Champion. He was also smart. He knew that if he kept racing long enough, the odds were grimly against him. Sooner or later, something would go wrong—something fatal. He had seen it happen all around him.

In fact, his first thoughts of retirement probably occurred the year after he won his first world championship. In that year, 1970, Jackie's good friend, Karl-Jochen Rindt, was killed in a terrible accident during practice at Monza. Stewart was badly shaken by his friend's death, but he went on racing.

He kept winning, earning money, and thinking about retirement. He decided he would get out of racing after the 1973 season. The last event of the year was the United States Grand Prix at Watkins Glen, New York. He would race in it and then quit.

By the time of the Watkins Glen race, Jackie Stewart had already clinched the 1973 World Championship. He could go easy in his final race. But his teammate couldn't. His teammate was the brilliant young French driver, Francois Cevert.

Cevert was a rising star—on his way to ranking fourth in the world that year, not far behind Stewart himself. He would never rank higher than fourth, though. On a practice run at Watkins Glen, Cevert lost control of his car. It crashed at high speed, killing the young driver instantly.

Stewart's team withdrew from the race. Heartbroken, Jackie retired as planned, one race short of completing the '73 season. He was at the very top of his form.

SUCCESS

Baseball

Dave Heaverlo, once a journeyman pitcher in the majors, on how he got the Oakland A's to trade him: "I tried growing a beard. That didn't work. I became the player rep. That didn't work. Then I bought a house. That worked."

SUCCESS

Baseball

Ruly Carpenter, former Philadelphia Phillies owner, on success: "I'm going to write a book, *How to Make a Small Fortune in Baseball*. First, you start with a large fortune. . . ."

SUCCESS

Baseball

Celebrities become experts. Magically. There's nothing new about it, and each new celebrity gets the treatment.

Oakland A's pitcher Vida Blue became a celebrity in the early 1970s. The media attention bewildered him. He said, "It's a weird scene. You win a few baseball games, and all of a sudden you're surrounded by reporters and TV men with cameras asking you about Vietnam and race relations."

SUCCESS

Football

"A tie," Bear Bryant used to say, "is like kissing your sister."

Bryant had plenty of experience to go by. He was a head coach in college football for 38 seasons, from 1945 through 1982. He led his teams to 323 wins against 85 losses and 17 sister-kissing ties. A recent biography is entitled *The Legend of Bear Bryant*, and no wonder. His life was the stuff of legend.

Think of it: In 38 seasons as head coach, Bear Bryant had one losing season. Just one. And that season—his first at Texas A&M—is itself the stuff of legend.

Here's the basic story. In 1954 Bryant had left the University of Kentucky in an ill temper after eight winning seasons. He had finally learned that in the State of Kentucky basketball (and Adolph Rupp) were bigger than football (and Bear Bryant).

He quit on short notice and inherited a Texas A&M team that was, plain and simple, bad. They lost their first game 41 to 9 to Texas Tech. Bryant had pushed his players to the limit and beyond in training, and he accepted full responsibility. "I took it away from them in practice," he said.

The next week, a revived A&M team held a strong Oklahoma State squad to 14 points, but they lost again, 14 to 6. This was a triumph of sorts, despite the loss, and a tribute to Bryant's ability to gain his players' respect in an hour of despair.

Looking at the schedule, there was still some doubt that A&M could win a game all year.

The next week, they played the Georgia Bulldogs in Athens. Sportswriters from Atlanta were astonished to find only 29 Aggies in uniform on the field. One writer asked Bear Bryant, "Coach, is this all the players you got?"

Bryant fired back, "No, these are the ones who want to play."

The fact is that the Bear's training program, conducted off campus in Junction, Texas, had driven player after player from the camp. Bryant pushed his players mercilessly—always pushed them. The Aggies weren't used to it, and even some potential stars quit on their new coach. For the Georgia game, there were 29 survivors.

The 29 survivors beat the tough Georgia Bulldogs 6 to 0. Bryant danced a jig in the locker room.

The A&M team never won another game the rest of the season, but they held their opponents close.

Two years later—only two—the Aggies were nine and zero, with one tie.

Pretty classy: from doormat to national power in two years—really in one year, because they were seven and two in Bryant's second year at A&M. It was a rebuilding effort of stunning effectiveness.

Twenty-five years down the road, all but seven of those 29 hardy A&M survivors of 1954 came to Junction, Texas, for a reunion with coach Bryant. It isn't often you have a nostalgic gathering of football players who won one game and lost nine a quarter of a century earlier. But this reunion was touching and appropriate. By then Bear Bryant was recognized as perhaps the best college football coach who ever lived.

SUCCESS

Mountaineering

George Mallory, a world-famous mountain climber, made a number of spectacular ascents in the Alps. He then tackled Mt. Everest, which at the time had never been successfully climbed. On his third expedition, some believe he may have succeeded, but he also disappeared.

Earlier he had written: "Have we vanquished an enemy? None but ourselves. Have we gained a success? That word means nothing here . . . We have achieved an ultimate satisfaction."

SURPRISE

Baseball

The College World Series in Omaha is always an exciting event. It's strictly amateur, although a few of the ballplayers each year make it to the majors. Some of the plays in the Series aren't ones you'd be likely to see in a major league game.

Take the Grand Illusion play. The University of Miami Hurricanes pulled it off against Wichita State. Here's how they did it.

With Wichita State's top base-stealer on first base, the Miami pitcher stepped off the rubber and faked a throw to first. The baserunner dived back. As he did, Miami's first basemen leapt over him, reaching—or so it seemed—for a bad throw. The Miami players on the field shouted and pointed toward the rightfield corner. Even the bat girl was pointing, looking upset. Players down the line in the Miami bullpen scattered as if to get out of the way of the errant throw.

The Wichita State baserunner jumped to his feet and took off for second. Miami's pitcher then tossed easily to second base for the putout.

One of the Miami players explained, "We only practiced it twice, because everyone was laughing too hard."

They didn't laugh very hard in the Wichita State dugout.

SURPRISE

Baseball

Bobby Mattick managed the Toronto Blue Jays for a while. He never had much success, and he found it easy to get discouraged. One day his team was far behind, which was nothing new. There were two outs in the inning.

Alfredo Griffin, the Blue Jays' shortstop, had reached second base and was dancing off the bag. But one run wouldn't mean anything at this point. The Jays needed a bunch of runs.

Mattick surveyed the scene without much hope. He crossed his arms in frustration.

On the next pitch, Alfredo Griffin sprinted for third. It startled the pitcher. It startled Bobby Mattick. Griffin slid into third safely. But the play made no sense. What did Griffin think he was doing?

As it turned out, Griffin was surprised too. So was the Blue Jays' third base coach, who had relayed the steal sign to him.

That's right. The steal sign that day was the manager's crossed arms in the dugout. Mattick, who was sometimes absentminded, had forgotten it.

SURPRISE

Baseball

One day Yogi Berra was standing outside Al Lang Field in St. Petersburg, Florida. It was a hot day, and Yogi was lightly attired in slacks and a polo shirt.

Two elderly ladies recognized Yogi, and one of them said, "Good afternoon. You look mighty cool today."

Yogi replied, "Thank you, ma'am. You don't look so hot yourself."

SURPRISE

Baseball/Football

Ron Luciano, the umpire with the fastest pen in baseball, once played pro football for the Detroit Lions. He was often injured and, partly because of that, he didn't have much of a football career. At one point he heard rumors that the Lions were moving him from tackle to guard or, possibly, center.

As Ron tells it, he went to head coach and told him he was willing to play wherever it would do the Lions the most good.

Luciano concludes ruefully, "It turned out to be Minnesota."

SURPRISE

Baseball

Among the great flakes of baseball was Frenchy Bordagaray, a Dodger outfielder of the '30s and '40s. Once in a dispute with an umpire, Frenchy took aim and spit at the offending arbiter.

The league found his action less than amusing and fined him five hundred dollars, which was big money in those days.

Frenchy said, "Okay, maybe I did wrong." But he thought the penalty was way too steep. He said, "The fine was more than I expectorated."

SURPRISE

Basketball

In a game between the New York Knicks and San Francisco Warriors, a flurry of fists under the basket left the Warriors' Rick Barry minus one tooth.

Play was stopped while everyone scouted around on the floor for the missing tooth. No one found it.

Barry put the blame for his misfortune on Walt Bellamy, but the Knicks knew better. Walt, or "Bells" as they called him, wasn't one to throw punches.

At half-time Willis Reed walked over to Knicks' trainer Danny Whelan. He held out his hand, and Danny looked at it.

"I think you need a dentist, not a trainer," Danny said with a smile.

Reed had played most of the first half with Rick Barry's tooth implanted in his knuckle.

SURPRISE

Fishing

Ernest Schwiebert, a noted fisherman and writer, tells this story about his boyhood days fishing the Little South Branch of the Pere Marquette River in Michigan.

He and his father awoke to discover a man and his two sons fishing worms just below their campsite. They decided to "Tom Sawyer" the trio— that is, to try to get them to fish someplace else.

"Had any luck this morning?" Schwiebert's father asked.

The bait-fisherman shook his head. "Nothing."

"Well, it's not good worm-fishing water."

That seemed to puzzle the man.

"It's pretty good dry-fly water," Schwiebert's father explained. He suggested there was better worm-fishing up at Baldwin.

The man seemed interested. "Where?" he wanted to know.

Young Schweibert had an answer for that. "Try the channel between the spillways," he advised. He'd once seen some good-sized brown trout there. He'd never caught any, and neither had his father, but they were there. Or had been.

"We're much obliged," the man said, and off he went with his two sons in their battered Plymouth.

Schweibert and his father settled down to their own dry-fly fishing. They did well and stayed for some time.

Later in the day, a car stopped by the river. A battered Plymouth. The man got out and shouted, "Sure want to thank you folks." He then started to walk toward the trunk of his car.

Schweibert and his father were a little nervous. They wondered what the man could be up to.

The man opened the Plymouth's trunk, yelled "Yessir!" and pulled out an eight-pound, 30-inch brown trout.

They had caught it under the spillway, exactly where they'd been told to fish.

"Can't thank you enough!" one of the boys shouted happily

SURPRISE

Football

Coaches like to feel in control. They can do without surprises. But sometimes they get surprised anyway, even if the surprise is only a practical joke.

One Friday, football coach John Madden was calling out the positions of the players on his punt return unit. This was the usual weekly meeting, and the players were simply shouting back their names.

Madden boomed, "Left end." The response should have been "Hendricks."

At that exact moment Ron Wolf, the club's director of operations, leaned into the room.

"John," he said, "you've got an important phone call."

Concerned, Madden grabbed a nearby phone and picked it up.

"Hendricks!" barked the left end's voice through the receiver.

SURPRISE

Football

General admission tickets to the first Rose Bowl game cost 50 cents. Box seats went for two dollars. And all 8,000 people who were there in Pasadena, California, on January 1, 1902, got their money's worth.

The game matched Stanford against the University of Michigan, with its "Point-a-Minute" offense and brick-wall defense. The temperature stood at almost 90 degrees as the game got underway. At first it looked as if Stanford might have a chance. The Michigan Wolverine's vaunted offense couldn't get going.

But Michigan had a new play ready. Eight Wolverines lined up to the right of the center. Only quarterback Boss Weeks and halfback Willie Heston were directly behind center. The ball was snapped to Weeks who pitched back to Heston.

The whole Michigan team swept right in what was supposed to look like an irresistible wave. Heston took one step with the wave, and then reversed and raced wide to the left. The shocked Stanford defense recovered, but not before Heston had ripped off 40 yards.

It was football's first bootleg play, and it set the pattern for the rest of the afternoon. With six minutes remaining in the game, Michigan led 49 to 0. The

Stanford captain announced that his team was exhausted. If Michigan would like to call it a day, Stanford was willing.

The Wolverines, who had played in blistering heat without a single substitution, were more than willing. Thus ended the first Rose Bowl game, and the only one that wound down with time still on the clock.

SURPRISE

Golf

There are a lot of stories about Jimmy Demaret, the great golfer. He was one of golf's more memorable characters.

Probably the most famous story involves his appearance on the '50s television show, "What's My Line?" On each show, a group of masked panelists would try to guess the identity of a celebrity guest.

Jimmy Demaret had been spending a few pleasant hours at Toots Shor's bar on West 52nd Street. Suddenly he remembered that he was scheduled to appear on "What's My Line?" He hurried over to the NBC building, where he had been told to take a special elevator. In his rush, he forgot the advice and took one of the main elevators.

When it was Jimmy's turn to appear before the masked panel, the first questioner asked immediately, "Are you Jimmy Demaret?"

The other panelists were amazed. The moderator, John Daly, couldn't believe it. How could this be? There had been no preliminary questions at all.

Daly wanted to know what had happened.

The panelist explained. "It was easy. When I was coming up here on the elevator, a man with a big smile stuck out his hand and said, 'Hi! I'm Jimmy Demaret.' "

SURPRISE

Golf

While qualifying for the National Open in 1964, Bobby Cupit teed off, and the ball connected in midair with a duck. The ball and the duck both took a nosedive and landed on the fairway.

The duck was stunned, but got up and flew away. The golf ball just lay there. Cupit played it and ended up two over par for the hole.

It was a case where the golfer got himself a birdie—but scored a double bogey.

SURPRISE

Hockey

Rodney Dangerfield claimed to be surprised. "I went to a fight last night," he said, "and a hockey game broke out."

SURPRISE

Horse Racing

Few horses ever came from farther back to win a race than Silky Sullivan. For a brief time in the late '50s, Silky Sullivan was the toast of American thoroughbred racing.

The horse was simply incredible. Bill Shoemaker remembered riding him at Santa Anita. The horse fell so far back in a nine-horse field that Shoe couldn't even see the eighth horse. In fact, Silky Sullivan was 35 lengths behind at that point. He was all by himself on the track and seemed to be hopelessly outclassed.

By the half-mile pole, though, the big horse began to move up. In the straightaway, he turned it on. Many years later Shoemaker would say that no other horse he ever rode made up so much ground. The crowd watched in awe as Silky Sullivan closed the huge gap, passing one horse after another, blazing across the finish line to win by half a length.

Later that year, in the Santa Anita Derby, a crowd of 61,000 watched Silky Sullivan almost duplicate his earlier effort. He galloped from 30 lengths back to win by three and half lengths.

The public looked for plenty of thrills in the Kentucky Derby that year. They were completely sold on this come-from-behind phenomenon. They placed more two-dollar bets on Silky Sullivan than on any other horse in Derby history. An exciting race and a breathtaking finish seemed assured.

CBS-TV used a split screen to show both the leader and the late-flying Silky Sullivan throughout the race.

Did the great horse disappoint his fans and the curious public? You bet he did. He finished 20 lengths back, beating out only two horses in the 14-horse field.

SURPRISE

Horse Racing

His wife had been suspicious for quite a while. She knew he had that little black book, and finally one morning she raided his trousers' pockets and went through it.

Most of the entries she found meant nothing, but she was intrigued by a one-page entry that read, "Melanie Rose, 943-2521."

"All right," she demanded, waking him up. "What does this mean? Who is this Melanie Rose?"

He rubbed the sleep from his eyes and reacted like a blooded pro. "Not who, honey—what? We're talking about Aqueduct, yesterday. Melanie Rose was a long-shot filly—won by a nose in the seventh race."

"Sure, Eddie," she said, fighting back tears. "Sure. And how about the 943—"

"Wait," he pleaded, rising to the occasion with a tired smile. "It's no big deal. My bookie lives at 943 Flatbush Avenue. The number's a reminder to me. That's all."

She grunted. "Uh-huh. And the 2521?"

"Just read it slow," he said in his kind and gentle way. "It means 25 to 1. This horse was no sure thing. Melanie Rose left the starting gate as a real long shot. You'll be happy, honey, when I tell you the rest of the story."

She didn't know just what to say, while he of the black book drifted back to sleep. An hour or so later the phone rang.

She answered it. She listened with a stone-cold expression on her face. She grabbed her husband by his striped pajama top and shouted, "Wake up, Eddie."

"What's the matter now?" he asked in a groggy voice.

"I'll tell you," she snapped. "Your horse is on the phone."

SURPRISE

Track and Field

Some records in track and field have long since been beaten, and yet they still have a certain glamour. One is the four-minute mile. Another is the 15-foot pole vault.

When Roger Bannister ran his four-minute mile, he had been training to do just that. So had a number of other fast milers. When Cornelius Warmerdam cleared 15 feet in the pole vault, however, it came as something of a shock.

It's true that Warmerdam, a Californian of Dutch background, held the indoor pole-vaulting record at 14 feet 6⅛ inches. But his name was hardly a household word. He was still just another good pole vaulter. At the Long Beach Relays in 1940, the best he could clear was 12 feet 6 inches.

So when he went next to an unimportant meet between California and Washington State at Berkeley, no one was expecting great things. They didn't get them either, not at first. Warmerdam cleared 14 feet 2 inches, but missed at 14 feet 5. He tried again and made it.

Then he had the bar moved up to 14 feet 8⅛ inches. At that height he sailed over the bar with ease. He was almost puzzled by his feat. It was the highest he had ever vaulted.

So he figured, why not? He asked the officials to raise the bar to 15 feet. He would go not only for the world record but for one of those invisible but very real track-and-field barriers of time or distance.

He missed at 15 feet, but he came close. He would try again.

From 140 feet out, he came sprinting toward the crossbar with the heavy bamboo pole poised. When he went up, the spectators held their breath. It looked as if he might be high enough. Off the pole and above the bar, he pulled his hands up just in time.

The crowd had come to see a more or less ordinary track meet. Instead they had witnessed a historic moment in sports—the world's first 15-foot pole vault. They were surprised. So was Warmerdam.

THOUGHTFULNESS

Auto Racing

Out on the Bonneville Salt Flats in Utah, the world's land speed record is broken every few years. Today they're going more than twice as fast as they did in the 1930s, which means that 300 miles an hour is really not much anymore. But it was fast driving back when Sir Malcolm Campbell, George Eyston, and John Cobb were trying to outdo one another.

This story concerns George Eyston, a retired British infantry captain. Stiff upper lip and all that. In 1937, driving a machine called *Thunderbolt*, he topped the old record with a speed of 311.42 miles per hour. He came back the following summer to try to break his own mark.

In trial runs it appeared likely that Eyston would set a new record. A few hundred tourists and fans were on hand for the attempt. So was the British press corps and the British Broadcasting Company. Live commentary, plus the impressive roar of *Thunderbolt*, would go out across the airwaves.

On the run for the record, everything went well for Eyston and his *Thunderbolt*. As he boomed past the timing tower, no one doubted that a new record was on the books.

The official timer that day was Art Pillsbury, an old pro. He looked down at the timing tape, and then looked again. He couldn't believe what he saw. There was no mark at all on it. The tape was blank.

Without a word, he climbed down from the tower and went to see Eyston. He began crying as he approached him, and he blurted out, "No, George—no record, no nothing." He tried to explain the problem with the timing equipment.

Eyston had to be bitterly disappointed. "What?" he gasped. He knew he had broken the world record speed, but there was no way to prove it.

When he addressed the press a few minutes later, he seemed to be in a better mood than than one might expect.

"Well, my good fellows," he said, "this was just a practice run. My car was running very well, and I am encouraged that I can break the record." He added that he expected to make a "formal attempt" in the near future.

No complaints, no recriminations.

And, in fact, he did make another attempt less than a month later. With the timing equipment working properly, he upped the world record by more than 45 miles an hour.

THOUGHTFULNESS

Baseball

In *The Umpire Strikes Back*, Ron Luciano tells about the time an unhappy fan fired a soda bottle at him from the Yankee Stadium stands.

Tommy John, with a look of deep concern, rushed out of his dugout to see if Luciano was all right. He was, and said so. The bottle had missed him by a whisker.

"Those fans," said Tommy, "they've got the worst aim in the world."

THOUGHTFULNESS

Basketball

Bob Knight, head basketball coach at Indiana University, suffered through his worst season ever in 1984–85. His team won 15 and lost 13 overall and had a losing 7–11 record in the Big Ten.

After being edged out by an undisciplined UCLA team in the NIT tournament, Bob Knight's Hoosiers returned to Indiana in a mood of deep depression.

No one was more depressed than Winston Morgan, a fine player who had gotten into trouble with a girl and was in Knight's doghouse. He had played only 58 seconds in the last 11 games. Although Morgan had one more year of eligibility, he wondered whether Knight wanted him back.

Knight didn't.

When the Hoosiers got back to Bloomington after the NIT loss, Knight talked to his team for a while in the small hours of the morning and then dismissed them. He asked Winston Morgan to stay behind. It was four a.m. when Knight told Morgan he was through at Indiana.

Knight's assistant coaches were present at this meeting. One of them, Jim Crews, had just accepted the head coaching job at the University of Evansville. This would be Crews' last meeting, just as it was Morgan's.

As bitterly disappointed as Morgan must have been, he stopped in front of Jim Crews on his way out.

"Coach," he said, "I want to thank you for working with me and wish you luck at Evansville. I know you'll do great."

When Bob Knight heard those words, he decided that maybe Winston Morgan wasn't such a bad kid after all. Knight, who always placed a high premium on a player's character as well as on his ability, decided to ask Morgan back.

He didn't do so immediately. But he finally did ask, and Winston Morgan became one of the mainstays of the successful 1985–86 Indiana basketball team.

THOUGHTFULNESS

Football

It's easy to lose your temper when somebody does something stupid. Even the great coaches and managers have been known to abandon their sense of humor after a bonehead play.

One coach who never seemed to get upset that way was Frankie Albert of the San Francisco 49ers. He took things in stride.

Albert had a great rookie prospect one year, a college All-American who was famous for his running. In his first game, the rookie took the opening kickoff deep in his end zone. He sprinted out to about the one- or two-foot line and then realized he should have downed the ball in the end zone for a touchback. That would have put it on the 20-yard line. The rookie could see from the charging defense that he'd never get that far by running.

So back he went into the end zone. He downed the ball and tossed it to the referee. The referee signaled a safety. Two points for the other team.

The rookie felt like a fool. But Coach Albert was calm and understanding. He put a hand on the rookie's shoulder and said, "Don't worry, son. It isn't everyone who can score the first time he carries the ball in the National Football League "

THOUGHTFULNESS

Horse Racing

The long-suffering wife stood before the divorce-court judge. "Your honor," she wailed, "my husband constantly ignores me. He isn't interested in anything except horse racing. Why, he can't even remember our wedding anniversary."

"Not true!" shouted her husband. "We got married two days after Seattle Slew won the Preakness!"

THOUGHTFULNESS

Sailing

In recent years the America's Cup Race has aroused a great deal of controversy and ill-will. It was not always that way. Back in the days when Sir Thomas Lipton, who was affectionately known as "Sir Tea," was challenging the New York Yacht Club for possession of the coveted trophy, the competition was a bit more gentlemanly.

For one thing, Sir Tea from Glasgow was a good sport, which was just as well, since he was never able to gain victory over the American entries. Five times he challenged for the Cup. Five times he lost. He suffered his final defeat in 1930 at the age of 80. "I canna win," he said sadly. "I canna win."

Even the victors felt sorry for him. Will Rogers, the Johnny Carson of his day, suggested that everyone send a dollar to the Lipton Cup Fund in care of the mayor of New York. The idea was to buy Sir Tea a consolation trophy.

Money poured in—$16,000 in the first week—and Tiffany's created a magnificent 18-carat gold cup. It was a far more elegant trophy than the actual America's Cup. When Sir Tea accepted it, he was deeply moved.

He promised that he would challenge for the America's Cup one more time. But it was not to be. He died unexpectedly within the next year.

TRUTH

Auto Racing

When drag racing turned respectable in the late 1950s, a few drivers rose quickly to the top ranks. Don Garlits was one. Tommy Ivo and Don Prudhomme were two others. And then in 1961, along came Pete Robinson.

Pete's hometown was Atlanta, Georgia, and he was a graduate of Georgia Tech in engineering. He went about designing his dragster in a cool, methodical way—just the way an engineer should. When he thought he was ready, he entered the national championships of the National Hot Rod Association.

No one in drag-racing circles had heard of him. So when on his first qualifying run he was clocked at 8.50 seconds, the officials hardly knew what to do. They thought the clock had malfunctioned. The best drivers in the world were having trouble breaking nine seconds.

What the officials decided to do was to withhold Pete's time slip. But on the second run, he did just as well. Now they were really puzzled. Still, they held up his time slip again and said nothing to the crowd.

At this point Bernie Partridge, the announcer, took off his official shirt and headed for the pits. When he found Robinson, he acted like a fan and asked him how things were going.

Robinson looked bothered. "Those damn officials won't give me my time," he said. "But I'm running about 8½ seconds."

He said it matter-of-factly, which surprised Partridge. "Did you ever run that fast before?" Partridge asked.

Pete assured him that he had. He said he ran about 8.50 on the dirt track back home. He thought he was doing just as well here, but the officials wouldn't tell him anything.

Partridge hurried back to the mike. The guy was for real after all. He was outrunning the best drivers in the world, and no one knew him.

When Pete's third pass was clocked at 8.60, Bernie Partridge went public with the news. He told why the earlier times had been withheld. He said that, yes, they were accurate, and, yes, Pete Robinson was leading all other drivers at the moment. The crowd went wild.

Robinson won the meet. And along with it he won his nickname, Sneaky Pete. He had snuck up on the world of drag racing—and had conquered it his first time out.

TRUTH

Auto Racing

Drag racing is a sport of explosive action. A dragster's time is measured in hundredths of a second. So drag racer Don Garlits is stating a fact, not using a metaphor, when he says, "A second is a long time on a drag strip."

TRUTH

Baseball

James Russell Lowell wrote that truth is forever on the scaffold. It certainly is when baseball players are trying to explain or deny some of their off-field activities.

Danny Murtaugh used to tell a story from his playing days. It seems that he and his roommate Ernie White had gone on the town one night during spring training and never returned to their motel room. The two of them looked more ready for bed than baseball when they reported to the ballpark the next morning.

"You boys have a good night's sleep?" the manager asked.

"Sure, Skip," lied Murtaugh.

"That's good," the manager said. "I was afraid you might have been disturbed by the tractor-trailer that crashed through your room in the middle of the night."

TRUTH

Baseball

There are so many Yogi Berra stories that it's hard to say which one is the best known. A good candidate for the honor is a true story—a lot of the Berra stories aren't. In this case, though, you could look it up, as Casey Stengel would say.

Early in Berra's playing career, his old friends and neighbors from St. Louis gave him a night at Sportsman's Park. The Yankees were playing the Browns for the last time that season.

The fans would expect Yogi to give a brief thank-you speech after he had received some gifts, including a new car. Berra was a 22-year-old kid with very little experience in public speaking.

His friend, third baseman Bobby Brown, offered to write a brief speech for him. Brown wrote it—just two sentences and 22 words—and Yogi proceeded to memorize it. The final word in the speech, at least as Brown had written it, was the word *possible*.

Yogi was sure he had everything right by the time his big night came. Even so, he was nervous as he approached the mike in front of all those people, and he stammered a bit.

He said: "I'm a lucky guy, and I'm happy to be with the Yankees. I want to thank everyone for making this night necessary "

TRUTH

Boxing

Benny Leonard boxed his way to the lightweight championship of the world and held the title for eight years. Before he became champ, he had lost a few fights—one of them to a boxer six inches shorter than he was.

A fan asked him, "How did you let that guy beat you—he only came up to your chin?"

"Yeah," said Benny, "but he came up to it too often."

TRUTH

Fishing

Not many people would argue with this observation by Patrick F. McManus, the outdoorsman and humorist: "Scholars have long known that fishing eventually turns men into philosophers. Unfortunately, it is almost impossible to buy decent tackle on a philosopher's salary."

TRUTH

Fishing

A fisherman stood at the bar of justice.

The judge said, "You're charged with catching three more rainbow trout than the law allows. How do you plead? Guilty or not guilty?"

"Guilty, your honor."

"That'll be twenty-five dollars and costs," the judge ruled. "Next case."

"Wait," the fisherman said. "How do I get copies of the court record to show my friends?"

TRUTH

Football

Most people can think of a story or two about how a real event differed from the newspaper accounts of it. There are those well-documented tales of the Vietnam War being observed from a Saigon bar. Not long ago there was a chatty, intimate society column about a glittering party that the columnist hadn't bothered to attend

One of the great sports stories on this theme concerns a wartime Army-Navy football game. The year was 1944. Army's Glenn Davis and Doc Blanchard led their team to a 23–7 win over Navy. The game took place in Baltimore, where the stadium resembled a swamp because of recent rains.

After the game the Army players were given exactly one hour *inside* the stadium to see their friends and relatives. Then they had to march a grueling six miles back to the troop transport that had brought them down to Baltimore. Once on board, the cadets were treated to a fine meal and a party.

No sooner had they finished eating and partying than a gusty storm came up on Chesapeake Bay. Many of the boys were land-lubbers, and they weren't prepared for this. The ship pitched and rolled. The men rushed for the railings. They came back a pale and sickly green. The night passed slowly.

It was still raining when the troopship docked at West Point the next morning. The cadets marched up the hill, away from the water, happy to be on firm ground again.

That night a cadet was reading one of the New York Sunday papers. He could hardly believe his eyes. The by-line belonged to a well-known New York sportswriter, and the story opened with this sparkling gem:

Quote: "There were West Point cadets celebrating and reveling into the wee hours in Baltimore's famous downtown streets following Army's 23–7 victory over Navy. . . ."

TRUTH

Football

Giants coach Bill Parcells didn't like the way his offensive line had protected quarterback Phil Simms against the San Francisco 49ers.

"My quarterback took too many shots in the mouth," he told them.

Phil Simms had to agree, but he didn't offer his opinion. He said, "My mouth was too sore for me to yell."

TRUTH

Golf

Mrs. O'Keefe had always wondered about the propriety of her husband playing golf on the Lord's Day. She decided to ask Father Donnelly, her parish priest.

"Father," she said, "is it a sin for my husband to play golf on Sunday?"

He smiled sympathetically. "Mrs. O'Keefe," he replied, "the way your husband plays golf, it's a sin for him to play any day of the week."

TRUTH

Horse Racing

Elbert Hubbard, an inspirational writer at the turn of the century, had words of truth—but none of inspiration—for those who bet on the horses.

"The only man who makes money following the races," he said, "is the one who does so with a broom and shovel."

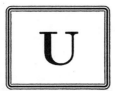

UNDERSTANDING

Baseball

It sometimes seems as if the superstars are more understanding than lesser-known athletes. Take Casey Stengel. He could be harsh on players, harsh on sportswriters, harsh on fans—especially when they deserved it. But he could also be kind, and not always when you'd expect it.

Robert Lipsyte, the journalist, tells about his days covering the early Mets. The team was playing in the grim confines of old Colts Stadium in Houston. The Mets were taking infield practice, looking every bit as bad as they actually were. Casey scowled and cursed.

A man leaned across the railing and touched Casey's arm. "I wonder if you remember me, Case?" he asked. The man gave his name. "I pitched against you in Kankakee."

Lipsyte expected a quick put-down as Casey turned and saw the middle-aged man, shabbily dressed, and holding the wrist of a teenaged boy. The kid looked embarrassed.

To Lipsyte's surprise, Casey clapped the man on the shoulder, smiled, and treated him like a man he'd been waiting a long time to see. "The old fireballer himself . . . glad when you quit the league . . . never could hit you a-tall."

Onward and upward soared the Stengalese. Good old Kankakee. Those long-ago days in the minors. The ballplayers, the games, the life.

And then it was "gotta go now," followed by "send that boy around if he can throw like you."

Lipsyte went after the ambling Casey to find out more about the encounter. He got nowhere. Casey just shrugged. The question was unasked and unanswered. Maybe Casey knew the guy, and maybe he didn't. And maybe it didn't matter.

UNDERSTANDING

Baseball

Not everyone liked the way Leo Durocher managed his ballclubs, but Willie Mays did. He could never forget how Leo lifted his spirits when Mays first joined the New York Giants in 1951.

After spending a year in Class B ball, Mays at the age of 19 went up to the Triple-A Minneapolis Millers, one step from the majors. After 35 games he was batting an awesome .477, and Durocher brought him up to the New York Giants.

Mays didn't want to go. Despite his .477 average, he didn't think he could hit major league pitching. Leo wanted him on the Giants anyway.

To everyone's surprise, Willie got off to a terrible start—a dismal 1-for-25 at the plate. That's a batting average of .040. Mays was sure he would be sent down. He felt terrible.

He was sitting alone next to this locker, crying, when Durocher came up to him and put an arm around his shoulders.

"Mr. Leo," he bawled, "I can't hit up here."

At that Durocher pointed to his uniform. "Willie," he said, "see what's printed across my jersey? It says Giants. As long as I'm the manager of the Giants, you're my center fielder. You're here to stay."

Mays never forgot that moment. He said, "I needed somebody to lift my spirits, to give me the confidence I needed at that low point. Leo was that person."

UNDERSTANDING

Basketball

Milestones in one's career are usually thought of as times for celebration. But Tom Murphy, the highly successful basketball coach at Hamilton College, wasn't so sure. When people began applauding him on his team's 300th victory, he thought back over those lengthening years of wins and losses and said, "All it means is you're getting old."

UNDERSTANDING

Soccer

At the end of his book on what it's like to be a professional hockey player, Ken Dryden tells a story not about hockey but about soccer. It's a story with resonant overtones. Dryden, formerly a star goalie for the Montreal Canadiens, describes an unnamed hockey player—"number 7"—who represents a universal type.

Although the author doesn't say so, number 7 is precisely what Ken Dryden was not. Dryden was the quintessential goalie—consistent, dependable, cool under pressure, and able to make the big save. Not especially flashy, he was a solid, steady performer. His skills carried him all the way to the Hockey Hall of Fame.

Number 7, the soccer player for Cambridge United in the English league, Second Division, was none of these. He was energy in motion—quick, hardworking, always in on the action, and a great crowd pleaser. He'd miss a shot, and the crowd would forgive him. "Bad luck!" they'd cry. They loved him. They counted on him.

At some point in the game, Dryden, new to soccer but not to sports, began to have his doubts about number 7. All those cheerful misses. Somehow the pattern seemed a little familiar. Dryden had played hundreds of professional hockey games, and he felt he'd seen the man before . . . seen him many times before.

A friend with Dryden at the game never lost faith in the feisty favorite of the crowd. With Cambridge a goal behind, a long pass put number 7 in the clear. The fans were on their feet. Dryden's friend was shouting ecstatically, "Here it comes! Here it comes!"

Dryden smiled. He had no such faith.

Number 7, with the game on the line, missed the shot.

UNDERSTANDING

Tennis

When passions are high, it can be hard to act rationally. It can be especially hard for fans, who are caught up in a kind of mob psychology.

Back in 1937, when the Nazis controlled Germany, one of the top tennis players in the world was Baron Gottfried von Cramm, the very picture of a

German athlete. But Cramm was also an anti-Nazi, despite having the tall, blond, Nordic look that was greatly admired by Hitler's propagandists.

Although Cramm's political views were well known, many Americans felt obligated to protest Nazism that year. At a tournament in Los Angeles, attended by many in the movie industry, about four fifths of the box-seat holders had agreed to stand up and leave the stadium as soon as Cramm arrived on court for his first match.

Cramm came out to play. No one moved. Silence greeted the German player, but no one stood up, no one left. They found themselves unable to protest Nazi politics by walking out on an anti-Nazi athlete.

Time proved them right. A year later Cramm found himself in a Nazi prison. Eventually, he was released and sent to the Russian front as an enlisted man, even though by then the Nazis desperately needed officers with his background. Cramm survived the war, just as he surely would have survived a fans' boycott on that day in 1937. Fortunately, the walkout never came. The fans rose to the occasion, perhaps without really knowing why.

VERSATILITY

Baseball/Football

Many people feel that a great athlete can succeed in almost any sport. A number of athletes have certainly done well in two or more professional sports. Gene Conley was a fine pitcher at the major league level and a pretty fair pro basketball player for the Celtics and Knicks. Bo Jackson began his career in the pros by dividing his time between baseball's Kansas City Royals and football's L.A. Raiders.

A few athletes have switched from one pro sport to another at some point in their careers. Ken Strong made the switch because of medical malpractice. It's quite a story.

Ken Strong had starred in football at New York University. Tim Mara, owner of the football Giants, told one of his coaches to sign this dazzling halfback regardless of the cost. The coach failed, and Strong signed with the Staten Island Stapletons for the 1929 season.

Ken played for the Stapes that year, but he thought his future was in baseball. The New York Yankees agreed and signed Strong as an outfielder. In 1930 he played at Hazleton in the New York-Pennsylvania League. That year he batted .373 and hit 41 home runs, a league record that would not be tied for nearly 50 years. Next year he went to Toronto, one step from the majors in those days. He was hitting .340 in 118 games when a collision with an outfield wall smashed his wrist. It was a bad injury. A doctor recommended surgery.

The surgeon who operated made a terrible mistake. He removed the wrong bone from Strong's wrist. The damage could not be fixed, and Ken had to forget about a future with the Yankees. He could no longer make the sharp, snap throws required in baseball.

But he found he could still throw a good forward pass in football. He could also run, kick, block, and tackle. So he abandoned his baseball career and switched to football. When he retired from pro football in 1947, he stood number one in career points scored for the New York Giants. His record was later broken by Frank Gifford, but Strong's overall performance in the NFL was brilliant.

You won't find a plaque honoring Ken Strong in the Baseball Hall of Fame at Cooperstown. You might have found one, except for a bone surgeon gone wrong. Strong seemed to be that good a baseball player.

You will find him, though, in the Pro Football Hall of Fame at Canton, Ohio. Ken Strong not only made the transition from one pro sport to another, but he rose to the very top. And he did it with a permanently damaged right wrist.

VERSATILITY

Football

The Associated Press chose Jim Thorpe as the greatest male athlete of the first half of the 20th century. Few people argued. The American Indian star from rural Oklahoma could do just about everything on an athletic field. No, make that everything.

He's a member of the Pro Football Hall of Fame, and it's probably as a football player that he's best remembered. But Thorpe was also a major league baseball player, an outfielder, mostly for the New York Giants.

And we shouldn't forget track. Once in a dual collegiate meet, Thorpe scored more points than all the rest of the 47-man field combined. In the 1912 Olympics he won both the pentathlon and the decathlon.

Thorpe excelled in baseball, basketball, boxing, football, gymnastics, handball, hockey, lacrosse, swimming, track, and wrestling.

At the closing of the 1912 Olympic games in Stockholm, the King of Sweden said, "Sir, you are the greatest athlete in the world."

VERSATILITY

Golf

In an age of specialization, it's hard to excel in a whole galaxy of sports. A few high school athletes are still able to, but beyond that it's tough.

Because of this, we may never see another Babe Didrikson Zaharias. As you probably know, she was chosen by the Associated Press as the greatest female athlete in the first half of the 20th century. And no wonder. Babe could do it all: baseball, basketball, bowling, golf, javelin, tennis, track.

She first gained fame in high school basketball. Back in the low-scoring girls' contests of the early 1900s, she once poured in a hundred points in a game.

In 1932, Babe—who was then just Mildred Didrikson—competed in the AAU national track meet. She was a one-woman track team. During a spectacular weekend in Chicago, she entered eight events, scored points in seven, won five outright, and set three world records.

That same year she won two Olympic medals, one for the javelin throw, one for the hurdles.

As a baseball player, Mildred toured the country with a barnstorming team. She was the only woman on it, and the team played only against men. A good all-around player, she was noted for her strong throwing arm.

At some point, even Babe Didrikson Zaharias had to concentrate on a single sport. She chose golf. You won't be surprised to learn that she won more than 50 major tournaments, 17 of them in a row.

Babe died from cancer in her early 40s. Nearly everyone agrees that she was the greatest female athlete of the half century. Many also think she was the greatest female athlete who ever lived. With the specialization in modern sports, we may never know for sure.

VERSATILITY

Shooting

Károly Takács belonged to the Hungarian world championship pistol shooting team. One day, while serving in the army, a grenade exploded in his right hand, shattering it. His right hand was his pistol hand, and it looked as if Takács's shooting days were over.

He started to practice pistol shooting with his left hand.

By the time of the 1948 London Olympics, Takács was ready to compete as a left-hander in the rapid-fire pistol event. In fact, he was more than ready. Shooting left-handed, he won the gold medal for Hungary. Four years later in Helsinki, at the age of 42, he won his second gold medal as a left-handed shooter.

SPEAKER'S
366-DAY
SPORTS
CALENDAR

JANUARY

January 1 1929: Roy Riegels ran 69 yards the wrong way in a Rose Bowl game between Georgia Tech and California. Georgia Tech won, 8–7.

January 2 1961: Bobby Fischer won his fourth consecutive United States chess championship by drawing with the Hungarian grand master Pal Benko.

January 3 1939: Don Budge made his professional tennis debut before 16,000 fans at Madison Square Garden, New York City.

January 4 1947: Donald Campbell, former world speed champion for both land and water, was killed when his speedboat was destroyed on Coniston Lake in northwest England.

January 5 1934: National and American Leagues selected a standard base-ball to be used by both leagues, the first time in 33 years that both leagues would be using the same ball.

January 6 1925: Paavo Nurmi, the "Flying Ghost of Finland," running on boards for the first time, broke two world records with a new indoor mile mark of 4:13⅗ and a new 5,000-meter time of 14:44⅗ at the Finnish-American track meet, Madison Square Garden, New York City.

January 7 1897: Michael Eagan won the first national handball championship match for amateurs at Jersey City, New Jersey.

January 8 1955: Georgia Tech defeated the University of Kentucky's basketball team 59–58, Kentucky's first loss in 130 home basketball games.

January 9 1793: Jean Pierre Blanchard made the first United States free flight in a balloon at Philadelphia, Pennsylvania, an event witnessed by a large crowd including George Washington.

January 10 1950: Ben Hogan tied Sam Snead for first place in the Los Angeles Open in his first golf tournament appearance since his 1949 automobile accident; Hogan lost in a playoff.

January 11 1973: Owners of the 24 major league baseball teams voted to allow the American League to experiment with a tenth player, the "designated hitter," who could bat for the pitcher without forcing the pitcher to leave the game.

January 12 1969: Joe Namath and the New York Jets upset the Baltimore Colts 16–7, giving the American Football League its first major triumph over the NFL and its first Super Bowl win.

January 13 1933: Babe Didrikson (later Zaharias) made her first professional basketball appearance, scoring nine points as her team, the Brooklyn Yankees, defeated the Long Island Ducklings 19–16 in a game played in New York.

January 14 1941: Paul Brown, whose Massillon, Ohio, high school football teams had lost only one game in seven years, became head football coach at Ohio State University.

January 15 1967: Vince Lombardi's Green Bay Packers defeated the Kansas City Chiefs in the first Super Bowl game, played at the Los Angeles Coliseum.

January 16 1961: Mickey Mantle signed a $75,000 one-year contract with the New York Yankees, making him the highest-paid player in the American League.

January 17 1945: Gil Dodds, holder of the indoor record for the mile, informed the National Amateur Athletic Union that he was retiring from competition to assume full-time gospel work.

January 18 1941: Epinard, one of the great racehorses of his day, was found by Paris police being used as a delivery wagon horse, having been stolen during the German occupation of France.

January 19 1880: William Muldoon, America's most famous nineteenth-century wrestler, defeated Thieubaud Bauer in the Greco-Roman wrestling championship of America.

January 20 1892: Students at the International YMCA Training School in Springfield, Massachusetts, played the first official basketball game.

January 21 1951: Babe Didrikson Zaharias won the Tampa, Florida, Women's Open golf tournament. Her 288 total set a new women's golfing record for 72 holes of medal play.

January 22 1962: Jackie Robinson and Bob Feller were elected to the Baseball Hall of Fame, Robinson becoming the first black player to receive the honor.

January 23   1964: Warren Spahn, left-handed pitcher of the Milwaukee Braves of the National League, signed a one-year contract for $85,000, baseball's highest salary for a pitcher.

January 24   1930: Primo Carnera made his American ring debut before 20,000 in New York, knocking out Big Boy Peterson of Minneapolis in 1:10 of the first round.

January 25   1968: Bob Seagren cleared 17 feet 4¼ inches in a new world record for the indoor pole vault, in the Millrose Games, Madison Square Garden, New York City.

January 26   1913: Jim Thorpe admitted in a letter to the AAU that he played professional baseball in 1909 and 1910, disqualifying him from amateur competition; he had to return the medals he had won in the 1912 Olympic Games in Stockholm, Sweden.

January 27   1894: The University of Chicago, the first college to play a full basketball schedule, defeated the Chicago YMCA Training School 19–11 in its first game of the season.

January 28   1958: Roy Campanella, one of baseball's greatest catchers, was seriously injured in an auto accident on Long Island, ending his playing career.

January 29   1936: Ty Cobb, Walter Johnson, Christy Mathewson, Babe Ruth, and Honus Wagner became the first five players elected to the National Baseball Hall of Fame in Cooperstown, New York.

January 30   1960: Carol Heiss won the women's singles United States figure skating championship in Seattle, Washington.

January 31   1950: Paul Pettit, a left-handed pitcher who hurled six no-hitters for his Lomita, California, high school team signed with the Pittsburgh Pirates for about $100,000 in bonuses and guarantees, a record; Pettit won one game in the majors.

FEBRUARY

February 1   1929:   Charles Rigoulet, a 402½-pound French weightlifter, achieved the first 400-pound clean and jerk.

February 2   1970:   Pete Maravich of Louisiana State University became the first collegiate basketball player ever to score 3,000 points, tallying 49 in a game against Mississippi State.

February 3   1964:   Adolph Rupp gained his 700th victory in 33 seasons of college coaching as his University of Kentucky basketball team defeated Georgia 108–83.

February 4   1939:   Glenn Cunningham, world record holder for the mile, agreed with Brutus Hamilton, track coach at the University of California, that the four-minute mile was impossible.

February 5   1956:   Bill Milhalo of Hollywood, California, set a world professional record of two hours, 20 minutes, one second, for the 20-mile walk, in San Fernando, California.

February 6   1948:   Barbara Ann Scott of Canada won the women's Olympic figure skating title.

February 7   1947:   Jimmy Demaret equaled the all-time competitive golf record in a PGA-sponsored event with a 62 in the first round of the Texas Open golf tournament at San Antonio, Texas.

February 8   1896:   Faculty representatives of universities in the Midwest met to form the Western (Big Ten) Conference.

February 9   1963:   John Thomas defeated Valeri Brumel in the high jump for the first time, both men clearing 7 feet ¼ inches, with Thomas having fewer misses.

February 10   1962:   Jim Beatty became the first American to run an indoor mile in less than four minutes, doing so in 3:58.9 at Los Angeles, California.

February 11   1949:   Willie Pep regained the world featherweight boxing title by defeating Sandy Saddler in New York.

February 12   1878:   Frederick Thayer patented the baseball catcher's mask under Patent No. 200,358.

February 13   1920:   The National Negro Baseball League was organized.

February 14   1951:   Sugar Ray Robinson defeated Jake LaMotta in Chicago, Illinois, becoming the first welterweight boxer ever to dethrone a middleweight title holder.

February 15   1950:   An Associated Press poll named the top athletes of the past 50 years: among them, Bobby Jones, George Mikan, Jesse Owens, Babe Ruth, Jim Thorpe, Bill Tilden, Johnny Weissmuller, and Babe Didrikson Zaharias.

February 16   1972:   Wilt Chamberlain of the Los Angeles Lakers became the first player in the National Basketball Association to score 30,000 points, doing so in 940 regular season games.

February 17   1924:   Johnny Weissmuller swam the 100-yard freestyle in a world record time of 52⅖ seconds at Miami, Florida.

February 18   1922:   Kenesaw Mountain Landis resigned from the bench as a United States District judge in Illinois to devote all his time to baseball, he had been named Commissioner of Baseball in 1920.

February 19   1970:   Denny McLain, the American League's Cy Young Award winner for two years, was suspended from baseball by Commissioner Bowie Kuhn for his role in a bookmaking operation.

February 20   1958:   Eddie Arcaro rode the 4,000th winner of his career as a jockey, at Santa Anita racetrack in Arcadia, California.

February 21   1957:   Brooklyn Dodgers' President Walter O'Malley announced the acquisition of Philip Wrigley, Jr.'s Los Angeles baseball franchise in the Pacific Coast League.

February 22   1920:   The first United States dog track to use imitation rabbits opened in Emeryville, California.

February 23   1967:   Jim Ryun set an indoor half mile track record of 1:48.3 in a meet in Lawrence, Kansas.

February 24   1949:   Greta Andersen of Denmark swam the 100-yard freestyle in a world record time of 58.2 seconds in Copenhagen, Denmark.

February 25 1964: Muhammed Ali won the world heavyweight boxing championship from Sonny Liston in Miami Beach, Florida.

February 26 1946: Jorge Pasquel, president of the Mexican Baseball League, offered star American players contracts to jump to his league.

February 27 1942: Frank Leahy, Notre Dame's football coach, announced his intention of using the T-formation rather than the Notre Dame shift developed by Knute Rockne.

February 28 1971: Jack Nicklaus won the Professional Golf Association tournament for the second time, thus capturing each of the world's four major golfing titles at least twice.

February 29 1964: Frank Rugani drove a shuttlecock 79 feet 8½ inches in tests at San Jose, California.

MARCH

March 1 1942: Torger Tokle set an American ski jump record of 289 feet at Iron Mountain, Michigan.

March 2 1962: Wilt Chamberlain, playing for the Philadelphia Warriors, scored a record 100 points against the New York Knicks as the Warriors romped to a 169–147 victory.

March 3 1938: The American Bowling Congress tournament in Chicago, Illinois, attracted a record 24,765 entrants.

March 4 1967: Peggy Fleming fell in the freestyle event in the World Figure Skating Championship in Vienna, but went on to win the title.

March 5 1864: Oxford and Cambridge met for the first time in track and field competition, a milestone in intercollegiate athletics.

March 6 1926: In a supervised camel race at Tunis, Africa, a camel was clocked at 12 minutes over a 3⅛ mile course, averaging better than a four-minute mile.

March 7   1934:   Gustavus Kirby, former president of the AAU, stated in a speech that Germany would have to allow Jews on Olympic teams if it wanted the United States to look with favor on the 1936 Olympic Games in Berlin.

March 8   1887:   Everett Horton patented the telescoping-steel fishing rod under Patent No. 359,153.

March 9   1929:   Eric Krenz became the first man to throw the discus more than 160 feet, reaching 163 feet 8¾ inches at Palo Alto, California.

March 10   1913:   William Knox bowled the first perfect 300 game in an American Bowling Congress tournament, in Toledo, Ohio.

March 11   1967:   Jean-Claude Killy of France clinched the World Cup of skiing by winning the North American giant slalom in Franconia, New Hampshire.

March 12   1966:   Bobby Hull of the Chicago Black Hawks became the first professional hockey player to score more than 50 points in a season, scoring his 51st in a game with the New York Rangers in Chicago, Illinois.

March 13   1880:   *American Cricketeer*, a magazine founded in 1877 for cricket fans, decided to include boating, tennis, bicycling, and other outdoor sports.

March 14   1939:   Abe Greene, New Jersey's boxing commissioner, offered to cut the New Jersey state tax from ten to five percent to obtain the world heavyweight title bout between Joe Louis and Tony Galento for New Jersey.

March 15   1943:   Steve O'Neill, manager of the Detroit Tigers, banned poker playing on his team, threatening a $500 fine for violations.

March 16   1937:   The Brooklyn Dodgers hired Percy Beard, former world champion hurdler, to teach them how to run, since they had been having trouble running the bases and chasing fly balls.

March 17   1951:   Sam Bankhead became the first black manager in organized baseball when he was named to pilot the Farnham, Quebec, team of the Class C Provincial League.

March 18   1959:   Bill Sharman, guard for the Boston Celtics, began his string of 58 straight free throws sunk, a record for pro basketball.

March 19   1971:   Rod Laver scored a straight-set victory over Tom Okker in Madison Square Garden, New York, to complete his sweep of the 13-match Tennis Champions Classic.

March 20   1973:   Roberto Clemente was elected to the Baseball Hall of Fame eleven weeks after his death, the second player—after Lou Gehrig—to be elected without the required five-year wait.

March 21   1934:   Babe Didrikson (later Zaharias) pitched an inning of exhibition baseball for the Philadelphia A's against the Brooklyn Dodgers at Fort Myers, Florida. After walking one batter and hitting another, she retired the side on a triple play.

March 22   1947:   Bobby Riggs defeated Don Budge for the world professional indoor tennis title.

March 23   1972:   New York Yankees agreed to continue playing in New York City after the city approved a plan to buy and renovate Yankee Stadium in the Bronx.

March 24   1973:   Lou Spadia, president of the San Francisco 49ers, proposed an expansion of the National Football League to 30 teams.

March 25   1668:   A silver trophy, the first such award in America, went to the winner of a horse race at Hempstead, Long Island, the intent being to encourage horse racing and thus improve the American breed.

March 26   1972:   The Los Angeles Lakers ended their regular season play with a 69–13 won-lost record, the best winning percentage ever in the National Basketball Association.

March 27   1931:   John McGraw, long-time manager of the New York Giants baseball team, predicted that night baseball would never supplant major league baseball played in the daylight.

March 28   1957:   A National Curling Championship was held for the first time.

March 29   1917:   Man o' War, the most famous American racehorse of the first half of the 20th century, was foaled.

March 30   1930:   The Cannes International tennis championship ended in a fiasco when spectators learned that the finalists, including Bill Tilden and Elizabeth Ryan, had agreed to divide first place instead of playing.

March 31 1931: Knute Rockne, Notre Dame football coach, died in a Kansas plane crash.

APRIL

April 1 1930: Gabby Hartnett of the Chicago Cubs caught baseballs dropped from 800 feet and 550 feet from the Goodyear blimp in Los Angeles, California, breaking Gabby Street's old record of catching a ball dropped 504 feet from the top of the Washington Monument.

April 2 1955: Pancho Gonzales retained his U.S. Professional tennis title by defeating Pancho Segura in the finals of a tournament played under table tennis rules.

April 3 1967: The Austrian Interior Ministry announced that 113 East Europeans who attended the World Amateur hockey championships in Vienna had asked for political asylum.

April 4 1944: Rogers Hornsby quit his job as manager of the Vera Cruz, Mexico, baseball club because he was required to pay his own expenses on road trips.

April 5 1915: Jess Willard won the heavyweight championship in boxing by knocking out Jack Johnson in the 26th round of a fight at Havana, Cuba.

April 6 1958: Arnold Palmer won the Masters tournament for his first major golf victory.

April 7 1928: Lester Patrick, 45-years-old and long retired, took to the ice for the New York Rangers in the Stanley Cup finals against the Montreal Maroons (because of an injury to the Rangers' regular goalie) and saved the game for the Rangers.

April 8 1974: Hank Aaron of the Atlanta Braves hit his 715th career home run in the Braves' home opener against the Los Angeles Dodgers, breaking Babe Ruth's career record.

April 9 1962: President John F. Kennedy opened the American League baseball season by tossing out the first ball at Washington's new District of Columbia Stadium.

April 10 1961: Gary Player of South Africa became the first foreigner to win the Masters golf title.

April 11 1933: Joe Savoldi defeated Jim Londos in a disputed wrestling match in Chicago, Illinois, after which the Illinois State Athletic Commission banned pro wrestling indefinitely in the state.

April 12 1950: Wilhelm Herz of Germany established a world mark for two-wheel motorcycles by doing a measured mile at 180 mph on a super-charged 500cc NSU on the Munich-Ingolstadt autobahn.

April 13 1940: Cornelius Warmerdam became the first pole vaulter to clear the bar at 15 feet, performing this feat in a meet in Berkeley, California.

April 14 1969: The first major league baseball game played outside the United States took place in Montreal, Canada, between the Montreal Expos and the St. Louis Cardinals.

April 15 1947: Jackie Robinson played his first major league game for the Brooklyn Dodgers, a game against the Boston Braves at Ebbets Field, Brooklyn.

April 16 1940: Bob Feller pitched the first no-hit, no-run game ever thrown on opening day, beating the Chicago White Sox 1–0.

April 17 1983: Wayne Gretzky scored a record seven goals in one Stanley Cup playoff game. Two years later, on April 25, 1985, he tied his own record.

April 18 1966: Eddie Rommel became the first major league umpire to wear glasses, in a game between the New York Yankees and Washington Senators in Washington, D.C

April 19 1951: Shigeki Tanaka, a survivor of the atomic bomb blast at Hiroshima, won the Boston Marathon.

April 20 1949: Bill Shoemaker, America's greatest jockey, won his first race, riding Shafter V to victory at Golden Gate Fields in Albany, California.

April 21 1959: Alf Dean caught the largest fish ever taken by hook and rod, a 2,664-pound, 16-foot 10-inch white shark, near Ceduna, South Australia.

April 22 1876: Boston played Philadelphia at Philadelphia in the first official National League game, Boston winning 6–5.

April 23 1964: Ken Johnson of the Houston Colts pitched a no-hitter, but lost 1–0 to the Cincinnati Reds who scored on two errors; it was the first no-hit loss in major league history.

April 24 1930: Sacramento, California, Board of Education asked Sacramento Solons of the Pacific Coast League to stop admitting school children free to Friday afternoon games, since classrooms had become all but deserted on Friday afternoons.

April 25 1901: Detroit Tigers, trailing Milwaukee 13–4 going into the last of the ninth, staged one of the great comebacks in baseball history, scoring 10 runs to win 14–13.

April 26 1952: Patty Berg shot a 64 for 18 holes, a women's record for major golfing competition, in a tournament at Richmond, California.

April 27 1947: Babe Ruth Day was observed throughout the United States and Japan, with Ruth attending ceremonies in Yankee Stadium, New York.

April 28 1961: Warren Spahn, at the age of 41, pitched his second no-hit game for the Milwaukee Braves, defeating the San Francisco Giants 1–0.

April 29 1986: Roger Clemens, Boston Red Sox pitcher, struck out 20 Seattle Mariner batters in a 3–1 victory at Fenway Park, setting a one-game major league strikeout mark for a nine-inning game.

April 30 1939: Lou Gehrig played the last game of his 2,130 consecutive game streak, and of his career.

MAY

May 1 1923: Earl Sande, one of the greatest American jockeys, rode his first Kentucky Derby winner, Zev.

May 2 1953: Dark Star, a 25–1 long shot, won the Kentucky Derby, nosing out the favored Native Dancer

May 3 1810: Lord Byron swam the Hellespont in one hour and ten minutes.

May 4 1957: Bill Shoemaker misjudged the finish while riding Gallant Man in the Kentucky Derby; his mistake allowed Iron Liege, with Bill Hartack up, to win the race.

May 5 1904: Cy Young of the Boston Red Sox pitched a perfect game against the Philadelphia Athletics, beating Rube Waddell 3–0.

May 6 1954: Roger Bannister became the first man to run the four-minute mile, covering the distance in 3:59.4 at Oxford, England.

May 7 1957: Herb Score, star Cleveland pitcher, was hit in the face by a line drive off the bat of New York's Gil McDougald, causing serious eye damage and blighting his promising career.

May 8 1915: Regret became the first filly (and one of only three) to win the Kentucky Derby.

May 9 1970: Avery Brundage, president of the International Olympic Committee and one of the world's great curmudgeons, urged that ice hockey, Alpine skiing, soccer, and basketball be eliminated from Olympic competition.

May 10 1909: Fred Toney, pitching for Winchester, Kentucky, in the Class D Blue Grass League, worked 17 no-hit innings to win 1–0 over Lexington.

May 11 1972: Willie Mays was traded by the San Francisco Giants to the New York Mets.

May 12 1955: Sam (Toothpick) Jones of the Chicago Cubs became the first black to pitch a major league no-hitter, winning 4–0; in the ninth inning, he walked the first three hitters to load the bases, and then he struck out the next three to keep his no-hit game.

May 13 1888: DeWolf Hopper recited Ernest Lawrence Thayer's "Casey at the Bat" during the second act of *Prince Methusalem* in New York, thus beginning his long association with the poem.

May 14 1874: The football goal post was used for the first time in a game at Cambridge, Massachusetts, between Harvard and McGill University; in the same game, admission was charged for the first time at a collegiate sporting event

May 15   1952:   Johnny Longden became the second jockey in thoroughbred racing history to ride 4,000 winners, chasing home Fleet Diver at Hollywood Park racetrack, Inglewood, California.

May 16   1903:   George Wyman left San Francisco, California, on a motorcycle trip across the United States, which he completed less than two months later, the first man to accomplish the feat.

May 17   1939:   Television presented its first collegiate sports event, a baseball game between Princeton and Columbia at Baker Field in New York, broadcast by NBC over station W2XBS.

May 18   1942:   New York Police Commissioner Lewis Valentine ended night baseball games for the duration of World War Two, fearing that the glow of the ballpark lights would endanger shipping.

May 19   1973:   Secretariat, with Ron Turcotte aboard, won the Preakness on his way to thoroughbred racing's Triple Crown.

May 20   1925:   Tris Speaker scored the winning run from first base on a single as the Cleveland Indians pushed across six runs in the last of the ninth to defeat the New York Yankees 10–9.

May 21   1881:   The United States Lawn Tennis Association was formed in New York.

May 22   1884:   Hugh Daily, a one-armed pitcher for Chicago, fanned 13 Baltimore players in a Union Association game; on the same date in 1958, Bob Lightbody, a similarly handicapped pitcher for Great Falls, Montana, of the Pioneer League started a game against Boise.

May 23   1922:   Harry Greb handed Gene Tunney his only defeat in the prize ring, outpointing Tunney in a 15-round bout and winning the American light heavyweight championship.

May 24   1935:   The first major league night baseball game took place at Crosley Field in Cincinnati as the Cincinnati Reds defeated the Philadelphia Phillies 2–1.

May 25   1935:   Jesse Owens set or equaled four world records in less than an hour in a Big Ten Conference track meet at Ann Arbor, Michigan, winning the 100- and 220-yard dashes, the broad jump, and the 220-yard low hurdles.

May 26 1959: Harvey Haddix, pitching for the Pittsburgh Pirates at Milwaukee, completed twelve perfect innings, and then lost the game in the thirteenth inning, 1–0, on an error, a sacrifice, and Joe Adcock's double.

May 27 1931: Auguste Piccard and his assistant, Charles Kipfer, rose 51,775 feet in a 16-hour balloon flight after launching from Augsburg, Germany; a pressurized cabin was used for the first time.

May 28 1948: Patricia Canning Todd of La Jolla, California, the defending tennis champion, was eliminated from the French international championship by forfeit as a result of her refusal to play a semifinal match on a side court.

May 29 1951: Billy Joe Davidson of Marion, North Carolina, a high school pitcher, was signed by the Cleveland Indians for a then-record bonus of about $120,000. Davidson never played in the majors.

May 30 1986: Bobby Rahal became the first winner of the Indianapolis 500 auto race to average better than 170 mph.

May 31 1964: A new record for long major league baseball games was set in a 23-inning contest between the New York Mets and the San Francisco Giants, lasting seven hours and 23 minutes.

JUNE

June 1 1909: The first American transcontinental automobile race from New York to Seattle, Washington, began.

June 2 1954: Never Say Die won the Epsom Derby at Epsom, England, the first American-bred Epsom Derby winner since 1881.

June 3 1851: The Knickerbockers of New York became the first baseball team to wear uniforms, appearing on the field in blue trousers, white shirts, and straw hats.

June 4   1968: Don Drysdale of the Los Angeles Dodgers blanked the Pittsburgh Pirates 5–0 for his sixth straight shutout en route to a record 58⅔ scoreless innings—a record since broken by Orel Hersheiser, also of the Dodgers.

June 5   1935: The National Association of Professional Baseball Leagues advised the Albany, New York, club of the International League against signing Edwin (Alabama) Pitts, a Sing Sing convict about to be released from prison, fearing public resentment.

June 6   1890: The United States Polo Association was formed in New York.

June 7   1892: John Joseph Doyle became baseball's first pinch hitter, being used by the Cleveland Spiders against the Brooklyn Ward's Wonders in accordance with the 1891 baseball rules.

June 8   1950: Bobby Doerr's three homers, plus Ted Williams's and Walt Dropo's two homers each, led the Boston Red Sox to a 29–4 rout of the St. Louis Browns; Al Zarilla cracked four doubles.

June 9   1899: Jim Jeffries knocked out Bob Fitzsimmons at Coney Island, New York, to win the heavyweight boxing title.

June 10   1944: Joe Nuxhall, at 15 years, 10 months, became the youngest player in major league history when he pitched two thirds of an inning for the Cincinnati Reds in an 18–0 loss to the St. Louis Cardinals; his ERA for the appearance was 67.50.

June 11   1919: Sir Barton won the Belmont Stakes to become the first of the Triple Crown winners in American thoroughbred racing history.

June 12   1957: Paul Anderson lifted 6,270 pounds in a back lift (weight raised off trestles) at Toccoa, Georgia, for a new world record.

June 13   1935: James Braddock won the world heavyweight boxing title from Max Baer.

June 14   1901: The Myopia Hunt Club of Hamilton, Massachusetts, hosted the first professional open golf championship played under the rules of the United States Golf Association.

June 15   1938: Johnny Vander Meer of the Cincinnati Reds became the first pitcher in major league history to pitch two successive no-hit, no-run games, beating Brooklyn 6–0; he had pitched an 8–0 no-hitter against Boston on June 11.

June 16 1946: Byron Nelson lost the United States Open golf tournament to Lloyd Mangrum when his caddie accidentally kicked the ball, resulting in a penalty stroke.

June 17 1912: Wishing Ring, a 940–1 shot, came in first at Latonia Race Track in Kentucky.

June 18 1953: Gene Stephens got three hits and Sammy White scored three runs—all in one inning—as the Boston Red Sox pushed 17 runs across the plate in the bottom of the seventh en route to a 23–3 romp over the Detroit Tigers at Fenway Park.

June 19 1946: Joe Louis vs. Billy Conn became the first boxing match at which tickets sold for $100; the fight, at Yankee Stadium, was also the first heavyweight championship match to be televised.

June 20 1943: Gunder Haegg of Sweden outran Greg Rice, winner of 65 straight races, by 35 yards to win the 5,000-meter title at the National AAU track and field championships in New York.

June 21 1963: Bob Hayes set a world record for the 100-yard dash of 9.1 seconds.

June 22 1959: Eddie Lubanski bowled 24 strikes in a row, two perfect games back to back, in the Mixed Scotch Doubles tournament in Miami, Florida.

June 23 1917: Ernie Shore, a pitcher for the Boston Red Sox, turned in the greatest relief effort of all time; taking over for pitcher Babe Ruth with nobody out and a man on first, Shore got the baserunner stealing and then retired all 26 batters he faced, gaining a 4–0 win over Washington.

June 24 1952: Eddie Arcaro became the first American-born jockey to win 3,000 races.

June 25 1924: Emil Yde, pitching for the Pittsburgh Pirates in relief, hit a double in the ninth inning to tie the Chicago Cubs and then tripled in the 14th to win his own game.

June 26 1976: Toby Harrah of the American League Texas Rangers played an entire doubleheader at shortstop without having a chance to make any fielding plays.

June 27 1950: Charles McGinn, a West Point cadet, completed his swim of the 45-mile length of the Panama Canal; the swim required 36 hours of time in the water; he started on June 22.

June 28   1907:   Branch Rickey, an ineffectual New York Yankee catcher, had 13 Washington players steal on him as the Senators trounced the Yankees 16–5.

June 29   1897:   The Chicago White Stockings set an all-time record for runs scored in major league baseball as they tallied in every inning and ran up a 36–7 score against Louisville.

June 30   1859:   Blondin, a professional French acrobat, crossed Niagara Falls on a tightrope.

JULY

July 1   1950:   Bob Mathias became the first athlete to win the decathlon title of the Amateur Athletic Association three years in succession.

July 2   1921:   Jack Dempsey knocked out Georges Carpentier at Jersey City, New Jersey, in the first boxing match to attract a million dollar gate.

July 3   1912:   Rube Marquard of the New York Giants defeated Brooklyn 2–1 to run his season record to 19–0. (His win streak ended five days later against the Chicago Cubs.)

July 4   1943:   Barney Ross, a Marine sergeant and former lightweight and welterweight boxing champion, received the Silver Star for heroism on Guadalcanal.

July 5   1947:   John B. Kelly, Jr., of Philadelphia, whose father was barred from the event, won the Diamond Sculls of the Royal Henley Regatta in Henley-on-Thames, England.

July 6   1957:   Althea Gibson became the first black to win a Wimbledon singles tennis title.

July 7   1962:   Bill Hartack won his 3,000th horse race, riding Big Steve at Arlington Park in Chicago

July 8   1889:   John L. Sullivan and Jake Kilrain met in the last championship bare-knuckle fight; Sullivan won after 75 rounds.

July 9   1968:   The first baseball All-Star Game was played indoors at the Astrodome in Houston, Texas, with the National League winning 1–0 in this year of the pitcher; Willie Mays scored on a double play in the first inning.

July 10   1971:   Lee Trevino won the British Open golf tournament, joining Bobby Jones, Gene Sarazen, and Ben Hogan as the only golfers to win the United States and British Opens the same year.

July 11   1935:   John Cobb, an English wool broker, established six new world and twelve American automobile speed records in one hour at the Bonneville Salt Flats, Utah.

July 12   1954:   The Major League Baseball Players Association was organized in Cleveland, Ohio, to represent players in policy-making negotiations with club owners.

July 13   1896:   Ed Delahanty of Philadelphia became the second major league ballplayer (after Boston's Bobby Lowe in 1894) to hit four home runs in one game.

July 14   1969:   El Salvador invaded Honduras; growing tensions were aggravated by rioting over a series of regional soccer matches played as part of the World Soccer Cup competition.

July 15   1912:   Jim Thorpe won the decathlon in the Olympic Games at Stockholm, Sweden, and King Gustav, in closing ceremonies, hailed him as the world's greatest athlete.

July 16   1950:   The largest recorded crowd at any soccer match, 199,854, assembled at Rio de Janeiro, Brazil, for the World Cup finals between Brazil and Uruguay.

July 17   1941:   Joe DiMaggio's 56-game hitting streak was stopped by Cleveland Indians pitchers Al Smith and Jim Bagby before a crowd of 67,000 in a night game at Cleveland.

July 18   1927:   Ty Cobb collected his 4,000th major league hit, the first player in baseball history to reach that number.

July 19   1946:   Clarence (Pants) Rowland, president of the Triple-A Pacific Coast League, said it was inevitable the PCL would become the third major league; he foresaw a three-way World Series

July 20   1973:   Wilbur Wood of the Chicago White Sox started both games of a double-header against the New York Yankees, but he was knocked out of the box each time, losing both games.

July 21   1968:   Julius Boros, at the age of 48, became the oldest Professional Golfers' Association champion, winning the annual PGA tournament.

July 22   1950:   Stanley Sayers, in the speedboat Slo-Mo-Shun IV, beat Guy Lombardo's Tempo VI in a record time of 83.520 mph in the Gold Cup at Detroit, Michigan.

July 23   1972:   Eddie Merckx of Belgium, one of the greatest cyclists in the history of the sport, won his fourth consecutive Tour de France.

July 24   1973:   Mary Decker won the 800-meter run in the US-USSR track meet at Minsk, Russia, with a time of 2 minutes, 3.2 seconds; at age 14, she was the youngest competitor.

July 25   1930:   The Philadelphia Athletics executed a triple steal in the first inning against Cleveland and then came up with another one in the fourth inning, a feat unique in baseball history.

July 26   1950:   Ted Allen threw double ringers 36 times in a row, a record of 72 consecutive perfect pitches, in winning the world's horseshoe pitching title in Murray, Utah.

July 27   1912:   Carter Harrison, mayor of Chicago, banned the showing in Chicago of fight films of the Jack Johnson / Jim Flynn heavyweight championship bout held on July 4th in East Las Vegas, New Mexico, a contest stopped by police.

July 28   1973:   Ken Barnes of Bakersfield, California, captured his sixth world skeet shooting championship, in Savannah, Georgia, by outlasting five other marksmen who entered the playoff round with perfect scores.

July 29   1931:   Helen Wills Moody, the great woman tennis player, said in Seabright, New Jersey, that she approved of short skirts and no stockings on the tennis court, but that shorts would never make any headway among ranking women players.

July 30   1959:   Willie McCovey, just up from Phoenix of the Pacific Coast League, went 4-for-4 in his debut with the San Francisco Giants, including two triples.

July 31 1954: Joe Adcock, Milwaukee Braves first baseman, hit four homers and a double in a game in Brooklyn, setting a major league record for total bases, 18, as the Braves won 15–7.

AUGUST

August 1 1894: George Samuelson and Frank Harbo completed their crossing of the Atlantic in a rowboat, landing in England after a 3,000-mile trip that started in New York on June 6th.

August 2 1979: Thurman Munson, 32-year-old Yankee catcher, died when the Learjet he was piloting crashed at the Akron-Canton, Ohio, airport.

August 3 1852: Harvard and Yale held the first American intercollegiate rowing race in eight-oared boats on a two-mile course at Lake Winnepesaukee, Centre Harbor, New Hampshire.

August 4 1982: Joel Youngblood, New York Mets outfielder, drove in the winning run against the Cubs at Wrigley Field, Chicago; he then learned he had been traded to Montreal that day; catching a plane for Philadelphia, he appeared in right field for the Montreal Expos that night and hit a single.

August 5 1963: Craig Breedlove, driving the three-wheeled Spirit of America, became the first driver to top 400 mph in an auto, hitting 407.45 mph on the Bonneville Salt Flats, Utah.

August 6 1926: Gertrude Ederle became the first American woman to swim the English Channel.

August 7 1952: Satchel Paige, reputed to be 51 years old, pitched for Miami, Florida, in a Triple-A International League game and defeated the Columbus (Ohio) Clippers before a record minor league crowd of 57,000 in the Orange Bowl.

August 8 1950: Florence Chadwick swam the English Channel in 13 hours, 28 minutes from France to England, a new speed record, beating Gertrude Ederle's 14 hours, 31 minutes.

August 9   1957:   Lee Calhoun, the 1956 Olympic hurdles champion, lost his amateur status for having married Gwendolyn Bannister on the TV program *Bride and Groom* and accepting gifts on the show.

August 10   1944:   Red Barrett of the Boston Braves threw only 58 pitches in defeating the Cincinnati Reds 2–0 in a nine-inning game.

August 11   1923:   Enrique Tiraboschi of Argentina became the first person to swim the English Channel from France to England, completing the swim in 16 hours, 33 minutes and winning a $5,000 prize.

August 12   1964:   Mickey Mantle of the New York Yankees hit homers from both sides of the plate for the tenth and last time in his major league career.

August 13   1919:   Man o' War, the great thoroughbred, was defeated for the only time by a horse appropriately named Upset in the Stanford Memorial Stakes at Saratoga, New York.

August 14   1971:   The field for the 34th All-American Soap Box Derby run at Akron, Ohio, included five girls, the first to enter in Soap Box Derby history.

August 15   1939:   President Franklin D. Roosevelt caused wholesale alterations in the 1939 college football schedules by changing Thanksgiving from November 30 to November 23, since gate receipts would slump in games played on a non-holiday Thursday.

August 16   1960:   Joseph Kittinger, a parachutist, fell a record 84,700 feet, more than 16 miles, before opening his parachute, having ascended to that height in a balloon over Tularosa, New Mexico.

August 17   1938:   Henry Armstrong became the first boxer to hold three titles simultaneously by winning the lightweight championship from Lou Ambers in New York.

August 18   1922:   Gene Sarazen became the first golf champion to win the United States Open and the Professional Golfers Tournament the same year by winning the PGA tournament at Oakmont, Pennsylvania.

August 19   1951:   Bill Veeck used a 43-inch midget, Eddie Gaedel, as a pinch hitter for the St. Louis Browns' Frank Saucier. Detroit Tiger pitcher Bob Cain walked him, whereupon Jim Delsing was put in to run for Gaedel.

August 20   1974:   Nolan Ryan of the California Angels threw a pitch clocked at 100.9 mph, the fastest ever.

August 21   1947: D. Lee Braun became the first person in history to hold both the national skeet and trapshooting titles in one year as he won the North American clay target championship.

August 22   1851: *America*, a 191-foot yacht, won the first international yacht race over boats of the Royal Yacht Club at the Isle of Wight off the coast of England.

August 23   1982: Gaylord Perry, 43-year-old Seattle Mariners' reputed spitball pitcher, was ejected in the seventh inning for throwing a spitball; it was the first time he had been caught.

August 24   1963: John Pennel became the first man to pole vault 17 feet, clearing 17 feet ¾ inches, with a fiber glass pole at the Gold Coast track and field meet in Miami, Florida.

August 25   1962: Ted Campbell of San Jose, California, pitched a no-hitter in the Little League World Series in Williamsport, Pennsylvania; at 6 feet 1 inch, 210 pounds, Campbell was the biggest player ever to compete in this contest for 12-year-olds.

August 26   1951: Bernarr MacFadden, 83-year-old physical culturist, parachuted 2,000 feet from an airplane into the Hudson River near Yonkers, New York.

August 27   1982: Rickey Henderson of the Oakland A's broke Lou Brock's season stolen base record of 118 as he stole four bases against the Milwaukee Brewers; his season total was 130.

August 28   1926: Dutch Levsen, Cleveland Indians pitcher, hurled two complete-game wins over the Boston Red Sox, 6–1 and 5–1, striking out no one.

August 29   1972: Mark Spitz set a world record for the 200-meter freestyle swimming event in the Olympics at Munich, Germany, with a time of 1 minute, 52.78 seconds.

August 30   1905: Ty Cobb made his major league debut, collecting a double off Jack Chesbro of the New York Yankees to help the Detroit Tigers win 5–3.

August 31   1946: Rocky Marciano, former heavyweight boxing champion, died in a plane crash near Newton, Iowa.

SEPTEMBER

September 1   1972:   Bobby Fischer became the world chess champion by beating Boris Spassky of Russia.

September 2   1962:   Ken Hubbs of the Chicago Cubs, a rookie, set a fielding record for second basemen, playing his 74th straight game without an error, a record later beaten by Cincinnati's Joe Morgan.

September 3   1935:   Sir Malcolm Campbell became the first driver of an automobile to exceed 300 mph, reaching 301.13 mph in his Bluebird Special at Bonneville Salt Flats, Utah.

September 4   1953:   Casey Stengel and his New York Yankees won their fifth straight American League pennant, the first and only team to capture five flags in a row.

September 5   1972:   Eleven members of Israel's Olympic team were shot to death in Munich, Germany, by Arab terrorists.

September 6   1930:   Gallant Fox won the Lawrence Realization at Belmont Park race track in New York to become the leading money-winning thoroughbred racehorse of the day.

September 7   1970:   Bill Shoemaker rode his 6,033rd winner at Del Mar race track in California, breaking Johnny Longden's record for most wins by a jockey.

September 8   1965:   Bert Campaneris of the Oakland A's played all nine baseball positions, but had to leave the game after a ninth-inning collision with Ed Kirkpatrick of the California Angels; the Angels won in 13 innings.

September 9   1968:   Arthur Ashe became the first winner of the new United States Open tennis tournament by defeating Tom Okker of the Netherlands at Forest Hills, New York.

September 10   1960:   Abebe Bikila, an Ethiopian, ran barefooted in winning the Marathon at the Olympics in Rome, Italy.

September 11   1912:   Eddie Collins stole six bases for the Philadelphia Athletics against the Detroit Tigers; on September 22, Collins again stole six bases—both modern records

September 12 1976: Minnie Minoso of the Chicago White Sox singled in three plate appearances as a designated hitter; at 53 he was the oldest player to collect a hit in a regulation game.

September 13 1883: Hugh Daily, one-armed hurler for Cleveland, pitched a no-hit game against Philadelphia, winning 1–0.

September 14 1968: Denny McLain, Detroit Tigers pitcher, posted his 30th win of the season; his final mark was 31–6.

September 15 1930: Ely Culbertson won in a contract bridge challenge match in London between the United States and Great Britain, setting off a world craze for the game.

September 16 1960: Amos Alonzo Stagg announced his retirement at the age of 98 from coaching football.

September 17 1941: Stan Musial made his debut with the St. Louis Cardinals, going 2-for-4 in a win over the Boston Braves.

September 18 1830: Tom Thumb, the first locomotive built in America, lost a nine-mile race with a horse, over a course near Baltimore, Maryland.

September 19 1965: Tamara Press of Russia set a women's shot-put world record of 61 feet, at Kassel, Germany.

September 20 1973: Billie Jean King defeated Bobby Riggs in their $100,000 winner-take-all tennis match at the Astrodome in Houston; attendance was 30,492, the largest single crowd ever for a tennis match.

September 21 1934: Dizzy Dean of the St. Louis Cardinals pitched a 3-hit, 13–0 win over the Brooklyn Dodgers in the first game of a doubleheader; brother Paul then hurled a 3–0 no-hitter in the nightcap.

September 22 1927: Gene Tunney, aided by the famous "long count," defeated Jack Dempsey at Soldier Field, Chicago, winning the greatest purse to that time in boxing history: $990,446.

September 23 1908: Fred Merkle of the New York Giants made his famous "bonehead" play, failing to touch second base as the apparent winning Giant run crossed the plate against the Chicago Cubs; the game, declared a tie, was played over and the Cubs won.

September 24 1938: Don Budge became the first tennis champion to win four major titles—the Australian, French, British, and American—by winning the American title at Forest Hills, New York.

September 25 1928: Lucky, a German shepherd dog, finished a swim from Albany to New York City in 44 hours, 52 minutes, bettering by five hours the record held by George Creegan, a human being.

September 26 1981: Nolan Ryan, Houston Astros pitcher, hurled his fifth career no-hit, no-run game, a 5–0 victory over Los Angeles at the Astrodome.

September 27 1936: Walter Alston played in his only major league game as a late-inning substitute at first base for Johnny Mize of the St. Louis Cardinals; he struck out in his only time at bat.

September 28 1941: Ted Williams of the Boston Red Sox went 6-for-8 on the final day of the season against the Philadelphia A's, raising his batting average to .406.

September 29 1954: Willie Mays caught Vic Wertz's 440-foot center-field drive in the first game of the World Series between the New York Giants and Cleveland Indians at the Polo Grounds.

September 30 1927: Babe Ruth of the New York Yankees hit his 60th home run of the season to set a major league record.

OCTOBER

October 1 1961: Roger Maris of the New York Yankees hit his 61st home run of the season, breaking Babe Ruth's record, but earning an asterisk due to the greater number of games played.

October 2 1968: Bob Gibson of the St. Louis Cardinals established a new World Series record by striking out 17 Detroit Tiger batters in the opening game of the Series.

October 3 1951: Bobby Thomson hit "the shot heard 'round the world," a three-run homer in the bottom of the ninth inning off Ralph Branca to give the New York Giants a dramatic 5–4 playoff win over the Brooklyn Dodgers and the pennant.

October 4   1955:   Sandy Amoros, Brooklyn Dodger outfielder, made a sensational catch to help the Brooklyn Dodgers defeat the New York Yankees in the final game of the World Series.

October 5   1941:   Mickey Owen, Brooklyn Dodger catcher, dropped a third strike for what would have been the third out in a Dodger victory over the New York Yankees; instead the Yankees scored four runs to win the game, and eventually the Series.

October 6   1912:   Owen Wilson of the Pittsburgh Pirates set a major league record for three-base hits, 36, as he was nipped at the plate trying for an inside-the-park grand slam home run.

October 7   1916:   Georgia Tech trounced tiny Cumberland College in Atlanta, Georgia, in a football game by a score of 220–0.

October 8   1956:   Don Larson of the New York Yankees pitched the first and only perfect no-hit, no-run game in World Series history, beating the Brooklyn Dodgers 2–0.

October 9   1915:   President Woodrow Wilson attended the second game of the World Series in Philadelphia between the Phillies and the Boston Red Sox, the first U.S. President to attend a World Series game.

October 10   1920:   Bill Wambsganss, Cleveland Indians second baseman, made an unassisted triple play in a World Series game against the Brooklyn Dodgers, a unique record.

October 11   1919:   Belvin Maynard won the first transcontinental air race, a flight completed in San Francisco; the race had begun on October 8 at Mineola, New York.

October 12   1982:   Paul Molitor of the Milwaukee Brewers collected five hits, a World Series record, in the 10–0 Brewers' win over the St. Louis Cardinals in the Series opener.

October 13   1960:   Bill Mazeroski opened the bottom of the ninth inning with a home run off Ralph Terry of the New York Yankees to give the Pittsburgh Pirates a 10–9 win and the World Series title.

October 14   1905:   Christy Mathewson of the New York Giants blanked the Philadelphia Athletics 2–0 to give the Giants the World Series four games to one over the Philadelphia Athletics; it was Matty's third shutout in the Series, a record unlikely to be broken.

October 15   1917:   Eddie Collins scored the winning run for the Chicago White Sox in the World Series as the New York Giants left home plate unprotected, and third baseman Heinie Zimmerman could do no more than chase Collins futilely home.

October 16   1968:   Tommie Smith and John Carlos aroused a storm of criticism when they appeared shoeless and gave the Black Power salute during the playing of the National Anthem after winning medals for the U.S. in the 200-meter event of the Olympics at Mexico City.

October 17   1883:   A numerical scoring system was adopted for football, with five for a field goal, two for a touchdown, one for a safety, and four for a goal on the try after touchdown.

October 18   1924:   Red Grange of the University of Illinois turned in one of the greatest performances in college football by making four long touchdown runs in the first ten minutes of a game against Michigan; Illinois won the game 39–14.

October 19   1941:   Anna Lee Wiley became the first woman jockey to ride in a regular race at a recognized track in North America, narrowly losing in the Roamer Handicap at Agua Caliente, Mexico.

October 20   1931:   The *Harvard Crimson*, undergraduate daily newspaper at Harvard, urged that Army be eliminated from Harvard's football schedule because of the absence of interests common to Harvard men and West Point cadets.

October 21   1933:   Oregon State and the University of Southern California played to a 0–0 tie in a football game that saw five All-Americans on the field: Franklin and Schwammel for Oregon State; Rosenberg, Stevens, and Warburton for USC.

October 22   1797:   Andre Garnerin of France became the first person to parachute from a balloon, jumping out over Paris, France.

October 23   1930:   The first national open miniature golf tournament ended in Chattanooga, Tennessee, with J.K. Scott winning the men's title and J.E. Rankin the women's.

October 24   1901:   Anna Taylor, a 43-year-old widow from Bay City, Michigan, went over Niagara Falls in a barrel and survived.

October 25 1973: Chris Wills, a pre-med student from Santa Ana, California, won the first national hang-gliding championship in a competition held in the Angeles National Forest, Sylmar, California.

October 26 1960: The American League approved the transfer of the Washington Senators to Minnesota and announced that new franchises would be awarded to Washington and Los Angeles; this was the first major-league expansion in the 20th century.

October 27 1973: The University of Alabama football team set a total offense record of 828 yards in defeating Virginia Tech 77–6 at Tuscaloosa, Alabama.

October 28 1924: Fewer than 20 people attended an exhibition game in Dublin, Ireland, between touring baseball teams of the Chicago White Sox and New York Giants, evidently because the time of the game conflicted with church services.

October 29 1942: Branch Rickey was named president and general manager of the Brooklyn Dodgers, the team his St. Louis Cardinals had just defeated for the National League pennant.

October 30 1921: Centre College of Danville, Kentucky, defeated Harvard 6–0 in one of college football's great upsets.

October 31 1964: Kelso, a seven-year-old gelding, won the Jockey Club Gold Cup at Aqueduct racetrack in New York for the fifth straight time, raising his earnings to $1,803,362, a record at the time.

NOVEMBER

November 1 1950: Charles Cooper became the first black player in the National Basketball Association, playing his first game for the Boston Celtics in Fort Wayne, Indiana.

November 2 1934: Baseball fans in Tokyo, Japan, paralyzed traffic in their eagerness to shake hands with Babe Ruth, who was touring the Orient with an American League baseball team.

November 3 1957: Dick Buek, age 27, two-time national downhill ski champion, died in a plane crash at Donner Lake, California.

November 4 1924: Professional boxing was legalized in California by constitutional amendment, with a State Boxing Commission and strict restraints, after having been outlawed for ten years.

November 5 1938: Rutgers Stadium was dedicated, and Rutgers defeated Princeton for the first time since their historic first intercollegiate football game 60 years earlier.

November 6 1869: Rutgers defeated Princeton 6–4 at New Brunswick, New Jersey, in the first intercollegiate football game in America, each team having 25 players on the field.

November 7 1935: Stanford University's daily newspaper recommended that a standardized basis for paying college athletes be adopted before the "public gets wise to what's going on."

November 8 1970: Tom Dempsey, the New Orleans Saints' field goal kicker, born without a right hand and with only half a right foot, kicked a record 63-yard field goal to give the Saints a 19–17 victory over the Detroit Lions.

November 9 1912: Pop Warner, Carlisle football coach, first used his double wingback or T-formation in a game between the Carlisle team, featuring Jim Thorpe, and an Army team that included Dwight D. Eisenhower at right halfback; Carlisle won 27–6.

November 10 1940: Sammy Baugh, Washington Redskins quarterback, set a National Football League record by completing 23 passes in a game against the Brooklyn Dodgers, but the Dodgers still won, 16–14, over the previously undefeated Redskins.

November 11 1868: The first American amateur indoor track and field meet was held in New York by the New York Athletic Club.

November 12 1944: Army's football team, including Glenn Davis and Doc Blanchard, defeated Notre Dame 59–0; it was Army's first win over the Fighting Irish since 1931.

November 13 1939: Mrs. Riley Bryan, a teacher at Lincoln Rural School, was permitted to close school during the deer hunting season by the Board of Education in Coldwater, Michigan, after promising to make up lost time by opening school two weeks early

November 14   1943: Sid Luckman of the Chicago Bears became the first pro quarterback to throw seven touchdown passes in one game.

November 15   1973: Bobby Orr scored three goals and added four assists as the Boston Bruins defeated the New York Rangers 10–2.

November 16   1957: Notre Dame defeated Oklahoma 7–0 in a football game that was a highlight of Oklahoma's 50th anniversary of statehood celebration.

November 17   1968: In a televised football game, NBC cut away during the last minute to broadcast *Heidi*; Oakland then scored twice in nine seconds to come from behind and win the game 43–32.

November 18   1938: Jimmy Londos, 42-year-old Greek, claimed the world's heavyweight wrestling championship after defeating ex-football-player Bronko Nagurski of Minnesota before 10,000 fans at Convention Hall, Philadelphia.

November 19   1932: Joe Kershalla, halfback for West Liberty State College in West Virginia, scored 71 points in a football game against Cedarville College as West Liberty won 127–0.

November 20   1969: Pele scored his 1,000th goal in a soccer game held in Rio de Janeiro, Brazil.

November 21   1971: The New York Rangers scored eight goals in the final period, tying a record set in 1947; they won 12–1 over the California Golden Seals.

November 22   1986: Mike Tyson knocked out Trevor Berbick in the second round at Las Vegas to win the world heavyweight boxing title.

November 23   1934: Plans were announced for the conversion of a building of the Baldwin Locomotive Works in Philadelphia, Pennsylvania, into a huge indoor/outdoor stadium with a movable steel ceiling, permitting sports events regardless of weather.

November 24   1938: The National Semi-Pro Baseball Congress announced that the yellow baseball would be the official ball for the national semi-pro tournament at Wichita, Kansas, in 1939.

November 25   1961: Bob Cousy of the National Basketball Association Boston Celtics scored his 15,000th point, joining Dolph Schayes as the second professional basketball player to reach this mark

November 26   1961:   Don Carter of St. Louis, Missouri, won the World Invitational Bowling Tournament for his fourth victory in the tournament's five-year history.

November 27   1926:   The largest crowd ever to watch a high school football game, 57,000, saw Los Angeles and Polytechnic High Schools in Los Angeles play to a 7–7 tie in their annual Thanksgiving Day football game at the Coliseum.

November 28   1929:   Ernie Nevers scored all 40 points for the Chicago Cardinals as they defeated the Chicago Bears, an all-time one man/one game scoring record for big-time pro football.

November 29   1890:   The first Army-Navy football game was played at West Point, New York, with Navy winning 24–0.

November 30   1948:   The Negro National League was dissolved, leaving the Negro American League with its ten teams to continue black baseball.

DECEMBER

December 1   1973:   Jack Nicklaus won the Walt Disney World Open golf tournament in Lake Buena Vista, Florida, becoming the first player in golfing history to pass $2 million in career earnings.

December 2   1929:   Earl (Dutch) Clark accounted for all the scoring as Colorado College defeated the University of Denver 3–2 in a football game, being forced into a safety for Denver's two points and then kicking a field goal for his own team's three.

December 3   1968:   The Baseball Rules Committee announced that for the 1969 season the pitching mound would be lowered from 15 to 10 inches in an attempt to lessen growing pitcher dominance.

December 4   1954:   Bang Away of Sirrah Crest, a canine boxer, won best-of-show in Bronx County New York Kennel Club show, becoming the first American show dog to win 100 best-in-show awards.

December 5 1970: The Stanley Cup, the Conn Smythe Trophy, and the Bill Masterson Memorial Trophy were stolen from the Hockey Hall of Fame in Toronto; they were later recovered.

December 6 1951: Kenneth (Tug) Wilson, commissioner of the Big Ten, disclosed he had hired a former FBI agent to help enforce the conference's athletic code.

December 7 1963: Instant replay was used for the first time, by CBS, during the televising of the Army-Navy football game.

December 8 1943: The Boxing Writers Association of New York presented the Edward J. Neil Memorial Plaque for outstanding contributions to the ring sport to the 4,019 boxers in the armed services, the first time the award had not gone to an individual.

December 9 1788: George Washington's diary noted the sale of his racehorse Magnolia to Colonel Henry Lee for 5,000 acres of Kentucky land.

December 10 1810: Tom Molineaux, a black American, fought Tom Cribb for the world heavyweight title, losing on a fluke in 40 rounds at Copthall Common, England, the first interracial title bout in boxing history.

December 11 1947: Baseball's two existing major leagues rejected the application of the Triple-A Pacific Coast League for major league status.

December 12 1959: Bruce McLaren of New Zealand became auto racing's youngest grand prix winner, winning the U.S. Grand Prix at Sebring, Florida; his age was 22 years, 104 days.

December 13 1960: George Koltanowski of Belgium, a chess expert, played 56 opponents blindfolded, winning 50 matches, drawing six, and losing none, in 9¾ hours in a chess tournament at the Fairmont Hotel in San Francisco, California.

December 14 1943: Lou Little, whose football team at Columbia University did not win a game in eight starts, received the annual award of the Touchdown Club of New York for his outstanding contribution to the sport in perpetuating it during wartime.

December 15 1973: The International Hot Rod Association announced a drastic reduction in its 1974 schedule because of the energy crisis.

December 16 1973: O.J. Simpson became the first 2,000-yard rusher in professional football history, finishing a game in which the Buffalo Bills defeated the New York Jets 34–14 with a season total of 2,003 yards.

December 17 1979: Stan Barrett set the land speed record for a wheeled vehicle, driving the Budweiser Rocket 739.666 mph, or Mach 1.0106, at Edwards Air Force Base, California.

December 18 1949: Star girl jockey Wantha Davis, riding Northeast, beat veteran rider Johnny Longden on Gray Spook in a match race at Tijuana race track in Mexico as part of her campaign to have female jockeys be allowed to compete equally.

December 19 1950: The elimination of trigonometry and elementary physics from its entrance requirements brought the Naval Academy's standards into line with West Point's and improved Navy's chances of recruiting good football players.

December 20 1954: Ernestine Russell, a 16-year-old gymnast, won the Rose Bowl Trophy as Canada's best woman athlete of the year.

December 21 1937: Byron (Whizzer) White, All-American football back from the University of Colorado, the nation's leading scorer in 1937, and later a United States Supreme Court Justice, received a Rhodes Scholarship.

December 22 1877: The *American Bicycling Journal* began publication in Boston.

December 23 1968: The Kentucky State Racing Commission ruled that although Dancer's Image finished first in the Kentucky Derby, illegal drugs administered prior to the race had been, and the purse went to Forward Pass.

December 24 1950: Lou Groza kicked a field goal in the final 20 seconds to give the Cleveland Browns a 30–28 win over the Los Angeles Rams; the win gave coach Paul Brown his fifth straight professional title.

December 25 1894: The University of Chicago became the first Midwest football team to play on the West Coast, defeating Stanford 24–4 in a game played at San Francisco.

December 26 1960: Norm Van Brocklin, quarterback of the Philadelphia Eagles, played his last game, as the Eagles defeated the Green Bay Packers 17–13 to win the NFL championship.

December 27 1946: The United States tennis team in Melbourne, Australia, won the Davis Cup for the first time since 1938.

December 28 1958: The Baltimore Colts defeated the New York Giants 23–17 in an extra sudden-death period for the NFL championship in what some regard as the greatest football game ever played.

December 29 1937: Babe Ruth declined the offer of a baseball comeback as manager of the DeLand Reds of the Class D Florida State League.

December 30 1907: A commission headed by Abraham Mills IV, reporting on the origins of baseball, decided the game was an invention of Abner Doubleday at Cooperstown, New York, in 1839.

December 31 1972: Roberto Clemente died in a plane crash while taking food and medicine to earthquake victims in Nicaragua.

SPEAKER'S
CALENDAR
OF SPORTS STARS'
BIRTHDAYS

JANUARY

January 1/Hank Greenberg/1911/baseball

Home runs were the stock-in-trade of Detroit Tigers' first baseman Hank Greenberg. His 58 homers in 1938 fell only two short of Babe Ruth's highest total for a season. During the 1938 season, Greenberg hit two or more home runs in 11 games—the most two-or-more homers per game ever hit in one year.

January 2/Calvin Hill/1947/football

In his second start for the Dallas Cowboys, Calvin Hill broke the club's single-game rushing record. His 942 yards rushing that season earned him NFL Rookie of the Year honors. In 1972, he became the first Cowboys back to gain 1,000 yards in a season. Twice an All-Pro, Hill played in Super Bowls V and VI.

January 3/Bobby Hull/1939/hockey

One of the strongest, most opinionated men ever to play pro hockey, Bobby Hull battled the NHL over the use of the curved blade (which he favored) and fought the management of the Chicago Black Hawks over his salary (which he always thought was too low). Hull led the NHL in goals seven times.

January 4/Floyd Patterson/1935/boxing

Floyd Patterson became the first heavyweight boxing champion to regain the title after losing it. He kayoed Ingemar Johansson of Sweden in the fifth round in New York City to win back the title he had lost to Johansson less than a year earlier.

January 5/Riggs Stephenson/1898/baseball

When Joe McCarthy became manager of the Chicago Cubs in 1926, he obtained "Old Hoss" Stephenson to join Hack Wilson and Kiki Cuyler in one of the hardest hitting outfields of all time. Stephenson's .444 led Cub batters in the 1932 World Series, and his lifetime batting average was a hefty .336.

January 6/Early Wynn/1920/baseball

Very few baseball players have had major-league careers spanning four decades. Early Wynn is one who did. He appeared in three games for the Washington Senators in 1939 and closed out his career in 1963 with a lone victory for the Cleveland Indians. He won exactly 300 games in the majors.

January 7/Maurice McLoughlin/1890/tennis

Dubbed the "California Comet," Maurice McLoughlin burst upon the tennis scene by winning both the national singles and doubles (with Thomas C. Bundy) in 1912 and 1913. Red-haired and aggressive, McLoughlin pioneered the serve as an offensive weapon, thus changing the nature of tennis dramatically.

January 8/Walker Cooper/1915/baseball

Catcher Walker Cooper and his brother, pitcher Mort Cooper, were at their best during the wartime years of 1942 to 1944. They starred as a brother battery for the St. Louis Cardinals. With Mort pitching and Walker catching, the Cards won the National League pennant each of those years.

January 9/Bart Starr/1934/football

When Vince Lombardi took over as head coach of the Green Bay Packers, he made Bart Starr his starting quarterback. Starr, one of the stellar passers in the game, spent his entire 16-year career at Green Bay. He holds the all-time record for most passes attempted without an interception: 294.

January 10/Willie McCovey/1938/baseball

Willie McCovey shares honors with Willie Mays as the best power hitter in San Francisco Giants history. His 521 lifetime homers put him well up on the all-time list, not far behind the other Willie. Seven times an All-Star first baseman, McCovey was the NL's Most Valuable Player in 1969.

January 11/Elmer Flick/1876/baseball

A swift, steady outfielder for the Phillies and Indians, Elmer Flick was involved in a classic might-have-been trade with the Detroit Tigers. After the 1907 season, the Tigers offered their young star Ty Cobb in exchange for Flick. Strange as it seems today, the Indians nixed the deal.

January 12/Ray Harroun/1879/auto racing

The Indianapolis 500 automobile race was a brand-new event in 1911. At the wheel of the winning car was the otherwise little-known Ray Harroun, who roared around the track at an average speed of 74.59 miles per hour.

January 13/Art Ross/1886/hockey

Although Art Ross was a fine hockey player, putting in 14 years with teams from Manitoba to Quebec, he is best known as the promoter who brought hockey permanently to Boston. He coached the Bruins to three Stanley Cups and, as an inventor, is credited with the kind of nets and puck now in use in the NHL.

January 14/Smead Jolley/1902/baseball

Smead Jolley put in four years as a major league outfielder. He did all right as a hitter, batting .305, but in the outfield, he was Mr. Awkward. He pulverized pitchers in the high minors, especially for San Francisco of the Pacific Coast League, where in 1927 and 1928 he led all hitters with .397 and .404.

January 15/Randy White/1953/football

A superb defensive lineman for the Dallas Cowboys, Randy White was selected to every Pro Bowl from 1975 through 1985. Nicknamed "The Monster," he and Harvey Martin were voted co-MVPs in Super Bowl XII when the Cowboys defeated the Denver Broncos 27–10.

January 16/Dizzy Dean/1911/baseball

One day Dizzy Dean, who needs no introduction, pitched a three-hitter in the first game of a doubleheader. His brother Paul, a Cardinal teammate, pitched the second game and threw a no-hitter. "Shucks," said Diz, "if I'd known Paul was gonna pitch a no-hitter, I'd a pitched one too."

January 17/Jacque Plante/1929/hockey

A great goalie and a sensible man, Jacques Plante introduced the face mask into widespread use in the NHL. He got the idea for it when a fan sent him a welder's mask. Plante later turned to manufacturing hockey face masks in Magog, Quebec.

January 18/Muhammad Ali/1942/boxing

Muhammad Ali, born Cassius Clay, won his first National AAU boxing title in Toledo, shouting, "I am the prettiest and greatest!" One of his most famous heavyweight championship bouts was the "Thrilla in Manila," October 1, 1975, a classic fight in which Ali kayoed Joe Frazier in the 14th round.

January 19/Chick Gandil/1888/baseball

An authentic sports villain, Chick Gandil, the leathery first baseman of the Chicago White Sox, is generally identified as the ringleader and paymaster in the infamous scheme to throw the 1919 World Series. Along with seven other of the "Black Sox," he was banned from organized baseball for life.

January 20/Carol Heiss/1940/figure skating

Carol Heiss captured the world women's figure skating championship four straight times as a teenager. At 16, she won a silver medal at the 1956 Winter Olympics, losing by a close margin to fellow American Tenley Albright. In the 1960 Olympics at Squaw Valley, she took the gold.

January 21/Jack Nicklaus/1940/golf

The greatest golfer in the history of the game, Jack Nicklaus has been both the youngest and the oldest player to win the prestigious U.S. Masters tournament. Overall, Nicklaus has won more major championships than any other golfer, and his total is thought to be unapproachable.

January 22/Mike Bossy/1957/hockey

An opposing goalie said of him, "You're always looking for Bossy, wondering where he is. Sometimes you never see him until he's scored on you." It was that come-from-nowhere ability that earned Mike Bossy the nickname "the phantom of the rinks" and helped him score a record 53 goals as an NHL rookie.

January 23/Jerry Kramer/1936/football

A guard on the Green Bay Packers in their glory days of the 1960s, Jerry Kramer played in the first two Super Bowls, both of which the Packers won. But he is probably better known as an author specializing in—what else?—football. His book *Instant Replay* is one of the best inside depictions of the pro game.

January 24/Giorgio Chinaglia/1947/soccer

When Giorgio Chinaglia, an Italian soccer star, joined the renowned Pelé on the New York Cosmos, fans knew they could count on plenty of shooting and scoring. They weren't disappointed. Chinaglia quickly established himself as the leading scorer in the North American Soccer League.

January 25/Lou Groza/1924/football

They called him "The Toe," and no wonder. After 17 years in the NFL, Lou Groza had scored just one touchdown—six points. But he had kicked 641 extra points and 234 field goals. Add those to his totals, and he comes out with 1,349 points. Among his many records are three field goals in each of 21 games.

January 26/Wayne Gretzky/1961/hockey

Every now and then a player comes along who is so dominant that he rewrites the record book. In hockey that player was Wayne Gretzky. For eight straight years Gretzky, playing for the Edmonton Oilers, led the league in scoring. He was named the league's Most Valuable Player in each of those years.

January 27/Joe Perry/1927/football

One of pro football's great running backs, Fletcher Joseph Perry played for the San Francisco 49ers from 1948 to 1960 and again in 1963, with a two-year stopover as a Baltimore Colt. He was among the first blacks in modern pro football—and the first runner ever to gain 1,000 yards in consecutive seasons.

January 28/Parry O'Brien/1932/track and field

Parry O'Brien pioneered the step-back style of shot putting. He would start with his back in the direction of the throw, something no one had ever done before. And it worked. O'Brien won Olympic gold medals in 1952 and 1956 and a silver medal in 1960. He broke the world shotput record 14 times.

January 29/Barney Oldfield/1878/auto racing

A noted bicycle racer, Barney Oldfield answered Henry Ford's call for a racing car driver in 1902. He had never driven a car before, but after two weeks of practice he won the Detroit five-mile classic, averaging nearly 60 miles an hour. Before the race, he said, "Well, the chariot may kill me, but. . . ."

January 30/Therman Gibson/1917/bowling

In 31 years of bowling, Therman Gibson's American Bowling Congress average was 198. He rolled six 1900s and was three times a member of the ABC championship team in the '50s. He had two sanctioned 300 games and four 299s.

January 31/Jackie Robinson/1919/baseball

Jackie Robinson, the man who integrated major league baseball, was more than a sports hero. He was also a significant historical figure. But civil rights aside, he was a superb ballplayer. Rookie of the Year for the Brooklyn Dodgers in 1947, he won the National League batting championship in 1949 with a .342 average. He also won the MVP Award that year.

FEBRUARY

February 1/Nat Holman/1896/basketball

In the 1920s, sportswriters viewed Nat Holman as pro basketball's greatest star. He played forward for the Original Celtics of New York City, a team that won 720 of 795 games. Today he is most often remembered as head basketball coach of CCNY, where his teams racked up a .689 winning percentage

February 2/George Halas/1895/football

The National Football League and George (Papa Bear) Halas are practically synonymous. A fine athlete as a youth—in fact, MVP of the 1919 Rose Bowl game and briefly a New York Yankee—he founded the team that became the Chicago Bears. He served the Bears as player, coach, and owner for 63 years.

February 3/Fran Tarkenton/1940/football

When Fran Tarkenton took over as quarterback of the Minnesota Vikings, they were a first-year expansion team. Their pass protection was none too good, and Tarkenton pioneered (and apparently named) "scrambling." His technique often demanded ball carrying and thus added to the duties of the quarterback.

February 4/Byron Nelson/1912/golf

Byron Nelson began in golf as a fellow caddie with Ben Hogan. His first year on the pro tour gave no hint of what was to come; he won $12.50. As he improved, he became a key figure in the evolution of the golf swing. His "one-piece" motion was emulated by pro and amateur golfers across America.

February 5/Hank Aaron/1934/baseball

At the age of 40, Hank Aaron, a quiet outfielder for the Atlanta Braves, broke Babe Ruth's lifetime record for most home runs. Number 715 came on April 8, 1974, against the L.A. Dodgers' Al Downing. And Hammering Hank wasn't through yet. When he retired as a player in 1976, his total stood at 755

February 6/Babe Ruth/1895/baseball

One of the most quoted remarks in sports history came from the immortal Babe. When reminded that he was earning more money than President Hoover, he quipped, "I had a better year than he did." The Sultan of Swat had a lot of good years, and fans of his era fully expected Ruth's home run records to endure forever

February 7/Charlie Jamieson/1893/baseball

Although his name is less familiar than that of the superstars, Charlie Jamieson was a brilliant left fielder for the Cleveland Indians for 14 seasons in the '20s and '30s. A lifetime .303 hitter, he was noted for bunting the ball hard down the first base line and then screening it with his feet while running.

February 8/Boo Smith/1920/football

If you've never seen the 1942 Columbia Pictures' release, *Smith of Minnesota*, you're not alone. The subject of the film, Bruce (Boo) Smith, was briefly a pro with the Green Bay Packers. He gained fleeting fame as a superb halfback for the University of Minnesota, winning the Heisman Trophy in 1941 and a closetful of other college awards.

February 9/John (Brooms) Abramovic/1919/basketball

The first college player to score 2,000 points, Brooms Abramovic (his father owned a broom factory) played for tiny Salem College. He was an All-American and the nation's leading scorer for two years. He netted 57 points in one game, a record at the time. Abramovic played pro basketball for a number of teams.

February 10/Bill Tilden/1893/tennis

A tall, thin right-hander, Big Bill Tilden injected high drama into tennis. Often he did this unintentionally, by falling far behind in an important match. Tilden would then bear down hard and come back to win. He did this well enough and often enough to take an unprecedented six straight U.S. tennis titles

February 11/Tommy Hitchcock/1900/polo

A graduate of Harvard, Tommy Hitchcock became a World War One aerial hero with the Lafayette Escadrille. Between the wars, he established himself as probably the outstanding polo player of all time. He was killed in an airplane crash in England in World War Two while commanding a U.S. fighter plane group.

February 12/Bill Russell/1934/basketball

When Bill Russell took over as coach of the Boston Celtics, he became the first black to head a major professional sports team. As a player for the Celtics, Russell changed the nature of the game by putting a new emphasis on defense. He won the NBA's Most Valuable Player award five times.

February 13/Patty Berg/1918/golf

Patty Berg won more than 80 tournaments in her pro golfing career. In 1951, she went to England with Babe Zaharias and Betty Jameson to challenge the British women pros. Winning easily, they were then matched against a group of men, two of whom were Walker Cup players. The women took every match.

February 14/Johnny Longden/1910/horse racing

Only ten jockeys in the history of thoroughbred racing have ridden Triple Crown winners. One of them was Johnny Longden, who was aboard Count Fleet in 1943. Longden was no stranger to the winner's circle. In his long career, the British jockey rode 6,032 winners and was the first ever to top 5,000.

February 15/Graham Hill/1929/auto racing

Sad but true—many top auto racing drivers die on the racetrack. Graham Hill was an exception—he died in a 1975 plane crash. A handsome and reserved Londoner, Hill won the Grand Prix championship in 1962 and 1968, and the Indianapolis 500 in 1966

February 16/John McEnroe/1959/tennis

He was called "Superbrat," "the Incredible Sulk," and so on, but no one could deny that for a while John McEnroe was the best tennis player in the world. He first won the U.S. Open in 1979. In 1981, he beat Bjorn Borg at Wimbledon, but his oncourt outbursts were such that the Wimbledon committee for the first time refused to make their new champion a member

February 17/Jim Brown/1936/football

Drafted out of Syracuse University, running back Jim Brown of the Cleveland Browns won eight NFL rushing championships in nine seasons. Never carrying the ball fewer than 200 times a season, Brown set many NFL records. After leaving the game, he appeared in a number of movies, including *The Dirty Dozen*.

February 18/George Gipp/1895/football

"Win one for the Gipper" said Knute Rockne (maybe) and Ronald Reagan (for sure). George Gipp was a gifted athlete but a self-destructive carouser. A brilliant runner and kicker for four years at Notre Dame, he became a national legend after his early, tragic death from pneumonia.

February 19/Eddie Arcaro/1916/horse racing

Eddie Arcaro was the premier American jockey prior to Bill Shoemaker. Arcaro rode 4,779 winners, five of them in the Kentucky Derby, six in the Preakness, and six in the Belmont Stakes. He rode two Triple Crown winners, Whirlaway in 1941, and Citation in 1948.

February 20/Phil Esposito/1942/hockey

"I don't get people excited," Phil Esposito was quoted as saying. Maybe not, but the Canadian-born center led the NHL in scoring five times and was named MVP twice. A steady, patient man with the puck, Esposito played for the Chicago Black Hawks, Boston Bruins, and New York Rangers.

February 21/Ron Clarke/1937/track

Australian track star Ron Clarke was the finest distance runner never to win a major championship. He set 17 distance records from 2-miles to 20,000-meters. Favored to win the 10,000-meter race at the 1964 Tokyo Olympics, Clarke ran well but finished third—one of the great upsets in Olympic history.

February 22/Julius Erving/1950/basketball

The famed "Dr. J," Julius Erving first attracted attention on the playgrounds of Harlem. A player with scintillating moves, he became the ABA's leading scorer in his second season with the Virginia Squires. He was MVP in the ABA three times and in the NBA once. Erving's stylish play made him a drawing card.

February 23/Elston Howard/1930/baseball

Elston Howard, a quiet, capable catcher, became the first black player on the New York Yankees, joining the team as a rookie in 1955. The Yankees won four consecutive pennants from 1955 to 1958. At the time, Howard was in the outfield and Yogi Berra was still a fixture behind the plate. Howard took over as Yankee catcher in 1960.

February 24/Honus Wagner/1874/baseball

Now and then someone will name Honus Wagner as the greatest baseball player of all time, and most experts consider him the game's best shortstop. The Flying Dutchman, as he was called, won eight batting titles in his 21-year career. He became one of the five original inductees of the Baseball Hall of Fame.

February 25/Bobby Riggs/1918/tennis

Although Bobby Riggs had been the U.S. Open Champion in 1941, he is remembered best for his challenge, at the age of 55, to women's champion Billie Jean King. His contention was that even an old man like him could beat a top woman in her prime. On September 20, 1973, Ms. King demolished Riggs, 6–4, 6–3, 6–3.

February 26/Grover Cleveland Alexander/1887/baseball

Grover Cleveland Alexander's finest hour came in game seven of the 1926 World Series. With St. Louis leading the Yankees 3 to 2, the Yanks loaded the bases. The Cards called in their 39-year-old righthander to face rookie slugger Tony Lazzeri. Old Pete, who had pitched the Cards to a Series-tying victory the day before, struck out Lazzeri to save the Series.

February 27/Gene Sarazen/1902/golf

Gene Sarazen, at five-feet-five-inches, was the shortest major championship golfer. When he first won the U.S. Open, he was the youngest ever, winning the last round with a 68—at that time, the record closing round by a champion. Sarazen is generally credited with inventing the modern sand iron.

February 28/Mario Andretti/1940/auto racing

Mario Andretti could race anything on four wheels—and win. One of the most versatile of racing car drivers, he drove Indianapolis cars, grand prix cars, stock cars, sports cars, sprint cars, midgets—and was competitive in all of them. He won the Daytona 500 in 1967, the Indy 500 in 1969, and the grand prix championship in 1978.

February 29/Pepper Martin/1904/baseball

Pepper Martin and Dizzy Dean were the head entertainers on the St. Louis Cardinals' colorful Gashouse Gang. Martin raced midget autos until Branch Rickey persuaded him to give it up. As a ballplayer, he was no slouch. His .418 batting average in three World Series (22 hits in 53 at-bats) is the highest ever.

MARCH

March 1/Duke Keats/1895/hockey

A native of Montreal, Gordon (Duke) Keats might better have been nicknamed "Suitcase." Although he played only three years in the NHL—for Boston, Detroit, and Chicago—he achieved lasting fame with various pro and amateur teams across western Canada. Keats was elected to the Hockey Hall of Fame in 1958.

March 2/Mel Ott/1909/baseball

Mel Ott played 35 major league games as a 17-year-old. He hit the first of his 511 career home runs when he was 18. From beginning to end—22 seasons in all—the durable Ott patroled right field for the New York Giants. His odd batting style, with a raised right foot while striding, was unmistakable.

March 3/Herschel Walker/1962/football

Big, lightning-fast running back Herschel Walker set innumerable records in high school, college, and pro football. He led his University of Georgia team to the national championship in 1980 and won the Heisman Trophy in 1982. Walker had great seasons with the New Jersey Generals and Dallas Cowboys.

March 4/Knute Rockne/1888/football

One of the most famous sports personalities of his day, Knute Rockne not only coached Notre Dame's football team, but he also wrote books, ran coaching clinics, and gave inspirational speeches. Led by this master of psychology, the Notre Dame team lost only 12 games in the 13 years he was head coach.

March 5/Milt Schmidt/1918/hockey

Milt Schmidt spent his entire NHL career, 1936 through 1955, with the Boston Bruins, playing on one of the strongest forward units ever. A hard-hitting center, Schmidt won the league scoring title in 1940. While serving with the Royal Canadian Air Force in World War Two, he played for the Ottawa Hurricanes.

March 6/Willie Stargell/1941/baseball

Willie Stargell was a mainstay of the powerful Pittsburgh Pirates of the 1970s. Playing the outfield and later first base, he led what he called "an amazing bunch of people" to six league Championship Series and two World Series. A powerful hitter and consistent performer, he was pretty amazing himself.

March 7/Franco Harris/1950/football

Famous for his "immaculate reception" of a deflected "Hail Mary" pass that defeated Oakland in the 1972 playoffs, Franco Harris, a running back for the Pittsburgh Steelers, went on to star in the Super Bowl that year—and in three more Super Bowls. Harris's postseason play was often spectacular.

March 8/Jim Rice/1953/baseball

An outfielder for the Boston Red Sox, Jim Rice contributed much to the awesome offense of that team. In '79, he and teammate Fred Lynn shared top-five American League honors for batting average, home runs, RBIs, slugging average, and total bases. Both came close to the Triple Crown, but missed.

March 9/Bobby Fischer/1943/chess

In 1958 Bobby Fischer became the youngest international grand master in the history of chess. His highly publicized match with Russian grand master Boris Spassky took place in Reykjavik, Iceland, in 1972. After losing the first game, Fischer came back to win. He resigned the title in 1974.

March 10/Marques Haynes/1926/basketball

Marques Haynes, the "world's greatest dribbler," played guard for the Harlem Globetrotters from 1947 to 1953. Haynes, along with Goose Tatum and Meadowlark Lemon, helped to make the team internationally famous. Haynes left the Globetrotters to form his own touring club, the Fabulous Magicians.

March 11/Louise Brough/1923/tennis

Louise Brough, a brilliant volleyer, won the women's singles title at Wimbledon three straight years and the U.S. singles title once. She shared honors in American women's doubles for ten years, 1944 to 1950 and 1955 to 1957. Like Doris Hart and Margaret Osborne duPont, she lost her singles' dominance to Maureen Connolly.

March 12/Dale Murphy/1956/baseball

Ted Turner's cable television network made it possible for much of the nation to watch Atlanta Braves baseball. But all too often, the only Brave worth watching was center-fielder Dale Murphy, who put together back-to-back MVP seasons in 1982 and 1983.

March 13/Doug Harvey/1940/hockey

A consistent NHL All-Star defenseman, Doug Harvey was a master at controlling the tempo of the game. He played for the Montreal Canadiens in a period of near-invincibility, when they skated to five Stanley Cup championships in a row, from 1956 through 1960. He was the team's acknowledged leader.

March 14/Wes Unseld/1946/basketball

One of the great debuts in sports history—that was Wes Unseld's with the Baltimore Bullets in 1969. Only six-feet-eight, Unseld in the pivot combined with Earl (The Pearl) Monroe to lead the Bullets from last place to first in NBA's Eastern Division. Unseld was named Rookie of the Year and MVP.

March 15/Norm Van Brocklin/1926/football

Norm Van Brocklin starred as quarterback for the Los Angeles Rams and Philadelphia Eagles. At first he had a tough time getting starting assignments at L.A., since the great Bob Waterfield was also on the team. In his last year, "the Dutchman" led the Eagles to the NFL championship.

March 16/Pat O'Dea/1872/football

The kicking game owes a lot to Pat (Kangaroo Kicker) O'Dea. Born in Australia, O'Dea starred for four years at the University of Wisconsin. A formidable dropkicker and placekicker, he dropkicked a 60-yard field goal one year against Minnesota and placekicked a 57-yarder against Illinois.

March 17/Bobby Jones/1902/golf

Until Jack Nicklaus came along, Bobby Jones had a good claim on the title of best golfer ever. No more. But Bobby Jones certainly did dominate the game in his era, 1923 to 1930. In 1930, he won each of the major tournaments he was qualified to enter Uninterested in the pro game, he retired at age 28

March 18/Ingemar Stenmark/1956/skiing

Ingemar Stenmark, hailing from a village of 700 people just below the Arctic Circle, dominated men's downhill skiing in the late 1970s. Stenmark won gold medals in the slalom and giant slalom at the 1980 Winter Olympics in Lake Placid, New York. His victory in the giant slalom was his 15th straight in world-level competition.

March 19/Richie Ashburn/1927/baseball

One of the Philadelphia Phillies' "Whiz Kids" of 1950, Richie Ashburn won the NL batting title twice, in 1955 and 1958. A Phillie for 12 years and a Cub for two, Ashburn ended his career as one of the few still-effective players on the 1962 expansion Mets. He hit .306, just two points off his career average.

March 20/Bobby Orr/1948/hockey

The Boston Bruins signed Bobby Orr, a native of Parry Sound, Ontario, when he was 14 years old. While playing junior hockey for the Oshawa Generals, ads screamed, "See Boston's $1,000,000 Prospect Bobby Orr!" He was as good as the hype, winning the NHL's Norris Trophy for best defenseman eight years in a row.

March 21/Joe Carveth/1918/hockey

From Regina, Saskatchewan, forward Joe Carveth played for the Detroit Red Wings, Boston Bruins, and Montreal Canadiens in his 11 years in the NHL. In three of those seasons, he scored 20 or more goals. Overall, he had 171 goals and 205 assists in 573 regular-season and playoff games.

March 22/Easy Ed Macauley/1928/basketball

After leading St. Louis University to an NIT basketball title in 1948, Ed Macauley (called "Easy" for his smooth play) went on to star for the Boston Celtics and St. Louis Hawks. The Hawks, with Ed Macauley and Bob Pettit, usually won the NBA Western Conference championship and then lost to the Celtics.

March 23/Donald Malcolm Campbell/1921/boat racing

A British automobile and boat racer, Donald Malcolm Campbell followed in the footsteps of his father, Sir Malcolm Campbell, who had set a number of land speed records. The younger Campbell died in his jet-powered boat *Bluebird* as he tried to crack the 300-mph mark on water

March 24/George Sisler/1893/baseball

There have been many great first basemen. All of the later ones except Lou Gehrig have played in the shadow of George Sisler. Never mind his .420 batting average for the St. Louis Browns in 1922. His 1920 stats, including a major-league-record 257 hits, were even better—and he was a fielder par excellence.

March 25/Howard Cosell/1920/sportscaster

He may not have been the best radio and TV sportscaster in the business, but he was probably the best known. Trained as a lawyer, the opinionated, polysyllabic Cosell was exceptionally good in his coverage of boxing—a sport he later concluded should be outlawed.

March 26/Wayne Embry/1937/basketball

Six-foot-seven-inch Wayne Embry set seven major basketball records at Miami of Ohio. Then he played for Cincinnati, Boston, and Milwaukee in the NBA. His best years were with the Royals. After his playing days, he became general manager of the Milwaukee Bucks, the first black executive in pro basketball.

March 27/Cale Yarborough/1939/auto racing

Stock car racing drivers are a hardy lot. Take Cale Yarborough. He won the Daytona 500 in 1968, came back to win again in 1977, and then twice more in 1983 and 1984. Yarborough, who turned down a number of offers to play pro football, was the NASCAR Grand National Champion three times in the late '70s.

March 28/Rick Barry/1944/basketball

Rick Barry, NBA Rookie of the Year in 1966, was the man who broke Wilt Chamberlain's string of seven straight seasons as the league's scoring leader. Barry averaged 36.5 points a game in 1967, playing for the San Francisco Warriors. With Golden State in 1975, he was named MVP in the NBA playoffs.

March 29/Cy Young/1867/baseball

When minor league pitcher Cy Young was offered to the majors for $500, the Cleveland Spiders took a chance on him. Over the next 23 seasons, the rawboned country boy from Ohio racked up 511 major league wins. The record is unlikely to be broken. Except for Walter Johnson, with 416, no one else ever exceeded 400.

March 30/Jerry Lucas/1940/basketball

As a high school star in Middletown, Ohio, Jerry Lucas led his team to 76 straight wins and two state titles. Recruited by 150 colleges, the six-foot-eight Lucas chose Ohio State, where the Buckeyes with Lucas put together a 78–6 record over three years. He went on to a career as a frequent All-Star pro.

March 31/Gordie Howe/1928/hockey

Gordie Howe's career in hockey spanned five decades. When he retired in 1980, he had played for 32 seasons and had set many all-time scoring records. He won countless honors and awards. His career almost ended in 1950 when, playing forward for the Detroit Red Wings, he had a near-fatal collision on the ice.

APRIL

April 1/Joseph Alexander/1898/football

As a lineman at Syracuse, Joseph Alexander once made 11 straight tackles against Colgate. He played pro football briefly and then quit to pursue a medical career. When Tim Mara established the New York Giants, however, Dr. Alexander was the first player he signed. Soon afterwards, he signed Jim Thorpe

April 2/Luke Appling/1908/baseball

A shortstop for 20 years with the Chicago White Sox, Luke Appling compiled a .310 lifetime batting average. He was never much of a home run hitter, but in a 1982 old-timers' game at RFK Stadium in Washington, D.C., the 75-year-old Appling slammed a Warren Spahn pitch out of the ballpark. By then he had been a Hall of Famer for nearly two decades.

April 3/Bernie Parent/1945/hockey

As a goalie for the Toronto Maple Leafs, Bernie Parent shared time on the ice with his boyhood hero, Jacques Plante. In 1974 and 1975, while playing for the Philadelphia Flyers, Parent won the Vezina Trophy as leading goalie and the Conn Smythe Trophy as MVP in the Stanley Cup playoffs.

April 4/Tris Speaker/1888/baseball

The prematurely gray Trip Speaker (thus his nickname "The Gray Eagle") was the standout center fielder of the 1910s and 1920s. He was also quite a hitter for the Boston Red Sox and Cleveland Indians, compiling a .344 lifetime average. He hit more doubles than anyone else in history, even Pete Rose.

April 5/Pop Warner/1871/football

Glenn (Pop) Warner's actual coaching record is less important than his many innovations and contributions to the game of football. He developed the single-wing and double-wing formations. He designed the reverse. He initiated the spiral punt, the hidden ball trick, play numbering, the first huddle, and more.

April 6/Mickey Cochrane/1903/baseball

Although he never won a batting title, Mickey Cochrane of the Philadelphia A's and Detroit Tigers was one of the finest hitting catchers ever. A left-handed batter, his lifetime average was .320. A great team leader, Cochrane's playing career ended suddenly in 1937 when a pitch fractured his skull

April 7/Tony Dorsett/1954/football

Winner of the 1976 Heisman Trophy, Tony Dorsett rewrote the football record book at the University of Pittsburgh. In 1973, he gained 303 yards in 23 carries against Notre Dame, a showing that Irish coach Dan Devine called the finest he had seen in 28 years of coaching. In the pro ranks, Dorsett became a Dallas Cowboys superstar.

April 8/John Havlicek/1940/basketball

The durable John Havlicek starred at Ohio State with Jerry Lucas and Larry Siegfried. As a pro, he put in 16 seasons as a forward and guard with the Boston Celtics. A first-team NBA All-Star four times, Havlichek was named MVP for his contribution to the Celtics' playoff victory over Milwaukee in 1974.

April 9/Curly Lambeau/1898/football

Lambeau Field in Green Bay, Wisconsin, is named for Earl (Curly) Lambeau, a Notre Dame dropout and hard working entrepreneur. A big-spender in his later years, he organized the semipro Green Bay Packers in 1919, earning just $16.75 the first year. Lambeau's pioneering pro Packers became an enormous success.

April 10/Chuck Connors/1938/basketball, baseball

Tall, lantern-jawed Chuck Connors starred in basketball and baseball at Seton Hall and then played pro basketball for two seasons with the Boston Celtics. After that he emerged as a first baseman for the Chicago Cubs. A .239 batting average turned him toward showbiz. He starred for years in TV's *The Rifleman*.

April 11/Stella Walsh/1911/track

Stella Walsh was living (or dead) proof that you just never know. Under her hard-to-pronounce Polish name, Walsh won the 1932 Olympic 100-meters. A track superstar, she set many world sprint records and won 41 AAU titles. When she was found shot dead in a Cleveland, Ohio, parking lot in 1980, imagine everyone's surprise to learn that *she* was really a *he*.

April 12/Joe Lapchick/1900/basketball

One of the early basketball greats, Joe Lapchick was a center for the Original Celtics in the 1920s. He played pro ball until 1936, after which he coached at St. John's University. His teams won four National Invitation Tournament titles. Lapchick also coached the New York Knicks in the NBA.

April 13/Bob Devaney/1915/football

Coach Bob Devaney took the University of Nebraska football team from last place to first in the Big Eight Conference. Over an 11-year period, his Cornhuskers had 101 wins, 20 losses, and 2 ties. They captured eight Big Eight Conference championships and two national titles, 1970 and 1971.

April 14/Pete Rose/1942/baseball

"Who's that Charlie Hustle?" people asked about the Cincinnati Reds' young and intent Pete Rose. They soon learned. When Rose's playing days were over, he owned a record that many baseball fans thought untouchable. He had grabbed first place in lifetime hits—4,256—away from Ty Cobb. He also set a host of other records.

April 15/Jim Jeffries/1875/boxing

When Jim Jeffries retired from the ring in 1905, he had been the undefeated heavyweight champion of the world for five years. In 1908, the black boxer Jack Johnson won the title, and Jeffries was persuaded to make a comeback. It was a mistake. In a fight at Reno, Nevada, Johnson kayoed Jeffries in 15 rounds.

April 16/Kareem Abdul-Jabbar/1947/basketball

In high school and college, he was Lew Alcindor, a basketball phenomenon. With the seven-foot Alcindor on the court, UCLA swept to a 30–0 season and three straight NCAA championships. He was just as spectacular for Milwaukee and Los Angeles in the NBA, winning the MVP title six times.

April 17/Cap Anson/1851/baseball

Baseball's first superstar—and later, as a manager, the father of spring training—Cap Anson's professional life revolved around Chicago's National League team. An adequate first baseman, Anson had lightning reflexes as a hitter. He won four batting championships, and as a manager, he led his team to five pennants

April 18/Pete Gogolak/1942/football

The brothers Gogolak, Pete and Charlie, were born in Hungary and graduated from Ivy League schools—Pete from Cornell, where his 44 consecutive points after touchdown set a record, and Charlie from Princeton, where his 50 straight PATs broke older brother Pete's record. Both became outstanding kickers in the NFL.

April 19/Bucky Walters/1909/baseball

In 1939, the year that Johnny Vander Meer pitched back-to-back no-hitters, the ace of the Cincinnati Reds' staff was not Double No-Hit Johnny. It was Bucky Walters, who won 27 games, lost 11, and, along with right-hander Paul Derringer, pitched the Reds to a pennant.

April 20/Don Mattingly/1962/baseball

Yankee first baseman Don Mattingly batted .343 in his first full season in the majors. The next year he drove in 145 runs. The year after that he banged out 232 hits. All these figures were league-leading totals. In addition, Mattingly fielded with Gold Glove precision.

April 21/William Knox/1887/bowling

Bowling goes back to ancient Egypt, but it was not until 1895 that the American Bowling Congress was formed to standardize rules. Modern bowling dates from then. William Knox, a Hall of Fame bowler, rolled the first 300 game in ABC tournament history in 1913. Knox's 22-year ABC tourney average was 191.

April 22/Spencer Haywood/1949/basketball

In the 1968 Olympics in Mexico City, the U.S. basketball team lacked some expected black stars. It was a time of racial protest. Prospects looked slim for the U.S. to retain its long unbeaten streak. But it did, as unsung Spencer Haywood, from Trinidad State Junior College, led the attack, beating out Yugoslavia for the gold. Haywood went on to play in the NBA.

April 23/Warren Spahn/1921/baseball

"Spahn and Sain and pray for rain," they said in 1948 when the Boston Braves were pennant-bound. Warren Spahn appeared in only three World Series. But it wasn't his fault. He won 20 or more games in 13 of his 21 seasons in the majors. His 363 lifetime wins are the most for a left-hander.

April 24/Mike Michalske/1903/football

The first guard elected to the Pro Football Hall of Fame, Mike Michalske had been an All-American fullback at Penn State. As a pro, he played guard for the New York Yankees of the old AFL and was named All-NFL in 1927 and 1928. Joining the Green Bay Packers, he made All-NFL the next three years too. Michalske pioneered linebacker blitzes.

April 25/Fred Haney/1898/baseball

Fred Haney managed the newly enfranchised Milwaukee Braves to pennants in 1957 and 1958. A utility infielder in his playing days, Haney got high praise for his managing of the Braves. But when the team snatched defeat from the jaws of victory in 1959, finishing second to the L.A. Dodgers, Haney was gone.

April 26/Sal Maglie/1917/baseball

Called "The Barber" because of his tendency to "shave" batters with high inside pitches, Sal Maglie stands eighth on the all-time won-lost-percentage list with .657. A shrewd right-hander, his best years were 1950 and 1951. Pitching for the New York Giants, he went 18–4 and 23–6 those two seasons.

April 27/Rogers Hornsby/1896/baseball

In 1924 Rogers Hornsby, second baseman for the St. Louis Cards, established a modern record by batting .424 for the season. From 1921 to 1924, his overall batting average was .402. Hornsby is regarded as the best right-handed hitter of all time. He managed various teams for many years, but with only modest success.

April 28/Frank Cavanagh/1876/football

After earning a law degree, Frank Cavanagh turned to coaching football at Holy Cross and Dartmouth prior to World War One. After the war, he coached Boston College (8–0–0 in 1920) and then Fordham, where he gained his greatest fame, and where his defensive linemen of 1929–30 won the name of "The Seven Blocks of Granite."

April 29/Jim Ryun/1947/track

In 1964, while still a student at Wichita East High School, Jim Ryun made the Olympic track team. As a young middle-distance runner in the late '60s, he set record after record. At the 1968 Olympics in Mexico City, the high altitude, a hamstring injury, and a recent fever probably cost him a gold medal.

April 30/Don Schollander/1946/swimming

Don Schollander's technique on front crawl has been called the best ever developed. It helped him set nine world records in the 200-meter freestyle. At the 1964 Olympic Games in Tokyo, he became the first swimmer to win four gold medals in one Olympics, a record eclipsed in 1972 at Munich by Mark Spitz's seven golds.

MAY

May 1/Steve Cauthen/1960/horse racing

Few jockeys have ever peaked as fast as Steve Cauthen. He was the most successful apprentice in racing history. In 1977, his first full year of racing, he ranked as the leading money winner among all jockeys. The year after that, he rode Affirmed to the Triple Crown.

May 2/Eddie Collins/1887/baseball

Eddie Collins played second base for the Chicago White Sox for many years. His salary was twice that of any other player on the team, which caused resentment. At shortstop was Swede Risberg; at first base was Chick Gandil. These two "Black Sox" players never spoke to Collins, but it didn't seem to affect his play. Ty Cobb called him the best second baseman he ever saw.

May 3/Sugar Ray Robinson/1921/boxing

Sugar Ray Robinson's boxing career spanned 25 years, and he lost a few fights along the way. But as one writer said, he was "the ultimate in ring class." Welterweight champion, middleweight champion, light-heavyweight challenger, Sugar Ray did it all—with artistry, showmanship, and fighting spirit.

May 4/Betsy Rawls/1928/golf

Betsy Rawls won the U.S. Women's Open Championship four times, in 1951, 1953, 1957, and 1960. She was the special nemesis of Jackie Pung. In 1953, Rawls defeated Pung in an 18-hole play-off. Then in 1957 Pung had actually won the Open by one stroke, but was disqualified because of a scoring error.

May 5/Chief Bender/1883/baseball

Charles Albert (Chief) Bender is the only American Indian ballplayer elected to the Baseball Hall of Fame. Bender, a Chippewa from Minnesota, was an outstanding right-handed pitcher for the Philadelphia Athletics. His best year was 1910, when he was 23 and 5 with a 1.58 earned run average.

May 6/Willie Mays/1931/baseball

One of the game's master outfielders, "Say Hey" Willie Mays was the ballplayer every manager dreams about having on his team. A New York and San Francisco Giant (literally and figuratively), he could do everything— hit for average, hit for power, steal bases at a league-leading clip, and make those impossible catches.

May 7/Johnny Unitas/1933/football

In the 1958 title game, the Baltimore Colts defeated the New York Giants 23–17 in overtime. Colt quarterback Johnny Unitas led his team on two memorable 80-yard drives, the first for a tying field goal, the second for the winning touchdown. The game has been called the greatest in pro football history.

May 8/Francis Ouimet/1893/golf

A 20-year-old shop assistant from Brookline, Massachusetts, Francis Ouimet shocked the sports world by winning the U.S. Open in 1913. In those days, Britishers usually won, and Ouimet's main challengers were British: Harry Vardon and Ted Ray. Ouimet's win did much to popularize golf in the United States.

May 9/Pancho Gonzales/1928/tennis

The highlight of his game was a cannonball service, but Pancho Gonzales was a superb all-around player. He won the U.S. singles title in 1948 and 1949. In the '49 final, he lost the first two sets to Ted Schroeder, but came back to win the next three. As a pro, he won a record eight U.S. singles titles.

May 10/Jimmy Demaret/1910/golf

One of the best golfers never to win the U.S. Open, Jimmy Demaret won many other tournaments—44 in all. He was the leading money winner in 1947. But golf didn't pay much in those days, and for a time Demaret was a band singer in night clubs. A colorful player, he was a close friend of Ben Hogan.

May 11/Charlie Gehringer/1903/baseball

Of the quiet Charlie Gehringer, his manager at Detroit in 1935, Mickey Cochrane, observed: "He says hello on opening day and goodbye on closing day, and in between he hits .350." Actually, through 19 seasons the smooth-fielding second baseman's lifetime average was .320. He's a Hall of Famer.

May 12/Yogi Berra/1925/baseball

All joking aside, Yogi Berra was a catcher any team would be proud of. He was a powerful hitter, although, yes, he swung at bad pitches now and then. He played in 14 World Series for the New York Yankees, setting many records for the fall classic. In response to comments on his appearance, he said, "I hit with a bat, not with my face."

May 13/Joe Louis/1914/boxing

No one held the heavyweight title longer than Joe Louis. He successfully defended his crown 25 times, and by no means were all of the contenders members of his so-called "Bum of the Month Club." Louis was nearly beaten by Billy Conn in 1941, but in 1946, after the war, Louis kayoed Conn in eight rounds.

May 14/Ed Walsh/1881/baseball

Once upon a time, the spitball was legal. Big Ed Walsh, one of 13 children from the anthracite region of Pennsylvania, perfected 14 variants of it. In 1908, pitching for the Chicago White Sox, he won 40 games—two times a 20-game winner in one season. His lifetime 1.82 ERA is the lowest ever.

May 15/George Brett/1953/baseball

In the 1980 season, Kansas City Royals' third baseman George Brett flirted seriously with a .400 batting average. He missed by ten percentage points, just as Rod Carew had missed by 12 in 1977. If Carew and Brett—and perhaps Wade Boggs—fail to crack the barrier, does Ted Williams reign forever as the last .400 hitter?

May 16/Billy Martin/1928/baseball

Billy Martin's brouhahas as a manager tend to make people forget Billy Martin's occasional triumphs as a player. One example: In the 1953 World Series between the Yankees and the Dodgers, Yankee second baseman Billy Martin collected 12 hits and drove in eight runs as the Yanks won it in six games.

May 17/Sugar Ray Leonard/1956/boxing

Ray Leonard, America's boxing hero at the 1976 Olympic Games, turned pro the next year. Handsome, articulate, and a superb boxer, he won the welterweight crown with victories over Roberto Duran and Thomas (Hit Man) Hearns. The Duran fight ended in the eighth round with Duran's unexpected *"No mas!"*

May 18/Reggie Jackson/1946/baseball

The World Series slugging average of "Mr. October" was higher than either Babe Ruth's or Lou Gehrig's. As a Yankee, Jackson put on his greatest show in the sixth and final game of the 1977 World Series. He hit three successive first-pitch home runs off three Dodger pitchers to lead the Yanks to victory.

May 19/Dolph Schayes/1928/basketball

One of the best all-around players in pro basketball, Dolph Schayes held a number of NBA records when he retired in 1964, most of which have since been broken. Schayes starred for NYU before joining the Syracuse Nationals. He led Syracuse to three Eastern Conference titles in the early 1950s.

May 20/Bud Grant/1927/football

Bud Grant won nine letters at the University of Minnesota. After graduation, he played pro basketball for the Minneapolis Lakers and then switched to pro football with the Philadelphia Eagles. He starred on both teams. Later, Grant became known as the long-time winning coach of the Minnesota Vikings.

May 21/Glenn Curtiss/1878/motor racing

Glenn Curtiss held a variety of air speed records in the early days of aviation. He was both an inventor and an active aviator. He developed the seaplane (or "flying boat," as he called it) and the hydroplane. In 1910, Curtiss made a daring and dramatic flight from Albany to New York City.

May 22/Al Simmons/1902/baseball

He never looked like much of a hitter, but he certainly was one. A lifetime .334 batter, Simmons could hit for power—and do it in key situations. Said Clark Griffith to Connie Mack, Simmons's manager at Philadelphia: "He hit 14 homers in the eighth and ninth innings, and every one figured in the ball game."

May 23/John Newcombe/1943/tennis

John Newcombe, brilliant Australian tennis player, won three Wimbledon titles and the U.S. Open championship—all before he managed to take the Australian title. His competition in Australia included all-time greats Rod Laver and Ken Rosewall

May 24/Suzanne Lenglen/1899/tennis

There are marvelous 1920s photographs of Suzanne Lenglen leaping through the air in a full-length dress to make her shots. One writer said, "Her feet seemed rarely to touch the ground." She was called the "Pavlova of Tennis." Six times singles and doubles champion at Wimbledon, she was literally unbeatable in her era.

May 25/Gene Tunney/1898/boxing

Whenever the subject of great boxers comes up, Jack Dempsey's name is sure to be mentioned. If Gene Tunney's is suggested, someone is sure to mutter, "Long count." The fact is that even if an alert Dempsey *might* have beaten Tunney in their title rematch, he didn't. Tunney decisioned Dempsey twice.

May 26/Jack Root/1876/boxing

Born Janos Ruthaly in Austria, but boxing out of Los Angeles, Jack Root won the first light heavyweight championship. He took the title by winning a 10-round decision over Kid McCoy. After retiring from boxing, Root established a chain of move theaters and became a millionaire.

May 27/Sam Snead/1912/golf

As a winner on the U.S. Tour, Sam Snead had no rivals. In 15 seasons, he missed being among the top seven players only twice. Yet he never won the U.S. Open. Snead was the leading money winner in 1938, 1949, and 1950. In 1979, he became the first player to beat his age in a full U.S. Tour event, with a 66 at age 67.

May 28/Jim Thorpe/1888/all sports

In 1950, the Associated Press named Jim Thorpe the American athlete of the half century. Winner of the 1912 Olympic pentathlon, standout in all sports at Carlisle Indian School, professional baseball player for six seasons, pro football player for 20—he was truly *Jim Thorpe, All-American*, as in the Burt Lancaster movie of that name.

May 29/Al Unser/1939/auto racing

For two decades, Al Unser made the Indianapolis 500 his own. He finished first at Indy in 1970, 1971, 1978, and 1987. He finished second at Indy in 1967, 1972, and 1983. In a sport where many winners die young, Al Unser, along with his brother Bobby, established an ˜enviable a record of achievement—and survival.

May 30/Gale Sayers/1943/football

Gale Sayers, drafted by the Chicago Bears from the University of Kansas, set an NFL rookie record by scoring 22 touchdowns. He tied another by scoring six touchdowns in one game. Sayers might well have become the best pro halfback of all time, but injuries cut his career to a mere seven years.

May 31/Joe Namath/1943/football

Plagued by injuries throughout his playing days, Broadway Joe was one of the finest pure passers in pro football. He was the first to produce a 4,000-yard passing season. In his best single game, he threw for 496 yards against the Baltimore Colts. New York media hype and Namath's outgoing personality made him a larger-than-life figure.

JUNE

June 1/Alan Ameche/1933/football

Alan (The Horse) Ameche ranks among the greatest fullbacks in college and pro football. Two-time All-America at the University of Wisconsin, he won the Heisman Trophy in 1954. In 1955, with the Baltimore Colts, he was Rookie of the Year. Ameche scored the winning touchdown in the 23–17 sudden-death NFL title game against the New York Giants in 1958.

June 2/Johnny Weissmuller/1904/swimming

Better known as Tarzan in a series of popular jungle movies, Johnny Weissmuller had established himself as a swimming star before taking up with Jane and Boy. He owned five Olympic gold medals, one bronze, and had broken 24 world records. His high-riding stroke influenced the development of the crawl.

June 3/Hale Irwin/1945/golf

Winner of the U.S. Open in 1974 and 1979, Hale Irwin was a steady and consistent pro. Like all golfers, he was aware of the pressure. He once said, "On the football field you can blow off your emotion by belting someone. In golf, pressure just keeps building up within you, and there is no outlet. . . ."

June 4/Bob Fitzsimmons/1862/boxing

They misspelled the name on his tombstone, but Bob Fitzsimmons was quite a celebrity in his day. He held the middleweight boxing title 1891 to 1897, the heavyweight title 1897 to 1899, and the light heavyweight title 1903 to 1905. His tombstone, now corrected, stands 200 feet from Jack Johnson's in Chicago.

June 5/Jack Chesbro/1874/baseball

Right-handed pitcher Jack Chesbro, called "Happy Jack" for his sunny disposition, won 41 games in 1904. Those wins were all forgotten, though, when Chesbro uncorked a wild pitch that cost his New York Highlanders the pennant. His 28–6 record in 1902 for Pittsburgh combined with his 41–12 mark for New York gave him pitching titles in the both the National and American Leagues.

June 6/Ed Giacomin/1939/hockey

Ed Giacomin, a goalie, broke into pro hockey with the Providence Reds in 1960. He did so by presenting himself as his brother Rollo, whom the Reds had hired for emergency duty, sight unseen. A remarkably talented skater for a goalie, Giacomin put in four fine seasons for the New York Rangers.

June 7/Cazzie Russell/1944/basketball

A superstar at the University of Michigan, Cazzie Russell joined the New York Knicks accompanied by the usual media hype. He was good, but not good enough to live up to the oversell. After a disappointing rookie year, Russell began to score. His 15.1 lifetime point average was good, not great.

June 8/Herb Adderley/1939/football

One of the finest left cornerbacks who ever played the game, Herb Adderley of the Green Bay Packers made the first touchdown pass interception in a Super Bowl, grabbing an Oakland Raider pass in Super Bowl II and racing 60 yards to the end zone. Adderley had good hands and anticipated plays brilliantly.

June 9/Dave Parker/1951/baseball

As an outfielder for the Pittsburgh Pirates, Dave Parker played a major role in the team's success in the 1970s. Called "The Cobra," the six-foot-five Parker moved over to the Cincinnati Reds in 1984, where the next year he drove in 125 runs to lead the league.

June 10/Battling Levinsky/1891/boxing

Born Barney Lebrowitz, he broke into boxing as Barney Williams and then became Battling Levinsky in 1913. He beat Jack Dillon in 1916 for the light heavyweight title and held it for four years. Levinsky was knocked out by up-and-coming Jack Dempsey and decisioned by up-and-coming Gene Tunney.

June 11/Vince Lombardi/1913/football

The source of many hard-nosed quotes, coach Vince Lombardi of the Green Bay Packers symbolized America's obsession with professional football in the 1960s. Lombardi's impressive coaching record backed up his tough words and methods. In Lombardi's eight years at Green Bay, the team won five NFL championships and the first two Super Bowls.

June 12/Brick Muller/1901/football

Brick Muller was an all-around athlete at the University of California, Berkeley. Three times an All-America end on UCs undefeated Golden Bears (27–0–1 for his three years), Muller took time off to win a silver medal in the 1920 Olympics in Antwerp. He became an orthopedic surgeon in California.

June 13/Red Grange/1904/football

The first true football celebrity, Red Grange came to national attention by leading his University of Illinois team to a stunning upset over long-unbeaten Michigan. Upon joining the Chicago Bears, he endorsed Red Grange dolls, candy bars, and a ginger ale. He starred in two movies, *One Minute to Play* and *Galloping Ghost*, as well as for George Halas's Bears.

June 14/Eric Heiden/1958/skating

At the 1980 Winter Olympics in Lake Placid, nobody could touch America's Eric Heiden in the speed-skating events, not even the USSRs 500-meter record-holder. Heiden won the 500, 1,000, 1,500, 5,000, and 10,000—five gold medals. As icing on the cake, his sister Beth won a bronze in the women's 3,000-meter.

June 15/Billy Williams/1938/baseball

Billy Williams, classy outfielder for the Chicago Cubs, had batting stats resembling those of fellow Hall of Famer Ernie Banks. Williams won both the batting and slugging crowns in 1972, but like other Cub stars, he got into post-season play only when traded to another team—in his case, the Oakland A's.

June 16/Hank Luisetti/1916/basketball

"Stay with it, boy," Stanford basketball coach Johnny Bunn told his young player. The "it" was Hank Luisetti's one-handed shot, and in 1936 it was a marvel. Nobody shot with just one hand. But when Luisetti's Stanford team broke Long Island University's 45-game winning streak at Madison Square Garden, people paid attention to this revolutionary technique.

June 17/Elroy Hirsch/1924/football

He was called "Crazylegs" because of the elusive moves that made him tough to tackle. One of the first backs to make the transition to flanker, Hirsch set a record for pro receivers by catching scoring passes in 11 straight games. He appeared in three movies, including *Crazylegs*, a fictional biography.

June 18/George Mikan/1924/basketball

The sign on Madison Square Garden read, "Tonight: George Mikan vs. Knicks." They weren't kidding. In the late '40s and early '50s, when the Minneapolis Lakers were a dynasty, six-foot-ten center George Mikan was a living legend. Awkward and slow by today's standards, he proved what many doubted—that there was a place in basketball for the big, big man.

June 19/Lou Gehrig/1903/baseball

When Lou Gehrig made his farewell speech, there could hardly have been a dry eye in Yankee Stadium. He said: "Today I consider myself the luckiest man on the face of the earth." Gehrig, dying from lateral sclerosis, had played for years in the shadow of Babe Ruth. But first-baseman Gehrig's own records rank him among the best ballplayers who ever lived.

June 20/Glenna Collett/1903/golf

Glenna Collett (later Vare) had remarkable power for a woman golfer. At the age of 18, she hit a measured drive of slightly over 300 yards. There was no *Guinness* record book to check, but it was generally regarded as a women's record. Collett won the U.S. Women's Championship six times, also a record.

June 21/Brian Sternberg/1943/track and field

In 1963, at the age of 19, Brian Sternberg set three successive world pole vault records. He won the NCAA and AAU titles in June of that year. Then, after just three spectacular months, he suffered a terrible trampoline accident that left him paralyzed from the waist down and ended his sports activities.

June 22/Carl Hubbell/1903/baseball

After six seasons in the minors, left-hander Carl Hubbell was ready for the big time. He put in 16 years pitching for the New York Giants—five seasons in a row winning more than 20 games. His best-known exploit was striking out six batters in two innings of the 1934 All-Star game: Babe Ruth, Lou Gehrig, Jimmy Foxx, Al Simmons, Joe Cronin, and Lefty Gomez.

June 23/Wilma Rudolph/1940/track

As a child, Wilma Rudolph had double pneumonia and scarlet fever. Also suffering from paralysis, she did not learn to walk normally for a few years. But by the time she was 20, she was a world-class, record-setting track star. She won three gold medals in the 1960 Olympics: 100- and 200-meter dashes and 400-meter relay.

June 24/Jack Dempsey/1895/boxing

"Take it easy," Jack Dempsey once said, " and you let everyone down." Dempsey never took it easy. He pounded Jess Willard, "The Pottawatomie Giant," into submission to win the heavyweight championship. He finished off Luis Firpo, "The Wild Bull of the Pampas," in two rounds, after seven knockdowns—and after being knocked out of the ring himself.

June 25/Willis Reed/1942/basketball

At Louisiana's Grambling College (one of two colleges interested in him), Willis Reed led his team to a 110–17 record over four years. Later playing center for the New York Knicks, his finest hour came in the seventh game of the 1970 championship playoffs when, painfully injured, he came into the game against the L.A. Lakers and inspired the Knicks to victory.

June 26/Babe Didrikson/1914/all sports

Eighteen-year-old Babe Didrikson (later Zaharias) won the 80-meter and javelin gold medals at the 1932 Olympics. "She is beyond belief until you see her perform," wrote Grantland Rice. Didrikson pitched exhibition baseball against major-leaguers. She made a cross-country billiards tour. Then she settled down to win three U.S. Women's Open golf titles.

June 27/Willie Mosconi/1913/billiards

Technical adviser for the the filming of *The Hustler*, Willie Mosconi had been a child prodigy at pocket billiards and then retired at the age of seven. When he returned to it in his late teens, he made it his career. At one time, his high run of 526 balls stood as a world record. Mosconi helped to popularize billiards in the U.S. and make it reputable.

June 28/John Elway/1960/football

Named Southern California Athlete of the Year for his high school football and baseball, John Elway went on to star in both sports at Stanford. He became the first college player ever with at least 2,500 yards total offense for each of three seasons. Elway next became a standout quarterback for the Denver Broncos, guiding them into Super Bowls XXI and XXII.

June 29/Harmon Killebrew/1936/baseball

The name of Harmon Killebrew's game was home runs. Playing for the Washington Senators and Minnesota Twins, Killebrew slammed 573 home runs to put him near the top of the all-time list. Only two players in history had a higher percentage of homers per times at bat: Babe Ruth and Ralph Kiner.

June 30/Edward Wachter/1883/basketball

A great player from the earliest days of pro basketball, Edward Wachter played center for a Troy, New York, team that barnstormed across the country. Before that, from 1900 to 1902, he played for a Ware, Massachusetts, pro team. He helped to introduce pro basketball to the hinterlands.

JULY

July 1/Rod Gilbert/1941/hockey

Rod Gilbert, a native of Montreal, rejected a baseball offer from the Milwaukee Braves to play Junior A hockey at Guelph. He overcame two serious back injuries to become one of the top right-wingers in the NHL. In 16 seasons with the New York Rangers, he set a host of team scoring records.

July 2/Richard Petty/1937/auto racing

When Lee Petty's stock-car driving career ended in a serious but nonfatal crash at Daytona, his son Richard took over the driver's seat. Richard Petty won the Daytona 500 seven times and the NASCAR championship seven times. Early in his career he became the first stock car driver to win a million dollars.

July 3/Mike Burton/1947/swimming

When Mike Burton was 13, he had a serious cycling accident. Doctors said he would never be able to compete in sports, but they advised him to swim to strengthen his leg muscles. Burton went on to become the only swimmer in history to take two successive Olympic gold medals in the 1,500-meter freestyle.

July 4/Floyd Little/1942/football

Wearing number 44 at Syracuse University, the same number worn by Jim Brown and Ernie Davis, running back Floyd Little scored five touchdowns in his first college game. After starring at Syracuse, he signed with the Denver Broncos and went on to become one of the leading rushers in the NFL.

July 5/John McKay/1923/football

After playing football for Purdue and the University of Oregon, John McKay turned down a pro offer to enter college coaching. As head coach at the University of Southern California, his teams won four national championships—1962, 1969, 1972, 1974. McKay took eight teams to the Rose Bowl.

July 6/Brad Park/1948/hockey

Hockey Hall of Famer Brad Park came out of the Toronto Maple Leafs' junior system. When the Leafs left Park unprotected in an amateur selection round, the New York Rangers signed him. A rushing defenseman, Park starred for the Rangers almost at once. He played 17 seasons and was seven times an All-Star.

July 7/Satchel Paige/1923/baseball

Right-hander Satchel Paige, a major figure in black baseball, relied on speed and pinpoint control. Pitching for a number of barnstorming clubs, he became the richest black player of his era. When Paige joined the Cleveland Indians in 1948, he was long past his prime, but he went 6 and 1 that year anyway.

July 8/Harrison Dillard/1923/track

Harrison (Bones) Dillard won an unprecedented 82 straight indoor sprints and hurdles from May 1947 to June 1948. As a student at Baldwin-Wallace College, he won 201 out of 207 sprints and hurdles. Dillard earned two Olympic gold medals, one in 1948 and one in 1952.

July 9/O.J. Simpson/1947/football

O.J. Simpson was not an instant star. Few colleges recruited him, and he entered a junior college in San Francisco. After a good season, he transferred to the University of Southern California. The USC Trojans with Simpson as running back were 19–2–1, and O.J. won the Heisman Trophy. He also started slow for the pro Buffalo Bills, but then went on to star.

July 10/Arthur Ashe/1943/tennis

A cool, disciplined tennis player, Arthur Ashe found the on-court antics of some of his contemporaries "embarrassing." Ashe won the U.S. singles title in 1968, the first black player to do so. Seven years later, in a stunning upset, he demolished number-one-ranked Jimmy Connors at Wimbledon.

July 11/Ed Sadowski/1917/basketball

Big Ed Sadowski, out of Seton Hall University, put in seven solid seasons as a pro. But he couldn't find a permanent home. His best single season was 1947–48 with the Boston Celtics when he averaged 19.4 points a game. Sadowski played only that one season for the Celtics and then moved on

July 12/Otis Davis/1932/track

Otis Davis won a gold medal in the 400-meter dash at the 1960 Olympic Games in Rome. It was a photo finish in which all six finalists broke the prior Olympic record. Davis also anchored the U.S. 1,600-meter relay team that set an Olympic and a world record.

July 13/Mickey Walker/1901/boxing

Known as the "Toy Bulldog," Mickey Walker won the welterweight boxing title in 1922 and held it through 1926, when he captured the middleweight crown. He held that through 1931 while campaigning with some success (but no title) in the light heavyweight and heavyweight classes. Walker became a noted primitive art painter.

July 14/Lee Elder/1934/golf

It used to be asked why all the caddies were black at the U.S. Masters, but none of the players were. That question ended with the Masters appearance of Lee Elder. He waited a long time for his first Tour win, and it was sometimes frustrating. One of his losses in 1968 went to the fifth extra hole against no less a golfer than Jack Nicklaus.

July 15/Alex Karras/1935/football

Recruited by over a hundred colleges, Alex Karras chose the University of Iowa. A two-time All-America tackle, he helped lead Iowa to a Big Ten championship and a Rose Bowl win. He won All-Pro honors with the Detroit Lions, but was suspended for betting on NFL games. After reinstatement and retirement, Karras worked for ABC sports and appeared in TV and films.

July 16/Joe Jackson/1887/baseball

With the third highest lifetime batting average in major league history, .356, you'd expect Shoeless Joe Jackson to be in baseball's Hall of Fame. But he isn't. Jackson was one of the "eight men out" of organized baseball as a result of the 1919 Black Sox scandal. "Say it ain't so, Joe," pleaded a small boy. "I'm afraid it is, kid," said Shoeless Joe.

July 17/Lou Boudreau/1917/baseball

When shortstop Lou Boudreau became playing-manager of the Cleveland Indians, he was just 24 years old. His greatest season was 1948, when he was the American League MVP, an All-Star shortstop, and manager of the pennant-winning Indians. He led them to a World Series victory over the Boston Braves.

July 18/Dick Button/1929/figure skating

By the time he entered Harvard, Dick Button held every major figure-skating title in the world. He won Olympic gold medals in 1948 and 1952. A pioneer in skating techniques, Button developed and executed a number of innovative movements. He went on to become a well-known sports commentator for ABC.

July 19/Ilie Nastase/1946/tennis

Aptly nicknamed "Nasty," Rumanian tennis star Ilie Nastase became better known for his on-court temper tantrums than for his explosive, artistic play. Nastase reigned as U.S. singles champion in 1972 and men's doubles champion (with Jimmy Connors) in 1975.

July 20/Tony Oliva/1940/baseball

A superb natural hitter—three times winner of the American League batting crown—Tony Oliva played during an era of pitcher dominance. Even so he compiled a lifetime batting average of .304. Oliva, an outfielder, was a key factor in the powerful Minnesota Twins teams of the late '60s.

July 21/Gene Littler/1930/golf

Gene Littler, who conquered cancer in his early 40s, was asked if he was surprised to find himself still playing so well. He replied, "I'm surprised to be playing at all." Nicknamed "Gene the Machine," Littler did well on the U.S. Tour, but some felt he lacked the intensity to be a truly great golfer.

July 22/Sparky Lyle/1944/baseball

When the critical importance of relief pitching began to be recognized, Sparky Lyle was one of those who attracted notice. Lyle won 99 games in his 16-year major league career—every one of them in relief. His 2.88 lifetime ERA gives some idea of his effectiveness. In World Series play, his ERA was 1.23.

July 23/Pee Wee Reese/1919/baseball

The shortstop and captain on Brooklyn's great Boys of Summer team, Pee Wee Reese, a Southerner, gave Jackie Robinson moral support in breaking baseball's color line. Once after a death threat to Robinson in Atlanta, Reese said, "Jack, don't stand so close to me today. Move away, will ya?" Robinson smiled.

July 24/Doug Sanders/1933/golf

Doug Sanders burst upon the professional golf scene after winning the 1956 Canadian Open, the only amateur ever to do so. His missed putt on the 18th hole in the 1970 British Open is among the most famous in golf history. Sanders, the popular favorite, lost by a stroke to the imperturbable Jack Nicklaus.

July 25/Walter Payton/1954/football

Walter Payton, a running back for the Chicago Bears, broke the all-time pro rushing record, surpassing Jim Brown's earlier mark. From 1976 to 1981, Payton ran off a string of six straight 1,000-yard seasons. An explosive runner, he was also a superb pass receiver.

July 26/Hoyt Wilhelm/1923/baseball

Hoyt Wilhelm, a right-handed relief pitcher, appeared in 1,070 games, a record since broken by Kent Tekulve. His 123 wins in relief are a major league high. Wilhelm toiled on the hill for various teams in a 21-year career. He relied on a knuckle ball so unpredictable that baffled catchers began using bigger mitts to handle it.

July 27/Leo Durocher/1906/baseball

The teams The Lip managed didn't always win the pennant, but they were usually in contention. He managed four teams—the Brooklyn Dodgers, New York Giants, Chicago Cubs, and Houston Astros—for a total of 24 years. In only five of those years did his teams play less than .500 ball.

July 28/Bill Bradley/1943/basketball

Rhodes Scholar and U.S. Senator Bill Bradley wrote his name in the basketball record book at Princeton University and later with the New York Knicks. Three times All-America, he paced the U.S. Olympic team to a gold medal in 1964. Quick, intelligent, and unselfish, he helped the Knicks to two NBA titles.

July 29/Don Carter/1926/bowling

Don Carter played the infield and pitched for Red Springs, North Carolina, of the Class D Tobacco State League. Then he made a smart move. He switched to bowling. Known as "Mr. Bowling" in the late '50s and early '60s, Carter, although not a great stylist, became the first pro bowler to reach a six-figure annual income.

July 30/Casey Stengel/1891/baseball

Brooklyn traded Casey Stengel, a pretty fair outfielder, to Pittsburgh in 1918. In his first Ebbets Field at-bat as a Pirate, the fans jeered him loudly. Casey made a sweeping bow, lifted his cap—and a bird flew out. But Stengel was more than a clown. In 12 years of managing the Yankees, the Old Perfessor could point to ten pennants. (Forget his record with the hapless expansion Mets.)

July 31/Evonne Goolagong/1951/tennis

Australian and partly aboriginal, Evonne Goolagong was a happy-go-lucky player who captured the Wimbledon women's singles title in 1971. In singles competition in the United States, she was a consistent runner-up—to Margaret Court in 1973, Billie Jean King in 1974, and Chris Evert the next two years.

AUGUST

August 1/Jack Kramer/1921/tennis

Power tennis was Jack Kramer's game. His explosive serves and net smashes transformed tennis from its classic baseline-to-baseline form into something different. For a few years as an amateur, and later as a pro, he was all but invincible. "When a guy runs up a lead on me," he said, "I'm surprised. I think he's either playing over his head or lucky."

August 2/Johnny McDermott/1891/golf

He tied for the U.S. Open at the age of 19. He won the U.S. Open the next year and the year after that. In 1913, he left British stars Harry Vardon and Ted Ray 13 strokes back at the Shawnee Open. His future seemed assured, but a mental breakdown ended Johnny McDermott's promising career in 1915.

August 3/Lance Alworth/1940/football

"Bambi," as he was called, put in nine seasons with the San Diego Chargers and two with the Dallas Cowboys. Tall and slender, Alworth was a pass receiver par excellence. In 1978, he became the first player originally with the American Football League to be elected to the Pro Football Hall of Fame.

August 4/Maurice Richard/1921/hockey

Known as "The Rocket," Maurice Richard was the first player in NHL history to score 50 points in a season. That was in 1944–45. Once during the season, he spent the day moving into a new home and then went out that night and had five goals and three assists. A Montreal Canadien throughout his long career, he was one of the most renowned and fiery competitors in hockey.

August 5/Roman Gabriel/1940/football

An All-America quarterback for two years at North Carolina State, Roman Gabriel joined the Los Angeles Rams and made the NFL All-Rookie team. Then he rode the bench for three seasons until coach George Allen started him at quarterback. Gabriel's best season was 1969 when the Rams were 11–2–1 and he won the NFL's Jim Thorpe (MVP) award.

August 6/Helen Hull Jacobs/1908/tennis

Helen Hull Jacobs was six times a finalist at Wimbledon, but won only once, in 1936. She did better at Forest Hills, capturing the U.S. women's singles championship from 1932 to 1935. Later she turned to writing and produced a number of children's books and historical novels.

August 7/Alan Page/1945/football

A defensive lineman and one of the famed "Purple People Eaters" of the Minnesota Vikings, Alan Page earned All-Pro honors from 1970 to 1977. In his 15-year career, including four with the Chicago Bears, he set records in safeties and blocked kicks. A law graduate of the University of Minnesota, Page took active roles in educational, civic, and charitable affairs.

August 8/Esther Williams/1923/swimming

Esther Williams had Olympic swimming aspirations, but World War Two intervened. Williams, the 100-meter women's freestyle champion in 1939, became an aquatic film star instead. When Johnny Weissmuller picked her from among 75 candidates for the 1940 San Francisco World's Fair Aquacade, she was on her way.

August 9/Bob Cousy/1928/basketball

In a career lasting from 1950 to 1963, Bob Cousy was a sparkling ball handler and playmaker for the Boston Celtics. The six-foot-one-and-a-half-inch "Cooz," a guard, along with big man Bill Russell, led the Celtics to six NBA championships. Cousy, who had starred at Holy Cross, was a ten-time NBA All-Star.

August 10/Steve Nagy/1913/bowling

Bowler of the year in 1952 and 1955, Steve Nagy became well known to TV fans when he rolled 300 in a 1954 on-screen match. Nagy held ABC records for the best two-, three-, and ten-year averages—224, 221, and 208 respectively. His 24-year tourney average was 197, and he rolled six sanctioned 300s.

August 11/Charlie Paddock/1900/track

A popular sprinter noted for his flying leaps at the tape, Charlie Paddock won the gold medal for the 100-meters in the 1920 Olympics. Paddock set a number of world records in the 1920s. In World War Two, he served as a captain in the Marine Corps. Upon his death in 1943, a ship was named for him.

August 12/Christy Mathewson/1880/baseball

One of the first five inductees into the Baseball Hall of Fame, right-hander Christy Mathewson had pinpoint control in addition to his celebrated "fade-away," or screwball. In 391 innings one season, he walked only 42 batters while striking out a league-leading 249. Matty spent virtually his entire 17-year career with the New York Giants.

August 13/Annie Oakley/1860/shooting

From the time she was a child in Darke County, Ohio, Annie Oakley was a dead shot with a rifle. In a contest, the 15-year-old Annie defeated Frank E. Butler, a touring exhibition shooter. Within a year the two were married, and soon they were stars in the Buffalo Bill Wild West Show. Annie, "Little Sure Shot," performed astonishing feats of marksmanship.

August 14/Magic Johnson/1959/basketball

Earvin (Magic) Johnson set a number of all-time NBA playoff records and All-Star Game records for most assists. Joining the Los Angeles Lakers out of Michigan State, the six-foot-nine Johnson established himself immediately as a star for the powerful and often-NBA-champion Lakers.

August 15/Lionel Taylor/1936/football

One of the finest receivers in AFL history, Lionel Taylor played for the Denver Broncos and Houston Oilers. In one game against the Buffalo Bills, Taylor snatched three touchdown passes and 199 total yards. He served as assistant coach on the staffs of the Pittsburgh Steelers and Los Angeles Rams.

August 16/Amos Alonzo Stagg/1862/football

Many consider Amos Alonzo Stagg the greatest figure in football history. He put in 71 years of coaching, was named Coach of the Year at age 81, and retired from active coaching at the age of 98. Most notably at the University of Chicago and the College of the Pacific, "The Grand Old Man of the Midway" created a galaxy of innovations and earned countless honors.

August 17/Guillermo Vilas/1952/tennis

A top-ranking tennis player for a brief span in the '70s, Guillermo Vilas, an Argentinian romantic and spare-time poet, won the U.S. and French Opens in 1977. During that year, the left-handed Vilas put together a 50-match winning streak.

August 18/Roberto Clemente/1934/baseball

When the Brooklyn Dodgers left Roberto Clemente unprotected in the player draft, Pittsburgh picked up his contract for $4,000. It was quite a bargain. Clemente starred for the Pirates for 18 seasons, collecting exactly 3,000 hits and batting .317. He died on a plane bound for Nicaragua with food, clothing, and medical supplies for earthquake victims.

August 19/Bill Shoemaker/1931/horse racing

Bill (which he always preferred to Willie) Shoemaker set many records as a jockey. He rode his first Kentucky Derby winner, Swaps, in 1955. Thirty-one years later he rode his fourth Derby winner, Ferdinand. With a career that long, it's not surprising he became the leading money winner as well as the winning jockey on the most mounts.

August 20/Al Lopez/1908/baseball

When baseball fans talk about Hall of Fame catchers, they tend to forget Al Lopez. They shouldn't. For 19 years, Señor Lopez was one of the best in the NL, playing for Brooklyn, Boston, and Pittsburgh. Next he became a premier manager in the AL, putting in 17 years with Cleveland and Chicago. In 1954, his Indians won 111 games and lost 43 for a .721 mark.

August 21/Wilt Chamberlain/1936/basketball

Wilt (The Stilt or The Dipper) Chamberlain is often cited to show that a phenomenally good big man—seven-one, 275 pounds—doesn't guarantee a championship team. Still, Chamberlain played for some winners, notably the Philadelphia Warriors of the mid-'60s and L.A. Lakers of the early '70s. He was the first player in NBA history to exceed 30,000 career points.

August 22/Carl Yastrzemski/1939/baseball

He had the challenging task of taking over for Ted Williams in the Boston Red Sox outfield, and he rose to the occasion. He put in 23 years with the Red Sox, playing almost as many games as Pete Rose. Yaz won three American League batting titles and in 1967 captured the triple crown with 44 homers, 121 RBIs, and a .326 batting average.

August 23/Sonny Jurgensen/1934/football

Sonny Jurgensen, one of the most impressive passers in NFL history, threw only six touchdown passes in three seasons at Duke University. The Blue Devils relied on a running game. As a pro with the Philadelphia Eagles and Washington Redskins, he set many passing records, including 288 completions in 1967.

August 24/Harry Hooper/1887/baseball

Harry Who? Harry Hooper was one of those good but not great ballpayers who slipped into the National Baseball Hall of Fame via the Veterans' Committee. Hooper was a right fielder for the strong Boston Red Sox club that had Tris Speaker in center and Duffy Lewis in left. Hooper's forte was classy fielding.

August 25/Althea Gibson/1927/tennis

Althea Gibson was the first black tennis player to win a major tournament. She was also the first black ever to play at Forest Hills. In 1957 and 1958 Gibson, tall and powerful, dominated the women's game, winning both the U.S. and Wimbledon titles.

August 26/Duke Kahanamoku/1890/swimming

Sheriff of Honolulu for 36 years and once described by *The New York Times* as "Hawaii's best-known citizen," Duke Kahanamoku gained fame as both a surfer and a swimmer. He pioneered tandem surfing, wind-surfing, and wake-surfing. As a swimmer, he won four gold medals and three silvers in four Olympiads.

August 27/Eulace Peacock/1914/track

If Jesse Owens had not been competing, Eulace Peacock would be a familiar name today. Even with Owens making headlines and records, Peacock did all right. In 1935, he defeated Jesse Owens three out of five times in outdoor meetings. He beat Owens in the AAU 100-meters with a wind-aided 10.2 and outjumped him in the AAU long jump with a 26'3" leap.

August 28/Andy Bathgate/1932/hockey

Andy Bathgate, a right-winger, began his pro career with the New York Rangers and then played on various NHL teams. He was a brilliant playmaker who led the league four times in assists. His best season was 1958–59 with the Rangers when he won the Hart Trophy as the league's Most Valuable Player.

August 29/Wyomia Tyus/1945/track

When Wyomia Tyus won the 100-meter dash at the 1968 Olympic Games, she became the first athlete, male or female, to win a gold medal twice for a sprint event. In 1964, she had won the same event, tying Wilma Rudolph's record time. In 1968, she set a world record of her own—11 seconds for the 100-meters.

August 30/Jean-Claude Killy/1943/skiing

A French skier, Jean-Claude Killy gained international fame for winning three gold medals for Alpine skiing at the 1968 Winter Olympics in Innsbruck, a feat that matched that of Austria's Toni Sailor eight years earlier. Killy turned pro, but remained in the public eye more through endorsements than by skiing.

August 31/Ted Williams/1918/baseball

"I do four out of ten jobs right," Ted Williams told a friend, "and they call me a great hitter." The Boston Red Sox outfielder had just batted .406 for the 1941 season—the last .400 to date. One of Williams's most dramatic moments came in the 1941 All-Star Game when, with two out in the ninth, he hit a three-run homer to give the American League a 7-5 victory.

SEPTEMBER

September 1/Rocky Marciano/1924/boxing

Failing to make it as a baseball catcher, Rocky Marciano tried boxing. In his first 15 pro fights, he scored 15 knockouts, nine of them in the first round. When Marciano retired as heavyweight champion in 1956, he was undefeated in 49 fights. A crude fighter with little ring finesse, he could not be kayoed. He won consistently on power and determination.

September 2/Jimmy Connors/1952/tennis

Jimmy Connors, one of the early bad boys of tennis, matured into a shrewd, controlled player. He had a long and brilliant career. His first big year was 1974, when he captured the U.S. and Wimbledon titles. Highly ranked through 1984, Connors won five U.S. titles in all, and two at Wimbledon.

September 3/John Roosma/1900/basketball

Basketball Hall of Fame player John Roosma led his West Point team to a 31–0 season in 1922–23, receiving All-America notice. As a high school player, he had starred for Ernest Blood's Wonder Five at Passaic (New Jersey) High School, a school that put together a winning streak of 159 games.

September 4/Tom Watson/1949/golf

As a golfer, Tom Watson could do it all—and did it all in short order. Four-time winner of the British Open, he won the U.S. Masters in 1977 and 1981 and the U.S. Open in 1982. One secret of his rapid emergence and dominance was his superb putting. Another was that he had no discernible weaknesses.

September 5/Nap Lajoie/1875/baseball

When Nap Lajoie went 8-for-8 in the final doubleheader of the 1910 season to challenge Ty Cobb for the batting title, the American League president suspected skullduggery. It didn't matter—Cobb won the title anyway. But Lajoie was no slouch as a hitter. He won four batting titles, one on a .422 average with the Philadelphia A's and three with Cleveland.

September 6/Red Faber/1888/baseball

The spitball was outlawed in 1920, but established major leaguers who relied on it could use it for the rest of their careers. Red Faber was one such pitcher. A right-hander, Faber spent 20 seasons with the Chicago White Sox, winning 254 regular-season games. He missed the 1919 Black Sox World Series because of an ankle injury.

September 7/Louise Suggs/1923/golf

After playing brilliantly as an amateur, Louise Suggs turned pro. In her first pro season, she won the U.S. Women's Open convincingly, defeating Babe Zaharias by a record 14 strokes. She said of her contests with Zaharias and Patty Berg that it was like "watching three cats fight over a plate of fish."

September 8/Duffy Daugherty/1915/football

Named head football coach at Michigan State in 1954, Duffy Daugherty guided the Spartans for 19 seasons. During those years, his teams were ranked in the top ten seven times. Daugherty's best Spartan teams were those of 1965 and 1966, both of which went undefeated in ten regular season games.

September 9/Frankie Frisch/1898/baseball

Frankie Frisch, the Fordham Flash, a star infielder for the New York Giants and St. Louis Cardinals for 19 years, had a lifetime batting average of .316. He played in eight World Series. As a manager he put in 16 years, leading the Cards' Gashouse Gang to a pennant and the world championship.

September 10/Arnold Palmer/1929/golf

Arnold Palmer was more than a golfer. He was a phenomenon. Although no longer among the top money winners of all time, he was the golfer, more than any other, who brought big money to the game. His great years were the 1960s. A four-time U.S. Masters champion, he was golf's first million-dollar winner.

September 11/Bear Bryant/1913/football

Paul Bryant was nicknamed "Bear" because as a kid he wrestled a bear for money at Fordyce, Arkansas. Bryant, who starred in high school and college football, made his name coaching at the University of Alabama, his alma mater, after eight seasons at Kentucky. He guided Alabama to six national championships.

September 12/Jesse Owens/1913/track

The Associated Press's U.S. track star of the first half of the 20th century, Jesse Owens had two moments of supreme triumph: the first when he broke three world records and tied one—all in less than an hour at a Big Ten meet in 1935; the second at the 1936 Berlin Olympics, when he won four gold medals plus the hearts of German spectators despite Hitler.

September 13/Clint Frank/1915/football

He was Frank Merriwell come to life—a sensational All-America tailback for Yale University who led and inspired his team to victory after victory. His greatest year was 1937, when he won the Heisman Trophy and led the Elis to routs of Brown and Princeton. After graduation, he entered the advertising field.

September 14/Kid Nichols/1869/baseball

Kid Nichols, a right-handed pitcher for Boston from 1890 to 1901, was consistently among the National League's leading pitchers. When Nichols retired after 15 years in the majors, he had won 360, lost 203, and posted an ERA of 2.94. Some of his toughest duels were against New York Giant ace Amos Rusie.

September 15/Merlin Olsen/1940/football

A member of Phi Beta Kappa and an All-America defensive tackle at Utah State, Merlin Olsen played 15 years with the Los Angeles Rams. He was chosen to the Pro-Bowl a record 14 times. Olsen remained in the public eye after retirement, most notably as an actor in TV's "Little House on the Prairie" and as a sports commentator on NBC-TV.

September 16/Elgin Baylor/1934/basketball

Elgin Baylor led all forwards in scoring for 12 seasons, during which he also led the Lakers to the playoffs every year. Baylor turned the Laker franchise around. From a dismal 19–53 pre-Baylor season, the Lakers jumped to the play-offs, upset St. Louis, but lost to the mighty Celtics.

September 17/Maureen Connolly/1934/tennis

One of the most popular tennis champions of all time, "Little Mo" Connolly led a star-crossed life. She sparkled as a teenager, dominating the women's game in the early 1950s. In 1953, she became the first woman to win the Grand Slam—U.S., France, England, and Australia. A horseback riding accident ended her career before she was 20. She died at 35.

September 18/Harvey Haddix/1925/baseball

Left-hander Harvey Haddix had a solid 15-year pitching career, including two wins and no losses in Pittsburgh's 1960 World Series upset of the New York Yankees. But he will always be best remembered for one game against Milwaukee on May 26, 1959, when he pitched 12 perfect innings, only to lose his no-hitter—and the game—on a Joe Adcock double in the 13th.

September 19/Al Oerter/1936/track

As Al Oerter got older, he got better. He earned his first Olympic gold medal in 1956 with a then-record discus throw of nearly 185 feet. He upped his discus throw to 192 feet in 1960, topped 200 feet in 1964, and 212 feet in 1968. In each of these four straight Olympics, Al Oerter won the gold medal.

September 20/Red Auerbach/1917/basketball

Red Auerbach's Boston Celtics dominated the pro game between 1956 and 1966. The Celtics of that era were one of basketball's great dynasties, winning eight straight world titles. Red Auerbach coached Bill Russell, Bob Cousy, John Havlicek, Bill Sharman, Sam Jones, and many other stars.

September 21/Howie Morenz/1902/hockey

When old-timers talk about the great hockey players, the name of Howie Morenz leads all the rest. U.S. sportswriters dubbed him "the Babe Ruth of Hockey." The Canadian press in 1950 named him the hockey player of the half century. Morenz, a fast, spectacular forward for the Montreal Canadiens, died at the age of 34 after suffering a broken leg in a game. His number 7 was retired.

September 22/Bob Lemon/1920/baseball

In the minors, they thought Bob Lemon was a third baseman. But by 1946 he became a starting pitcher in the majors, and by 1948 he was a 20-game winner. Lemon went on to win 20 or more games in seven of his 13 big-league seasons on the mound. His pitching, all for Cleveland, put him in the Hall of Fame.

September 23/Peter Thomson/1929/golf

Australia's greatest golfer, Peter Thomson won the British Open three straight times, five times in all. His low, running style of play did not prove successful in the U.S., but in Europe, Australia, and Asia he was a winner throughout the '50s. In later years he pursued golf architecture.

September 24/John Mackey/1941/football

John Mackey switched from halfback to end while playing for the Syracuse University team that featured the great Ernie Davis. Drafted by the Baltimore Colts in 1963, Mackey became the premier pass receiver for quarterback Johnny Unitas. Fast, strong, and sure-handed, he was a model tight end.

September 25/Bob McAdoo/1951/basketball

Basketball fans in Buffalo aren't likely to forget Bob McAdoo. He burst on the scene like a comet, winning Rookie of the Year honors in 1973. Then, to prove it was no fluke, he came back in 1974, 1975, and 1976 to lead all scorers in the league. In 1975, he was named the NBA's Most Valuable Player.

September 26/Frank Brimsek/1915/hockey

In a game dominated by Canadians, Frank Brimsek, born in Minnesota, stood out. His brilliant play as a goalie quickly earned him the nickname "Mr. Zero." As a rookie, he twice put together shutout strings of three games running. Brimsek spent most of his career with the Boston Bruins.

September 27/Kathy Whitworth/1939/golf

At the end of Kathy Whitworth's first season on the pro Tour, her stroke average stood above 80. It took her six months to win $30. Yet when she began winning, she won .   and won   and won. Her 83 U.S. victories topped Mickey Wright's previous career record. Whitworth's swing was not picture-perfect, but it worked.

September 28/Alice Marble/1913/tennis

A California tomboy, Alice Marble became the undisputed queen of American women's tennis in the late 1930s. She reigned as U.S. singles champion from 1936 to 1940, except for one year. Her finest showing at Wimbledon came in 1939. Inconsistent but aggressive, Marble suffered ill health throughout her career.

September 29/Sebastian Coe/1956/track

Sebastian Coe set three world track records in 1979—the 800-meters, the mile, and the 1,500-meters. The rivalry between Coe and his fellow British countryman and middle-distance runner Steve Ovett was one of the great match-ups in track history. Coe set durable world marks at 800 and 1,000-meters.

September 30/Robin Roberts/1926/baseball

It's a truism that a major league pitcher can't get by on just a fast ball, but Robin Roberts is a Hall of Famer. Pitching for the Philadelphia Phillies, who needed all the pitching they could get, Roberts won 20 or more games six seasons in a row, 1950 through 1955.

OCTOBER

October 1/Rod Carew/1945/baseball

Rod Carew, one of modern baseball's great hitters, played 19 seasons for the Minnesota Twins and California Angels. He led the American League in hitting seven times, compiling a .328 lifetime batting average. Carew appeared in four Championship Series but never in a World Series.

October 2/Maury Wills/1932/baseball

Base-stealing records have been among the least durable in baseball in recent years. Maury Wills's 1962 total of 104 steals was thought to be unapproachable. But Lou Brock stole 118 bases just 11 years later, and in 1982 Rickey Henderson stole 130.

October 3/Glenn Hall/1931/hockey

Glenn Hall, "Mr. Goalie," played in 502 consecutive games, an all-time NHL record for a goaltender. He was effective as well as durable, leading the league in shutouts six times and winning All-Star recognition 11 times. He played four seasons each with Detroit and St. Louis, two with Chicago.

October 4/Sam Huff/1934/football

Sam Huff is best remembered for a number of hard-fought games between the New York Giants and Cleveland Browns in which Huff, a linebacker, faced Jim Brown, one of the greatest running backs in pro football history. The Huff-led Giant defense more than held its own against the Cleveland attack.

October 5/Barry Switzer/1937/football

Talk about trouble. University of Oklahoma head coach Barry Switzer's .800+ won-lost record shrunk to the fine print in 1989 when the Sooners' starting quarterback was arrested for selling cocaine, three other players were charged with rape, and some Sooner players trashed their hotel rooms prior to the Citrus Bowl game. Maybe winning *isn't* the only thing.

October 6/Helen Wills/1905/tennis

The press called her "Little Miss Poker Face," and her style of play was intense and self-assured. She was a complete player who brought a new vitality and seriousness to women's tennis. Known for her green-lined eyeshade and mid-calf-length skirts, Helen Wills (later Moody) and Helen Hull Jacobs were perennial rivals in the 1920s and early 1930s.

October 7/Chuck Klein/1904/baseball

On July 10, 1936, Chuck Klein hit four home runs for the Philadelphia Phillies in a ten-inning game at Pittsburgh. He led the league in homers four times, although critics gave partial credit to Baker Bowl's 280-foot right-field fence.

Still, Klein's lifetime performance, including a .320 batting average, earned him a place in the Baseball Hall of Fame.

October 8/Billy Conn/1917/boxing

People tend to remember Billy Conn for only two fights—his first loss to Joe Louis in 1941 and his second loss to Joe Louis in 1946. It's too bad, because Conn was a classy light heavyweight champion from 1939 to 1941, a boxer who retired undefeated from that class. In 75 bouts, he was knocked out just twice—in his two fights with Louis.

October 9/Orville Moody/1933/golf

Orville Moody, an Army sergeant for 14 years, went on the pro Tour in 1967. In 1968, he finished 103rd on the money list. Things looked none too promising. But in 1969 he startled the golf world by winning the U.S. Open. Moody never came close to that peak again, and he remains the least known Open winner.

October 10/Martina Navratilova/1956/tennis

No player in tennis history, male or female, dominated the game for as long as Martina Navratilova. Born in Czechoslovakia, she won Wimbledon singles titles in 1978 and 1979. Then she came back to win the title every year from 1982 through 1987. Along the way, she also won four U.S. singles championships.

October 11/Willie Hoppe/1887/billiards

How many people have dominated a sport for 46 years in tournament competition? Not many. But if you're willing to classify three-cushion billiards as a sport, then Willie Hoppe accomplished the feat. Hoppe won his first world championship in 1906, his last in 1952.

October 12/Joe Cronin/1906/baseball

Joe Cronin was a rags-to-riches success story. He won the junior tennis championship of San Francisco at the age of 15. But it was baseball that propelled him upward. A superb, hard-hitting shortstop and fine playing-manager for the Washington Senators and Boston Red Sox, he became the Red Sox general manager and then president of the American League.

October 13/Eddie Matthews/1931/baseball

In his day Eddie Mathews set a lot of records at third base and at the plate. He led the league twice in home runs while playing for the Milwaukee Braves. He had over 30 homers for nine years in a row. He's a Hall of Famer, and his plan in baseball history is secure, though most of his records have been broken by Mike Schmidt.

October 14/John Wooden/1910/football

A three-time All-America guard at Purdue, John Wooden was elected to the Basketball Hall of Fame as a player. But it was as a coach at UCLA that he really came into his own. Under Wooden, UCLA won ten national titles in 12 years, 1964–75. He was reinducted into the Hall of Fame as a coach.

October 15/Jim Palmer/1945/baseball

The nemesis of Baltimore Oriole manager Earl Weaver, right-hander Jim Palmer was also the nemesis of the batters he faced. From 1970 through 1977, Palmer won 20 or more games every year but one. Baltimore either won the pennant or was in contention every one of those years.

October 16/Dave DeBusschere/1940/basketball

Dave DeBusschere pitched for the Chicago White Sox in 1962 and 1963. His real forte was basketball, though. When the Detroit Pistons asked him to become a player-coach at the age of 24, he said yes. "I was too young to handle men," he said later. But he was very good at handling a basketball, as fans discovered when he went to the media-saturated New York Knicks.

October 17/Candy Cummings/1848/baseball

Why is a little 120-pound pitcher who won 21 major league games and lost 22 in the Baseball Hall of Fame? One good reason is that he invented the curve ball. Cummings's career preceded the founding of the National League, so some of the teams he played for may sound unfamiliar—the Star of Brooklyn, the Live Oaks of Lynn, the Forest City of Cleveland.

October 18/Mike Ditka/1939/football

A first-round draft pick of the Chicago Bears, Mike Ditka became one of the earliest, and one of the best, tight ends in pro football. When he retired after 12 years, he went into coaching—first for Tom Landry at Dallas, and then in 1982 as head coach of the Bears. His 1986 team won the Super Bowl.

October 19/Three-Finger Brown/1876/baseball

His first name was Mordecai, and his nickname was inevitable. As a young-ster, Brown stuck his finger in a feed chopper on his uncle's farm and lost most of his right index finger. He never considered it a handicap. As the ace of the Chicago Cubs, he claimed it put a sharper break on his curve.

October 20/Mickey Mantle/1931/baseball

Baseball fans knew right away that Mickey Mantle was something special. When the teenager was busting fences for Joplin, Missouri, of the Class C Western Association, an opposing manager said, "We had pretty good luck against this Mantle kid last night; he got four hits, but they were all singles."

October 21/Whitey Ford/1928/baseball

Whitey Ford's great years on the mound coincided with the New York Yankees' dominant years in the standings. Ford's won-lost percentage was the third best in baseball history, and his World Series record—he pitched in 11 of them—ranked him first in eight separate categories, including most wins.

October 22/Jimmy Foxx/1907/baseball

Double X had awesome power at the plate. In 1932, he hit 58 home runs and would have topped Babe Ruth's 60 with ease except for the screens at Sportsman's Park, St. Louis (costing him five homers) and League Park, Cleveland (costing him three homers). Neither screen existed in 1927 when Ruth hit his 60.

October 23/Pelé/1940/soccer

Perhaps the greatest soccer player who ever lived, Brazil's Pelé became the highest paid athlete of his day. He led his Brazilian national team to World Cup championships in 1958, 1962, and 1970. Late in his career, he joined the New York Cosmos and helped popularize soccer in the United States.

October 24/Y.A. Tittle/1926/football

In the book *The Best of LIFE* there is a classic photograph of New York Giants' MVP quarterback Y.A. Tittle, dazed and bleeding, kneeling on the ground, trying to recover from a bone-crushing tackle. He was nearing retirement. Although Tittle starred for the Giants in the early '60s, his greatest triumphs had come earlier as a San Francisco '49er.

October 25/Dave Cowens/1948/basketball

At six-feet-eight-and-a-half-inches, Dave Cowens was small for a pro center. So Tom Heinsohn, Boston Celtics coach, built a new offense that made use of Cowens's speed and outside shooting skill. It worked. Cowens helped transform the Celtics into league champions once again.

October 26/Primo Carnera/1906/boxing

They called him the "Ambling Alp." He was a circus strongman who became the world heavyweight boxing champion. But Max Baer humiliated him in taking away his crown. Baer decked Carnera 11 times in the title fight and punctuated his knockdowns with such comments as, "Last one up's a sissy!"

October 27/Ralph Kiner/1922/baseball

In later years, people would think of Ralph Kiner as a genial broadcaster of New York Mets games. In his playing days, though, he packed a deadly wallop. Kiner, a Pittsburgh Pirate outfielder, led the National League in homers for his first seven seasons in the majors. In any given at-bat, only Babe Ruth was more likely than Kiner to unload a home run.

October 28/Bruce Jenner/1949/track

The United States has done well in the Olympic decathlon over the years, and 1976 was no exception. Bruce Jenner, of whom much was expected, delivered—and how. At the very top of his form, he put together the highest point total in Olympic history. In each of the first five of the ten events, he achieved personal best marks.

October 29/Denis Potvin/1953/hockey

The New York Islanders, hopeless in their first NHL season, got to choose first in the draft. They picked defenseman Denis Potvin, and they were on their way. Rookie of the Year in 1974, best defenseman for three seasons, Potvin was a stalwart on the Islanders team that took the Stanley Cup four years in a row.

October 30/Ed Delahanty/1867/baseball

He was the only player in history to lead both the American and National leagues in hitting. He hit .408 for the NL Phillies in 1899 and .376 for the AL Senators in 1902. The best of five major league Delahanty brothers, Big Ed met an untimely end. Drunk, he toppled off a railroad bridge into the Niagara River during the 1903 season.

October 31/Wilbur Shaw/1902/auto racing

One of the greats of auto racing, Wilbur Shaw won the Indy 500 three times—1937, 1939, and 1940. But his most vivid memory was of a race on the high-banked wooden track at Altoona, Pennsylvania. Children had climbed into holes in the rotting track surface, and each time Shaw roared into the stretch, he saw the kids' heads sticking up through the holes.

NOVEMBER

November 1/Gary Player/1935/golf

By the 1960s, Gary Player of South Africa had established himself as one of golf's Big Three, along with Jack Nicklaus and Arnold Palmer. Player's 1965 victory in the U.S. Open was the first in 45 years by an overseas golfer. At five-feet-seven he was not overpowering, but had great competitive spirit

November 2/Ken Rosewall/1934/tennis

The 1950s saw the emergence of a powerful coterie of Australian tennis players. One of them, Ken Rosewall, steady and consistent, never won a Wimbledon title, but he twice became the U.S. Open champion: first in 1956, then—far down the road—in 1970. In both of those years he was also the losing finalist at Wimbledon.

November 3/Bronko Nagurski/1908/football

One of pro football's early heroes, the almost legendary Bronko Nagurski did it all. He was a powerful runner, a solid linebacker, and a talented passer. The first great fullback in the NFL, Nagurski was a 60-minute player. When the Pro Football Hall of Fame opened in 1963, he was a shoo-in.

November 4/Jimmy Piersall/1929/baseball

When the name Jimmy Piersall comes up, people think of his autobiography, *Fear Strikes Out* (Anthony "Psycho" Perkins played Piersall in the movie version), and of the violent room at Westborough State Hospital. Piersall did have mental problems, but he also put in 17 seasons as a first-rate major league outfielder, mostly for the Red Sox and Indians.

November 5/Bill Walton/1952/basketball

At UCLA no one doubted that redheaded Bill Walton would be a superstar in the pros. He paced the Bruins—the "Walton Gang"—to two NCAA crowns as Player of the Year. But Walton had an Achilles heel, or rather two tendinitis knees. Injury-prone, he had some fine seasons for the Portland Trail Blazers, but never quite matched his promise. His radical political views made news.

November 6/Walter Johnson/1887/baseball

"You can't hit what you can't see," moaned Yankee outfielder Ping Bodie. A blazing fastball plus pinpoint control made Walter Johnson the second winningest pitcher of all time. Among his 416 major league victories were 101 shutouts. Nolan Ryan and Steve Carlton together got about that many shutouts.

November 7/Jim Kaat/1938/baseball

Jim Kaat was one of those rare players (Early Wynn was another) whose career spanned four decades. Left-hander Kaat pitched briefly for the Washington Senators in 1959, losing two games. Twenty-five years later, in 1983, he was still toiling in the majors. His best years were with the Minnesota Twins and Chicago White Sox.

November 8/Frank McGuire/1914/basketball

Frank McGuire starred in baseball and basketball at St. John's University. But his fame rests on his success as a college basketball coach. He coached his teams to more than 100 wins at each of three major universities—St. John's, North Carolina, and South Carolina. No one else has ever done it.

November 9/Bob Gibson/1935/baseball

In 1968, it was tough to get a hit off St. Louis Cards' right-hander Bob Gibson. He allowed only 198 hits in 305 innings. He struck out 268 batters while walking 62. He allowed just 38 earned runs all year, posting an ERA of 1.12—the lowest in major league history (for 300 or more innings). Gibson's 22–9 won-lost record suggests that his Cards weren't hitting.

November 10/Clyde (Bulldog) Turner/1919/football

He came out of little Hardin-Simmons College with enough talent to attract the attention of both the Chicago Bears and the Detroit Lions. The Bears got him in the 1940 draft, and he quickly became an All-Pro center. For 13 seasons Turner was both a great offensive lineman and a skilled linebacker.

November 11/Pie Traynor/1899/baseball

Until Brooks Robinson came along, Pie Traynor of the Pittsburgh Pirates was the finest fielding third baseman the game had ever seen (although his .945 lifetime fielding average seems unremarkable compared to Robinson's .971). But Traynor also contributed mightily with his bat, posting a .320 career batting mark (to Robinson's .267).

November 12/Nadia Comaneci/1961/gymnastics

Nadia Comaneci, a tiny 14-year-old girl from Rumania, startled the sports world at the 1976 Montreal Olympics when she became the first gymnast ever to be awarded a maximum 10.0 score in Olympic competition. She won three individual gold medals. Interestingly, her normal physical development took the edge off her skills, and she had less success at the 1980 games.

November 13/Earl Sande/1898/horse racing

He was the most successful jockey of the Golden Age of Sports. Sande started out as a broncobuster in Idaho, but it was aboard thoroughbreds that he gained his fame. He rode two Kentucky Derby winners in the '20s— Zev (1923) and Flying Ebony (1927). In 1930, he rode Gallant Fox to the Triple Crown.

November 14/Ted Meredith/1892/track

The man favored to win the 800-meters at the 1912 Stockholm Olympics was an American, Melvin Sheppard, who had won the gold medal in 1908. The gold stayed with the United States, but the surprising winner was 19-year-old James (Ted) Meredith, who set a world-record pace to nose out Sheppard by one tenth of a second.

November 15/Tommy Thomas/1898/football

Tommy Thomas, who roomed with the fabled George Gipp at Notre Dame, earned a law degree and then decided to try a year or so of coaching. He proved to be sensational at it, leading Alabama's Crimson Tide to three Rose Bowls, one Sugar Bowl, one Cotton Bowl, and one Orange Bowl. Thomas's teams won four, lost two. Overall he was 141–33–9, a .795 percentage.

November 16/Mel Patton/1924/track

American runners were expected to dominate the sprints at the 1948 London Olympics, and they did. Mel Patton won the gold in the 200-meter event, while Harrison Dillard was the surprising winner in the 100-meters. Barney Ewell, another great U.S. sprinter, took the silver medal in both races.

November 17/Elvin Hayes/1945/basketball

Elvin Hayes was a college standout at the University of Houston. His 39 points and 15 rebounds gave Houston a win over UCLA's till-then-unbeaten Lew Alcindor team. A durable, consistent performer, six-foot-nine Hayes put in three superb pro seasons with San Diego before joining the Washington Capitals.

November 18/Jack Tatum/1948/football

They Call Me Assassin is the title of his autobiography. "The name of the game is hitting," he said, and few have ever hit harder. Tatum's most famous hit was the one in an exhibition game that paralyzed Darryl Stingley from the neck down. Noted for his pass interceptions and fumble recoveries, Tatum played for the Oakland Raiders and Houston Oilers.

November 19/Roy Campanella/1921/baseball

Three-time MVP Roy Campanella was the catcher for the great Brooklyn Dodger teams that ruled the National League in the 1950s. After he was paralyzed in an automobile accident, a benefit night in the Los Angeles Coliseum (he never played for L.A.) drew 93,103 fans—the biggest crowd ever to assemble for a baseball game.

November 20/Kenesaw Mountain Landis/1866/baseball

He looked like an Old Testament prophet, and he sometimes acted like one. As commissioner of baseball after the Black Sox scandal, Landis fined and suspended players right and left, helping to restore the image of baseball. He despised Branch Rickey's farm system, but failed to curb it.

November 21/Stan Musial/1920/baseball

Stan Musial started out as a so-so minor league pitcher. When he switched to the outfield, he found a home. The St. Louis Cardinals kept him there for 23 years—and 24 All-Star games. His best year was 1948, when he led the league in almost every offensive department. A .331 lifetime hitter, The Man from Donora, Pennsylvania, was one of the great stars of the game.

November 22/Billie Jean King/1943/tennis

Billie Jean King won the women's singles title four times at Forest Hills and six times at Wimbledon. A fierce competitor on and off the court, she led the fight for the professionalization of women's tennis. Her circus-atmosphere defeat of 55-year-old Bobby Riggs aside, King's impact on women's tennis was profound.

November 23/Lew Hoad/1934/tennis

A spectacular shot-maker, Australian Lew Hoad took the singles title at Wimbledon in 1956 and 1957. In '56, he missed the Grand Slam of tennis by losing to Ken Rosewall in the finals at Forest Hills. Brilliant as he was at his peak, Hoad never won the U.S. singles title.

November 24/Oscar Robertson/1938/basketball

If you were looking for the perfect, all-around basketball player, you'd have to consider Oscar Robertson, called the "Big O" ever since his days at the University of Cincinnati. Actually, Robertson wasn't all that big—six-feet-five—but he had all the moves. For the Rochester Royals, he averaged more than 30 points a game in six of his first seven seasons.

November 25/Joe DiMaggio/1914/baseball

TV pitchman and one-time husband of Marilyn Monroe, Joe D, the Yankee Clipper, was a worthy successor to Babe Ruth and Lou Gehrig. A smooth, stylish hitter and fielder, he is best known for hitting safely in 56 straight games in 1941. In 1933, he had hit safely in 61 straight games for the minor league San Francisco Seals. Joe D's lifetime batting average—.325.

November 26/Hugh Duffy/1866/baseball

Little Hugh Duffy, an outfielder for the Boston Braves, came to bat 539 times in 1894. He rapped out 236 hits. That works out to a .438 batting average—the highest in history for a single season. Duffy went hitless in only 17 games of the 124 games he played that year. So pleased were the Braves with his performance that they raised his salary $12.50 a week.

November 27/Johnny Blood/1903/football

His real name was John McNally, but after seeing the Rudolph Valentino film titled *Blood and Sand*, he began calling himself Johnny Blood. His off-field swashbuckling matched his new name and angered Packers' coach Curley Lambeau. But Blood was a great pass receiver and a fine tackler. He was poor material for a head coach, though, as he proved at Pittsburgh.

November 28/Paul Warfield/1942/football

Once Paul Warfield had snagged a pass, it was hard to stop him. In 13 NFL seasons he averaged more than 20 yards a catch, the only player ever to do so. Warfield spent most of his career with the Cleveland Browns and Miami Dolphins. His best year was 1968 when he caught 50 passes for 1,067 yards.

November 29/Minnie Minoso/1923/baseball

Cuban-born Saturnino Orestes Armas Arrieta Minoso, better known as Minnie, batted over .300 for eight seasons. He played for various teams, but usually got bounced back to the Chicago White Sox. When he stepped to the plate as a pinch hitter for the White Sox on October 5, 1980, he was 57 years old.

November 30/Bo Jackson/1962/football, baseball

Many athletes have to make a choice when they enter the pro ranks— baseball or football? Bo Jackson refused to make the choice. He opted for both. Sportswriters grumbled when Jackson signed on as an outfielder for the Kansas City Royals and also as a running back for the Los Angeles Raiders. Could he make it work? Stay tuned.

DECEMBER

December 1/Lee Trevino/1939/golf

Lee Trevino played a lot of pro golf before anyone took much notice. Even after winning the U.S. Open in 1968, Trevino (not to mention his critics) doubted that he was a major golfer. He was, though. By 1970 he was the leading money winner on the Tour. He took the British Open in 1971 and 1972 and was PGA Champion in 1984.

December 2/Bob Pettit/1932/basketball

"This is a guy who knows his business," said Easy Ed Macauley of Bob Pettit. And indeed he did—but it was something he had to learn. Cut from his high school team, Pettit put in many hours of practice on his own. It paid off for him and for the Milwaukee and St. Louis Hawks. When he retired, he had scored 20,880 points in the NBA, a record at the time.

December 3/Bobby Allison/1937/auto racing

Bobby Allison of Hueytown, Alabama, established himself early as one of the top pros in stock car racing. He was driving and winning with Modifieds in the early 1960s. Later a winner of many superspeedway events, he won the Daytona 500 in 1978, 1982, and 1988.

December 4/Jesse Burkett/1868/baseball

Known as "The Crab," Jesse Burkett was one of three players in major league history to put together back-to-back .400 seasons. (The others were Ty Cobb and Rogers Hornsby.) Burkett did it for the Cleveland Spiders in 1895 (.423) and 1896 (.410). A diminutive left-handed outfielder, he showed the Boston Red Sox how to bunt when he was 70.

December 5/Jim Plunkett/1947/football

All-Everything as a quarterback at Stanford, Heisman Trophy winner Jim Plunkett was the first college football player to amass more than 7,000 yards. He started fast, as Rookie of the Year, for the New England Patriots.

Injuries seemed to have ended his career when, in 1981 and again in 1983, he came off the bench to lead his teams to the Super Bowl.

December 6/Otto Graham/1921/football

He attended Northwestern on a basketball scholarship, where football coach Pappy Waldorf saw him playing touch football. In 1943, Graham was All-American in both basketball and football. After playing pro basketball for the Rochester Royals, he signed on as a T-formation quarterback with the Cleveland Browns. Some regard Graham as the greatest passer of all time.

December 7/Johnny Bench/1947/baseball

Catcher Johnny Bench was one of the main cogs in Cincinnati's Big Red Machine of the 1970s. Superb at the plate as well as behind it, he drove in 1,376 runs for the power-packed Reds, 145 of them in 1970. But Bench built a towering reputation more on his play, especially his clutch play, than on his stats, which, while good, weren't eye-popping.

December 8/George Rogers/1958/football

Son of a convicted murderer and a welfare mother, George Rogers made his Horatio Alger leap as a running back. It took him all the way to the Heisman Trophy in 1980 and the NFL Rookie of the Year award with the New Orleans Saints. Cocaine use tarnished his image, but he continued to rack up impressive yardage.

December 9/Dick Butkus/1942/football

"Dick Butkus," said George Allen, "had a name that sounded like the man he was." Butkus was big, unfriendly, and formidable. A linebacker for the Chicago Bears, he made 11 unassisted tackles in his first game as a pro. Said Allen, "Players always were vowing to get even with Butkus, and no one ever did."

December 10/Ragnhild Hveger/1920/swimming

She was Denmark's "Golden Torpedo," and she broke 42 world records for various freestyle distances between 1936 and 1942. At age 15, she won a silver medal at the 1936 Berlin Olympics, but because of the war she missed her best chance at a gold. In 1938, she won the 400-meter European championship by an amazing 25 meters. Her 400-meter record held for 16 years.

December 11/Pierre Pilote/1931/hockey

During his first five seasons with the Chicago Black Hawks, Pierre Pilote never missed a game. He was one of the game's outstanding defensemen, winning the Norris Trophy three straight years. A member of the Hockey Hall of Fame, Pilote played in eight consecutive All-Star games.

December 12/Henry Armstrong/1912/boxing

Born in Columbus, Mississippi, Henry Armstrong grew up to become the only boxer in history to hold three world titles at the same time—featherweight, welterweight, and middleweight. He brought attention to the lower weight classifications of boxing and is considered one of the sport's great champions. After retirement, he became a Baptist minister.

December 13/Larry Doby/1924/baseball

The first black ballplayer in the American League, outfielder Larry Doby led the league twice in homers, once in RBIs. He starred on Lou Boudreau's triumphant 1948 Cleveland Indians. Like Jackie Robinson, he was subjected to many insults from players and fans, which he endured with composure. Doby managed the Chicago White Sox briefly in 1978.

December 14/Ernie Davis/1939/football

Ernie Davis's story is one of the saddest in football. A brilliant running back at Syracuse University, the Heisman Trophy winner in 1961, Davis was the first player selected in the 1961 NFL draft. He looked forward to joining the great Jim Brown in the Cleveland Browns backfield, but he was never to play pro ball, succumbing to leukemia at the age of 23.

December 15/Nick Buoniconti/1940/football

Drafted out of Notre Dame by the Boston Patriots, Nick Buoniconti, a linebacker, was named All-League four times before being traded to the Miami Dolphins. At Miami his passing, rushing, and tackling helped carry Don Shula's Dolphins to three Super Bowls.

December 16/Jack Hobbs/1882/cricket

Sir John Berry Hobbs was the first person in England, or presumably anywhere, to be knighted for playing cricket. Hobbs was quite a bloke. He made a record 197 hundreds in first-class cricket. In 1926, he made 316 for Surrey against Middlesex, the highest individual score at Lord's. You have to hand it to Jack Hobbs—at least if you know cricket.

December 17/Peter Snell/1938/track

Peter Snell, New Zealand's great track hero, played lawn tennis before taking up running at the age of 18. At the Rome Olympics in 1960, he won the 800-meters unexpectedly in a blazing finish and in an Olympic record time. Two years later in Tokyo, he won gold medals in both the 800- and 1,500-meters.

December 18/Ty Cobb/1886/baseball

This brawling, spike-filing outfielder for the Detroit Tigers had a burning desire to succeed. He practiced, he trained, and he sought every possible edge over his opponents. Cobb claimed that desire, not innate ability, was what enabled him to set record after record. From 1907 through 1919 he missed winning the AL batting title only once (1916, Tris Speaker).

December 19/Al Kaline/1934/baseball

You can almost count on one hand the baseball players who started in the major leagues with no prior minor league experience. Al Kaline was one of them. At the age of 20, he became the youngest player ever to win a batting crown. He went on to play 22 seasons for the Detroit Tigers, a consistently fine outfielder and hitter.

December 20/Branch Rickey/1881/baseball

How important was Branch Rickey to modern baseball? As the inscription at St. Paul's says of Christopher Wren, "If you seek a monument, look about you." Branch Rickey signed Jackie Robinson to a major league contract, bringing blacks to organized baseball. He established the farm system, ensuring (intentionally or not) that baseball, unlike football and basketball, would not rely on the colleges for pro training.

December 21/Chris Evert/1954/tennis

Chris Evert (later Lloyd, then Evert again), a cool perfectionist on the court, won four U.S. singles titles in a row, 1975 through 1978. She won four times at Wimbledon. A crowd favorite, Evert spent most of the 1980s in the shadow of the overpowering Martina Navratilova.

December 22/Steve Carlton/1944/baseball

At times it looked as if lefty Steve Carlton would pitch forever: seven years for the St. Louis Cardinals, 15 years for the Philadelphia Phillies. He challenged Nolan Ryan briefly for the all-time career strikeout record and then fell behind. But Carlton still had a firm grip on second place, one of two pitchers in history to strike out more than 4,000 batters.

December 23/Paul Hornung/1935/football

Paul Hornung's off-field escapades sometimes grieved Green Bay Packer coach Vince Lombardi, but on the field he was a brilliantly versatile back. He played on NFL championship teams in 1961, 1962, and 1965. In between he got himself suspended (in 1963 along with Alex Karras) for gambling on NFL games. After retirement he turned to sports broadcasting.

December 24/Red Sullivan/1929/hockey

Red Sullivan, a forward, broke into the NHL with the Boston Bruins in 1949–50. He shuttled between the Bruins and the Hershey Bears of the AHL, setting a league scoring record while with Hershey in 1953–54. Later he played for the Chicago Black Hawks and New York Rangers and then coached the Rangers briefly.

December 25/Larry Csonka/1946/football

It was obvious that Larry Csonka had quite a future. At Syracuse University he broke the rushing records of Jim Brown, Ernie Davis, Jim Nance, and Floyd Little. The Miami Dolphins grabbed him, along with other top prospects. Miami soon ruled the NFL. In the 1973 Super Bowl, Csonka carried 33 times for 145 yards, winning the MVP award

December 26/Carlton Fisk/1947/baseball

After six years in the minors, Carlton Fisk came up to the Boston Red Sox and checked in as AL Rookie of the Year. Afterwards he had a solid career, though one beset by injuries. The Bosox fans loved him for ten years, and the Chisox fans did later. In 1984, he caught a 25-inning game for Chicago. A .270 lifetime hitter, his 300+ home runs attest to his power.

December 27/Jim Tobin/1912/baseball

Pitchers like to talk about their hitting, but with rare exceptions they don't have much to say. Jim Tobin, however, had a tale to tell. On May 13, 1942, playing for the Boston Braves, he belted three home runs in a game he was pitching. The Braves needed them all, eking out a 6–5 win over the Cubs. Tobin's career batting average was a none too robust .137.

December 28/Terry Sawchuk/1929/hockey

A star goalie for the Detroit Red Wings, Terry Sawchuk reached his pinnacle in the 1952 Stanley Cup playoffs. He collected four shutouts in the minimum eight game series and allowed only five goals in all. He was a member of five NHL championship teams. Sawchuk also played for Boston, Toronto, Los Angeles, and New York. His 103 lifetime shutouts set a record.

December 29/Jess Willard/1883/boxing

They were willing to pay training and travel expenses, so big Jess Willard, six-feet-seven, 240 pounds, went down to Havana and fought Jack Johnson for the heavyweight championship. Surprisingly, the awkward Willard won. The cheering lasted through one title defense—a draw with Frank Moran. Then Jack Dempsey pummeled Willard mercilessly to take the crown.

December 30/Sandy Koufax/1938/baseball

At his best, Sandy Koufax was all but unhittable, but it took him some time to reach that point. Wildness was a problem for years. Then, starting in 1961, he found the groove. In his last five seasons—before an arthritic elbow ended his career at age 30—his earned run average led the league every time. In his last season he won 27 and lost 9, with a 1.73 ERA.

December 31/King Kelly/1857/baseball

When asked if he drank while playing, Mike (King) Kelly replied, "It depends on the length of the game." He had that reputation. He also had the reputation of being able to do everything well on a ballfield—hit, field, throw, run, play any position. "Slide, Kelly, Slide" became a popular song of the 1880s, and Kelly's book, *Play Ball*, sold far and wide.

BIBLIOGRAPHY

This is a list of books consulted in compiling the Speaker's Treasury. Only books are included, not periodicals, newspapers, or other published sources that provided information for a number of entries.

Adams, Joey. *Joey Adams' Encyclopedia of Humor*. Indianapolis: The Bobbs-Merrill Company, Inc., 1968.

Adams, Joey. *Joey Adams' Son of Encyclopedia of Humor*. Indianapolis: The Bobbs-Merrill Company, Inc., 1970.

Allen, George, with Ben Olan. *Pro Football's 100 Greatest Players*. Indianapolis: The Bobbs-Merrill Company, Inc., 1982.

Allen, Maury. *Voices of Sport*. New York: Grosset & Dunlap Publishers, 1971.

Allen, Mel, with Frank Graham, Jr. *It Takes Heart*. New York: Harper & Brothers, 1959.

Alliss, Peter. *The Who's Who of Golf*. Englewood Cliffs, NJ: Prentice-Hall, Inc., 1953.

Anderson, C.W. *Twenty Gallant Horses*. New York: The Macmillan Company, 1965.

Anderson, Scott. *The Funniest Baseball Stories of the Century*. Los Angeles: Price/Stern/Sloan, 1985.

Anderson, Scott. *The Funniest Football Stories of the Century*. Los Angeles: Price/Stern/Sloan, 1983.

Appel, Martin, and Burt Goldblatt. *Baseball's Best: The Hall of Fame Gallery*. 2nd ed. New York: McGraw-Hill Book Company, 1980.

Asimov, Isaac. *Isaac Asimov's Treasury of Humor*. Boston: Houghton Mifflin Company, 1971.

Auerbach, Red, with Joe Fitzgerald. *On and Off the Court*. New York: Macmillan Publishing Company, 1985.

Babcock, Havilah. *The Best of Babcock*. Selected and with an Introduction by Hugh Grey. New York: Holt, Rinehart and Winston, 1974.

Bartlett, Michael, and Bob Gillen. *The Tennis Book*. New York: Arbor House, 1981.

Beck, Fred. *89 Years in a Sand Trap*. New York: Hill and Wang, 1965.

Beddoes, Richard, Stan Fischler, and Ira Gitler. *Hockey!: The Story of the World's Fastest Sport*. New York: Macmillan Publishing Company, Inc., 1973.

Benagh, Jim. *Incredible Athletic Feats*. New York: Hart Publishing Company, 1969.

Besford, Pat. *Encyclopedia of Swimming*. New York: St. Martin's Press, 1976.

Blount, Roy, Jr. *About Three Bricks Shy of a Load*. Boston: Little, Brown and Company, 1974.

Boswell, Thomas. *Strokes of Genius*. Garden City, NY: Doubleday & Company, 1987.

Boswell, Thomas. *Why Time Begins on Opening Day*. Garden City, NY: Doubleday & Company, 1984.

Boyle, Robert H. *At the Top of Their Game*. Piscataway, NJ: Winchester Press, 1983.

Brasch, R. *How Did Sports Begin?: A Look at the Origins of Man at Play*. New York: David McKay Company, Inc., 1970.

Brondfield, Jerry. *Great Moments in American Sports*. New York: Random House, 1974.

Broun, Heywood Hale. *Tumultuous Merriment*. New York: Richard Marek Publishers, 1979.

Burrill, Bob. *Who's Who in Boxing*. New Rochelle, NY: Arlington House, 1974.

Camerer, Dave, ed. *The Best of Grantland Rice*. New York: Franklin Watts, Inc., 1963.

Carpenter, Harry. *Boxing: An Illustrated History*. New York: Crescent Books, 1982.

Carruth, Gorton, and Eugene Ehrlich. *The Harper Book of American Quotations*. New York: Harper & Row, Publishers, 1988.

Cutter, Robert, and Bob Fendell. *The Encyclopedia of Auto Racing Greats*. Englewood Cliffs, NJ: Prentice-Hall, Inc., 1973.

Davids, L. Robert, ed. *Minor League Baseball Stars*. Cooperstown, NY: Society for American Baseball Research, 1978.

Davis, Mac. *Great Sports Humor*. New York: Grosset & Dunlap, 1973.

Dickey, Charley. *Opening Shots and Parting Lines*. Piscataway, NJ: Winchester Press, 1983.

Ditka, Mike, with Don Pierson. *Ditka: An Autobiography*. Chicago: Bonus Book, 1986.

Drees, Jack, and Jim Mullen. *Where Is He Now?: Sports Heroes of Yesterday—Revisited*. Middle Village, NY: Jonathan David Publishers, 1973.

Dryden, Ken. *The Game: A Thoughtful and Provocative Look at a Life in Hockey*. New York: Times Books, 1983.

Dundee, Angelo, with Mike Winters. *I Only Talk Winning*. Chicago: Contemporary Books, Inc., 1985.

East, Ben. *Danger! Explosive True Adventures of the Great Outdoors*. New York: E.P. Dutton & Co., 1970.

Einstein, Charles. *The Fireside Book of Baseball*. New York: Simon and Schuster, 1956.

Eskensai, Gerald. *A Thinking Man's Guide to Pro Soccer*. New York: E.P. Dutton & Co., 1980.

Fadiman, Clifton, ed. *The Little, Brown Book of Anecdotes*. Boston: Little, Brown and Company, 1985.

Feinstein, John. *A Season on the Brink: A Year with Bob Knight and the Indiana Hoosiers*. New York: Macmillan Publishing Company, 1986.

Fetros, John G. *This Day in Sports: A Diary of Major Sports Events*. Novato, CA: Newton K. Gregg/Publisher, 1974.

Fischler, Stan. *Stan Mikita: The Turbulent Career of a Hockey Superstar*. New York: Cowles Book Company, Inc., 1969.

Fitzgerald, Ray. *Champions Remembered: Choice Picks from a Boston Sports Desk*. Brattleboro, VT: The Stephen Greene Press, 1982.

Fleischer, Nat. *The Heavyweight Championship: An Informal History of Heavyweight Boxing from 1719 to the Present Day*. New York: G.P. Putnam's Sons, 1961.

Fox, Larry. *Illustrated History of Basketball*. New York: Grosset & Dunlap, 1974.

Frayne, Trent. *Famous Hockey Players*. New York: Dodd, Mead and Company, 1973.

Frayne, Trent. *The Mad Men of Hockey*. New York: Dodd, Mead and Company, 1974.

Frewin, Michael, ed. *The International Grand Prix Book of Motor Racing*. Garden City, NY: Doubleday & Company, 1965.

Gallico, Paul. *The Golden People*. Garden City, NY: Doubleday & Company, 1965.

Garagiola, Joe. *Baseball Is a Funny Game*. Philadelphia: J.B. Lippincott Co., 1960.

Goldstein, Richard. *Spartan Seasons: How Baseball Survived the Second World War*. New York: Macmillan Publishing Co., 1980.

Gordon, Alison. *Foul Ball!: Five Years in the American League*. New York: Dodd, Mead & Company, 1985.

Greenspan, Bud. *Play It Again, Bud!* New York: Peter H. Wyden, Inc., 1973.

Hackett, Buddy. *The Truth about Golf and Other Lies*. Garden City, NY: Doubleday & Company, 1968.

Hanley, Reid M. *Who's Who in Track and Field*. New Rochelle, NY: Arlington House, 1973.

Heglar, Mary Schnall. *The Grand Prix Champions*. Newport Beach, CA: Bond/Parkhurst Books, 1973.

Heller, Peter. *In This Corner: Forty World Champions Tell Their Stories*. New York: Simon and Schuster, 1973.

Hershfield, Harry. *Laugh Louder, Live Longer*. New York: Grayson Publishing Corp., 1959.

Herskowitz, Mickey. *The Legend of Bear Bryant*. New York: McGraw-Hill Book Company, 1987.

Hickok, Ralph. *Who Was Who in American Sports*. New York: Hawthorn Books, Inc., 1971.

Higdon, Hal. *Finding the Groove*. New York: G.P. Putnam's Sons, 1973.

Hobbs, Michael. *In Celebration of Golf*. New York: Charles Scribner's Sons, 1982.

Hollander, Zander, ed. *The NBA's Official Encyclopedia of Pro Basketball*. New York: New American Library, 1981.

Holmes, Tommy. *Dodger Daze and Knights*. New York: David McKay Company, Inc., 1953.

Holzman, Red, and Harvey Frommer. *Red on Red*. New York: Bantam Books, 1987.

Holzman, Red, with Leonard Lewin. *A View from the Bench*. New York: W.W. Norton & Company, 1987.

Houlgate, Deke, and the Editors of *Auto Racing Magazine*. *The Fastest Men in the World—On Wheels*. New York: World Publishing, 1971.

Humes, James C. *Podium Humor: A Raconteur's Treasury of Witty and Humorous Stories*. New York: Harper & Row, Publishers, 1975.

Kanner, S. Lee. *The New York Times Sports Question Box*. New York: The Rutledge Press, 1981.

Klein, Gene, and David Fisher. *First Down and a Billion: The Funny Business of Pro Football*. New York: William Morrow and Company, Inc., 1987.

Kramer, Jerry, edited by Dick Schaap. *Instant Replay*. New York: The World Publishing Company, 1968.

Lasorda, Tommy, and David Fisher. *The Artful Dodger*. New York: Arbor House, 1985.

Lebow, Fred, with Richard Woodley. *Inside the World of Big-Time Marathoning*. New York: Rawson Associates, 1984.

Lee, Bill, with Dick Lally. *The Wrong Stuff*. New York: The Viking Press, 1984.

Lieberman, Gerald F. *3,500 Good Quotes for Speakers*. Garden City, NY: Doubleday & Company, Inc., 1983.

Lipsyte, Robert. *SportsWorld: An American Dreamland*. New York: Quadrangle/The New York Times Book Co., 1975.

Locke, Tates, and Bob Ibach. *Caught in the Net*. West Point, NY: Leisure Press, 1982.

Luciano, Ron, and David Fisher. *The Fall of the Roman Umpire*. New York: Bantam Books, 1986.

Luciano, Ron, and David Fisher. *Strike Two*. New York: Bantam Books, 1984.

Luciano, Ron, and David Fisher. *The Umpire Strikes Back*. New York: Bantam Books, 1982.

Lund, Morten, Bob Gillen, and Michael Bartlett, eds. *The Ski Book*. New York: Arbor House, 1982.

McConkey, Phil, and Phil Simms, with Dick Schaap. *Simms to McConkey: Blood, Sweat and Gatorade*. New York: Crown Publishers, Inc., 1987.

McManus, Patrick F. *Never Sniff a Gift Fish*. New York: Holt, Rinehart and Winston, 1983.

Madden, John, with Dave Anderson. *Hey Wait a Minute, I Wrote a Book*. New York: Villard Books, 1984.

Madden, John, with Dave Anderson. *One Knee Equals Two Feet (And Everything Else You Need to Know About Football)*. New York: Villard Books, 1986.

Maikovich, Andrew J., ed. *Sports Quotations: Maxims, Quips, and Pronouncements for Writers and Fans*. Jefferson, NC: McFarland & Company, 1984.

Mantle, Mickey. *The Quality of Courage*. Garden City, NY: Doubleday & Company, 1964.

Mays, Willie, with Lou Sahidi. *Say Hey: The Autobiography of Willie Mays*. New York: Simon and Schuster, 1988.

Mazer, Bill. *The Sports Answer Book*. New York: Grosset & Dunlap, 1966.

Mendel, Ronald L. *Who's Who in Basketball*. New Rochelle, NY: Arlington House, 1973.

Mendel, Ronald L., and Timothy B. Phares. *Who's Who in Football*. New Rochelle, NY: Arlington House, 1974.

Miller, Jerry. *Fast Company: The Men and Machines of American Auto Racing*. Chicago: Follett Publishing Company, 1972.

Moore, Kenny. *Best Efforts: World Class Runners and Races*. Garden City, NY: Doubleday & Company, Inc., 1982.

Nash, Bruce, and Allan Zullo. *The Football Hall of Shame*. New York: Washington Square Press/Pocket Books, 1986.

Navratilova, Martina, with George Vecsey. *Martina*. New York: Alfred A. Knopf, 1985.

Neasham, V. Aubrey. *Wild Legacy: California Hunting and Fishing Tales*. Berkeley, CA: Howell-North Books, 1973.

Nelson, Cordner, *Track and Field: The Great Ones*. London: Pelham Books, 1970.

Nelson, Kevin. *Baseball's Greatest Quotes*. New York: Simon and Schuster, 1982.

Nelson, Kevin. *The Greatest Stories Ever Told (About Baseball)*. New York: Perigee Books, 1986.

Nelson, Lindsey, with Al Hirschberg. *Backstage at the Mets*. New York: The Viking Press, 1966.

Noverr, Douglas A., and Lawrence E. Ziewacz. *The Games They Played: Sports in American History, 1865-1980*. Chicago: Nelson-Hall, 1983.

O'Brien, Michael. *Vince: A Personal Biography of Vince Lombardi*. New York: William Morrow and Company, Inc., 1987.

Okrent, Daniel, and Harris Lewine, eds. *The Ultimate Baseball Book*. Boston: Houghton Mifflin Company, 1979.

Olney, Ross R. *Daredevils of the Speedway*. New York: Grosset & Dunlap, 1966.

Pachter, Marc. *Champions of American Sport*. New York: Harry N. Abrams, 1981.

Parrott, Harold. *The Lords of Baseball*. New York: Preager Publishers, 1976.

Pepe, Phil. *The Wit and Wisdom of Yogi Berra*. New York: Hawthorn Books, 1974.

Pluto, Terry, and Jeffrey Neuman, eds. *A Baseball Winter: The Off-Season Life of the Summer Game*. New York: Macmillan Publishing Company, 1986.

Porter, David L., ed. *Biographical Dictionary of American Sports: Baseball*. New York: Greenwood Press, 1987.

Porter, David L., ed. *Biographical Dictionary of American Sports: Football*. New York: Greenwood Press, 1987.

Price, Charles. *Golfer-at-Large*. New York: Atheneum, 1982.

Pritchard, Anthony. *The World Champions: Giuseppe Farina to Jackie Stewart*. New York: Macmillan Publishing Company, 1974.

Prochnow, Herbert V., and Herbert V. Prochnow, Jr. *The Successful Toastmaster*. New York: Harper & Row, Publishers, 1966.

Reichler, Joseph L., ed. *The Baseball Encyclopedia*. 7th ed. New York: Macmillan Publishing Company, 1988.

Reidenbaugh, Lowell. *Cooperstown: Where Baseball Legends Live Forever*. St. Louis: The Sporting News, 1983.

Riggs, Doug. *Keelhauled: The History of Unsportsmanlike Conduct and the America's Cup*. Newport, RI: Seven Seas Press, Inc., 1986.

Robyns, Gwen. *Wimbledon: The Hidden Drama*. New York: Drake Publishers, Inc., 1974.

Roper, Steve, and Allen Steck. *Fifty Classic Climbs of North America*. San Francisco: Sierra Club Books, 1979.

Rosenthal, Harold *Fifty Faces of Football*. New York: Atheneum, 1981

Ross, John M., ed. *Golf Magazine's Encyclopedia of Golf.* New York: Harper & Row, Publishers, 1979.

Rowes, Barbara. *The Book of Quotes.* New York: E.P. Dutton & Co., 1979.

Salzberg, Charles. *From Set Shot to Slam Dunk: The Glory Days of Basketball in the Words of Those Who Played It.* New York: E.P. Dutton & Co., 1987.

Schaap, Dick. *Sport.* New York: Arbor House, 1975.

Schachter, Norm. *Close Calls: Confessions of a NFL Referee.* New York: Quill, 1983.

Schlossberg, Dan. *Baseball Laffs.* Middle Village, NY: Jonathan David Publishers, Inc., 1982.

Schrier, Eric W., and William F. Allman, eds. *Newton at the Bat: The Science in Sports.* New York: Charles Scribner's Sons, 1984.

Schulian, John. *Writers' Fighters and Other Sweet Scientists.* Kansas City: Andrews and McMeel, 1983.

Schwiebert, Ernest. *Death of a Riverkeeper.* New York: E.P. Dutton & Co., 1980.

Severn, Bill. *A Carnival of Sports.* New York: David McKay Company, Inc., 1974.

Sharnik, John. *Remembrance of Games Past: On Tour with the Tennis Grand Masters.* New York: Macmillan Publishing Company, 1986.

Shoemaker, Bill, and Barney Nagler. *Shoemaker: America's Greatest Jockey.* New York: Doubleday & Company, Inc., 1988.

Smith, Red, ed. *Press Box: Red Smith's Favorite Sports Stories.* New York: W.W. Norton & Company, Inc., 1976.

Smith, Red. *Red Smith on Fishing.* Garden City, NY: Doubleday & Company, Inc., 1963.

Smith, Red. *To Absent Friends.* New York: Atheneum Publishers, Inc., 1982.

Sports Greats: Past and Present. New York: Interlyth, Ltd., 1973.

Stephens, Woody. *Guess I'm Lucky: My Life in Horse Racing.* Garden City, NY: Doubleday & Company, Inc., 1985.

Stone, Herbert L., William H. Taylor, and William W. Robinson. *The America's Cup Races.* New York: W.W. Norton & Company, Inc., 1970.

Thorn, John, ed. *The Armchair Quarterback.* New York: Charles Scribner's Sons, 1982.

Thorn, John. *A Century of Baseball Lore.* New York: Hart Publishing Company, Inc., 1976.

Tingay, Lance. *Tennis: A Pictorial History.* New York: G.P. Putnam's Sons, 1973.

Trevino, Lee, and Sam Blair. *The Snake in the Sandtrap (and Other Misadventures on the Golf Tour).* New York: Holt, Rinehart and Winston, 1985.

Uecker, Bob, and Mickey Herskowitz. *Catcher in the Wry.* New York: G.P. Putnam's Sons, 1982.

Underwood, John. *Spoiled Sport: A Fan's Notes on the Troubles of Spectator Sports.* Boston: Little, Brown and Company, 1984.

Vare, Robert. *Buckeye: A Study of Coach Woody Hayes and the Ohio State Football Machine.* New York: Harper's Magazine Press, 1974.

Waitz, Grete, and Gloria Averbuch. *World Class.* New York: Warner Books, 1986.

Wallechinsky, David. *The Complete Book of the Olympics.* New York: Penguin Books, 1984.

Whittingham, Richard. *Saturday Afternoon: College Football and the Men Who Made the Day.* New York: Workman Publishing, 1985.

Wilde, Larry. *The Official Sports Maniacs Joke Book.* New York: Bantam Books, 1985.

Wind, Herbert Warren. *The Gilded Age of Sport.* New York: Simon and Schuster, 1961.

Wolf, Warner, with William Taaffe. *Gimme a Break!: Warner Wolf on Sports.* New York: McGraw-Hill Book Company, 1983.

Zern, Ed. *Hunting and Fishing: From A to Zern.* Piscataway, NJ: Winchester Press, 1985.

Zimmerman, Paul. *The New Thinking Man's Guide to Pro Football.* New York: Simon and Schuster, 1984.

INDEX